KNOWLEDGE AND IGNORANCE OF SELF IN PLATONIC PHILOSOPHY

Knowledge and Ignorance of Self in Platonic Philosophy is the first volume of essays dedicated to the whole question of self-knowledge and its role in Platonic philosophy. It brings together established and rising scholars from every interpretative school of Plato studies, and a variety of texts from across Plato's corpus – including the classic discussions of self-knowledge in the *Charmides* and *Alcibiades* I, and dialogues such as the *Republic, Theaetetus*, and *Theages*, which are not often enough mined for insights about this crucial philosophical topic. The rich variety of readings and hermeneutical methods (as well as the comprehensive research bibliography included in the volume) allows for an encompassing view of the relevant scholarly debates. The volume is intended to serve as a standard resource for further research on Plato's treatment of self-knowledge, and will highlight the relevance of Plato's thought to contemporary debates on selfhood, self-reflection, and subjectivity.

JAMES M. AMBURY is Assistant Professor of Philosophy at King's College, Pennsylvania. He has published articles in journals including *Ancient Philosophy, International Philosophical Quarterly, Proceedings of the Boston Area Colloquium in Ancient Philosophy, Dionysius*, and *Plato*.

ANDY GERMAN is Assistant Professor of Philosophy at Ben-Gurion University of the Negev in Be'er-Sheva, Israel. He is the editor of Stanley Rosen's *Platonic Production: Theme and Variations* (2015) and the author of articles in journals including the *British Journal for the History of Philosophy, Review of Metaphysics, Epoché*, and *Polis*.

KNOWLEDGE AND IGNORANCE OF SELF IN PLATONIC PHILOSOPHY

EDITED BY

JAMES M. AMBURY
King's College, Pennsylvania

ANDY GERMAN
Ben-Gurion University of the Negev

CAMBRIDGE
UNIVERSITY PRESS

CAMBRIDGE
UNIVERSITY PRESS

University Printing House, Cambridge CB2 8BS, United Kingdom

One Liberty Plaza, 20th Floor, New York, NY 10006, USA

477 Williamstown Road, Port Melbourne, VIC 3207, Australia

314–321, 3rd Floor, Plot 3, Splendor Forum, Jasola District Centre, New Delhi – 110025, India

79 Anson Road, #06–04/06, Singapore 079906

Cambridge University Press is part of the University of Cambridge.

It furthers the University's mission by disseminating knowledge in the pursuit of education, learning, and research at the highest international levels of excellence.

www.cambridge.org
Information on this title: www.cambridge.org/9781107184466
DOI: 10.1017/9781316877081

© Cambridge University Press 2019

First published 2019

Printed and bound in Great Britain by Clays Ltd, Elcograf S.p.A.

A catalogue record for this publication is available from the British Library.

Library of Congress Cataloging-in-Publication Data
NAMES: Ambury, James M., editor. | German, Andy R., editor.
TITLE: Knowledge and ignorance of self in Platonic philosophy / edited by James M. Ambury, Andy German.
DESCRIPTION: Cambridge, United Kingdom ; New York, NY : Cambridge University Press, 2018. | Includes bibliographical references and indexes.
IDENTIFIERS: LCCN 2018034470 | ISBN 9781107184466 (hardback : alk. paper) | ISBN 9781316635728 (paperback : alk. paper)
SUBJECTS: LCSH: Plato. | Self-knowledge, Theory of.
CLASSIFICATION: LCC B398.S45 K56 2018 | DDC 184–dc23
LC record available at https://lccn.loc.gov/2018034470

ISBN 978-1-107-18446-6 Hardback

Contents

v

Contributors

SARA AHBEL-RAPPE is Professor of Greek and Latin at the University of Michigan, Ann Arbor

JAMES M. AMBURY is Assistant Professor of Philosophy at King's College, Pennsylvania

JEREMY BELL is Lecturer of Philosophy at Emory University

SARA BRILL is Professor of Philosophy and the Director of the Classical Studies Program at Fairfield University, Connecticut

ANDY GERMAN is Assistant Professor of Philosophy at Ben-Gurion University of the Negev

LLOYD P. GERSON is Professor of Philosophy at the University of Toronto

DREW A. HYLAND is Charles A. Dana Professor of Philosophy Emeritus at Trinity College, Connecticut

DANIELLE A. LAYNE is Associate Professor of Philosophy at Gonzaga University

BRIAN MARRIN is Assistant Professor in the Department of Philosophy at the University of the Andes, Colombia

MARINA MCCOY is Associate Professor of Philosophy at Boston College

ERIC SANDAY is Associate Professor of Philosophy at the University of Kentucky

HAROLD TARRANT is Professor Emeritus at the University of Newcastle, Australia, and an Honorary Associate at the University of Sydney

THOMAS TUOZZO is Professor of Philosophy at the University of Kansas

Acknowledgments

The editors offer substantial thanks to Hilary Gaskin and the wonderful staff at Cambridge University Press for their impeccable professionalism and attentiveness in bringing this volume to press and to the anonymous reviewers of the manuscript, whose comments and criticisms informed and improved every chapter. In addition, they thank their contributors and express their deep appreciation for the superb work they have produced.

Andy German extends warmest thanks to James Ambury, who made the process of working on this volume into a paradigm of what fruitful philosophical collaboration can be. He also gratefully acknowledges the unstinting support and encouragement of his philosophical home, Ben-Gurion University, and of his colleagues there, without whom this volume would have been impossible. Ben-Gurion students in a seminar on "Soul and Self-Knowledge in Plato" had to endure Andy's first attempts to work through the ideas that planted the seeds of this project, and so heartfelt thanks are due to them and, finally and above all, to his wife and children, who had to endure him.

James M. Ambury acknowledges King's College for its institutional support of this and other ongoing research. He is grateful to have had the privilege of working with and learning from Andy German, whose steadfast enthusiasm for this volume has, from its inception, been as indispensable to its production as his trenchant and insightful intellect. Mindful that the philosophical roots of this project extend back much further than the conversation with Andy over which it was originally conceived, he thanks the inimitable Kevin Thomas Miles, for inspiring in him a love of wisdom; Andrea Tschemplik, for igniting his passion for Plato; and Clyde Lee Miller, for his doctoral direction and continued faith. He also extends deep gratitude to his colleagues and dear friends; William Irwin, for his editorial guidance and good humor; and Daniel J. Issing, for his wisdom and grace. Aware too, of the lifelong bonds essential for knowing oneself, he thanks Jason Roth, Natasha Franzen, Pavan Thimmaiah, Kierstyn Sharrow, and Chi Chi Wang. Finally, he dedicates this book to his parents, James and Carol, and his brothers, Jeffrey and Matthew, for the boundless love and infinite blessings they have bestowed upon him.

Abbreviations of Platonic Dialogues

Alc. I, II   Alcibiades I, II
Ap.   Apology
Chrm.   Charmides
Clit.   Clitophon
Cra.   Cratylus
Cri.   Crito
Criti.   Critias
Ep.   Letters
Epin.   Epinomis
Euthd.   Euthydemus
Euthphr.   Euthyphro
Grg.   Gorgias
La.   Laches
Lg.   Laws
Ly.   Lysis
Men.   Meno
Phd.   Phaedo
Phdr.   Phaedrus
Phlb.   Philebus
Plt.   Statesman
Prt.   Protagoras
R.   Republic
Smp.   Symposium
Sph.   Sophist
Thg.   Theages
Tht.   Theaetetus
Ti.   Timaeus

Introduction
Self-Knowledge as Thematic Intersection

Andy German and James M. Ambury

I.1

If any evidence were needed of a revived interest in Plato's treatment of self-knowledge and self-ignorance, the Bibliography at the back of this volume should be evidence enough. Papers, monographs, and symposia on the topic are increasingly thick on the ground.[1]

It would, however, be incorrect to say that self-knowledge has only now been discovered as an important Platonic theme. This is hardly plausible when dealing with a writer whose most famous literary creation describes his entire philosophical career as an act of interrogative obedience to the Delphic imperative, γνῶθι σαυτόν.[2] What is new is the discourse to which this volume explicitly aims to contribute – an interest in the systematic significance of self-knowledge in Plato's philosophical economy and its role in how his thinking and his work stand together. Doubtless, there has been a sea change in the three decades since Julia Annas' diagnosis that Plato's interest in self-knowledge "faded" as he graduated to a more mathematical conception of ἐπιστήμη and its objects.[3]

What, though, explains this change, this new focus on self-knowledge and self-ignorance even in dialogues where they are not dominant themes, as they had been in the *Charmides* or *Alcibiades* I? There are factors internal to the dynamic of academic Plato scholarship, surely. Among these are the difficulties that have hounded all attempts at a definitive chronological ordering of the dialogues, the struggle over relative priority of argument analysis and literary treatment of dialogue form, and so on. More

---

[1] A rebirth of interest in self-knowledge has also taken place in ancient philosophy broadly speaking. For just one example, see the recent volume of Seaford et al. (2017), in which one finds essays on Plato but also on Epicureanism, the Stoics, Plotinus, and others.

[2] *Ap.* 21b3–c2 and cf. with Aristotle, *Fragmenta*, F1 (in the 3rd Ross edition) and also with the similar remarks of Olympiodorus, *In Alc.* 11.1–3.

[3] Annas (1985, 135–136).

interesting for our present purpose, however, is the connection between this renewed interest and a transformation in the wider intellectual atmosphere of the age – a certain loss of confidence in modernity's philosophical conception of itself and, indeed, of "selfhood" as such.[4]

That self-conception was expressed in various ways. For example, it could be found lurking behind the popular dichotomy between the ostensibly reflective and fully self-conscious character of modern thought and the "naïve," still uncritical, ontological realism of antiquity. Even more emphatically, it was found in the widespread conviction that modernity represented an unprecedented break with the past, or rather a decisive advance upon it, laying down a floor below which philosophical and scientific thought would not "fall" again. Faith in these verities was nourished by a sense of the irreversibility of what Habermas once referred to as the "paradigm" of subjectivity or the philosophy of consciousness, viz., the modern attribution of a foundational role to the self-conscious – and therefore self-determining – subject.[5]

The cataclysms of the twentieth century have treated this paradigm to a sound drubbing, from various directions – philosophical, linguistic, political, psychological, and even, we are repeatedly told, neurological. We are still far too close to, and implicated in, these intellectual upheavals to judge their significance properly. But at least one philosophical result has become clear: a new, chastened openness to what Plato had to say, and what he chose not to say, about that intimate, but in many ways unfathomable, phenomenon of human life: our capacity for becoming, in some problematic way, an object of our own interior reflection and assessment. It has become increasingly worth our while to ask: How exactly *did* Plato get on – how did he do justice to this phenomenon – without our modern, now-questionable, concept of subjectivity? On several counts then, internal both to Platonic scholarship and to the broader philosophical universe, we have reason to think that a conspectus of essays on self-knowledge and self-ignorance, by a variety of readers of Plato studying a variety of Platonic texts, is ἔγκαιρος – right on time.

However, it is a much harder task to figure out just what self-knowledge and self-ignorance mean for Plato, since the topography of his thinking does not necessarily match the conceptual maps we bring to it. Does

---

[4] A very welcome recent summary volume that addresses self-knowledge throughout the history of philosophy – from Homer through the medievals to Descartes and Kant and into contemporary hermeneutics and analytic philosophy – is Renz (2016). For a recent interdisciplinary study, see Rossellini (2018).
[5] See, e.g., Habermas (1992, 31–44).

self-knowledge mean knowledge of one's own idiosyncratic personality, an exhaustive inventory of our peculiar character traits, and an account of how we came to acquire them? Usually, in Plato, it does not. Then again, sometimes it does: *Philebus* 48c3–49a5, for example, discusses the Delphic command as enjoining a correct assessment of our financial, physical, and ethical endowments alongside our capacity for wisdom. Is self-knowledge the introspective awareness of our mental states? This would seem a modern, "psychological" take, thoroughly alien to the Platonic context. And yet, at *Philebus* 21c1–d1, Socrates is able to point out that feeling pleasure without the realization, or awareness, that we are feeling it would be a life fit for jellyfish or mollusks, not human beings. In the *Apology*, Socrates famously describes his mission as motivated by an awareness of his own ignorance, his knowledge that he does not know. Elsewhere, though, he knows something very specific (and supremely important) about himself and others – the erotic arts.[6]

Then there are passages from which it is clear that self-knowledge in Plato cannot finally be captured by *any* categories familiar to modern thought. In the *Phaedrus*, we can only know who we are, what kind of character we have, by relation to how much our soul was able to see of the structure of true Being, of ὄντως ὄν. As for knowing what our soul is, that turns out to be inseparable from knowing at least the nature of all soul and its ontological status, and perhaps even the nature of the whole.[7] Similarly, as the whole second half of the *Charmides* demonstrates, any reflexive knowledge we might have – whether knowledge about knowledge itself or about the soul itself – cannot ultimately be detached from the question of knowledge of the Good. All this, finally, to say nothing of the great systematic thinkers who inherit and develop the Platonic worldview, not the least of which is Proclus, for whom self-knowledge was a kind of mystic rite of initiation that pointed toward the soul's purification and its 'ascent' to the divine.[8]

Given such a multiplicity of possible senses, the task facing scholarly research is not only to articulate what self-knowledge is for Plato – a task well under way – but also to integrate self-knowledge with other themes animating the dialogues, rather than merely adding it is as one more theme alongside others. How, for example, is self-knowledge related to the hypothesis of Forms, to Plato's political thought, his purported ethical "intellectualism," the psychic tri-partition, and his teaching on eros, to take only some examples?

---

[6] *Smp.* 177d8 and *Thg.* 128b4.   [7] See *Phdr.* 270c1–2.   [8] Proclus, *In Alc.* 5.3–12.

In this regard, it will be helpful to note a peculiar feature of self-knowledge when approached in the context of Platonic thought, viz., the way it quickly reduces to nonsense all our accepted interpretative categorizations about just what kind of philosophical question it is. At *Phaedrus* 229e4–230a7, for example, Socrates laments his inability to fulfill the Delphic injunction to know himself. The specific question that demands his further study is whether he is complex in form (πολυπλοκώτερον) or a simpler (ἁπλούτερον) creature. Let us see what happens when we actually try to follow Socrates and ask that question about just one aspect of ourselves – our capacity for thinking.

As is well known, Plato portrays the relationship between the intelligible objects of thought (τὰ νοητά) and the thinking soul, using a variety of (not entirely consistent) mythical or allegorical devices. He will speak of "glimpsing" or "seeing" the Forms with the "eye" of the soul[9] (but occasionally of "grasping" or coupling with them).[10] Often the relation is described as an act that occurs suddenly, in a moment of complete psychic transformation.[11] Elsewhere, however, the emphasis will be on a *discursive* relation to the Forms, or to the Good, which become accessible to "logos itself" via the power of "dialectic," an experience that is also likened to a prolonged battle.[12]

The nature of our thinking power would seem to be different in each of these two cases. In the first case, knowledge is not a propositional state in which we hold a correct belief which is about – which refers to – a known object. Rather, it is the *presence* of the known object to, or in, a soul having a structure so constituted as to be open and receptive to being absorbed in a nonperspectival view of that object.[13] Knowing is an event that happens to a soul, and *in* a soul, via its assimilation to the known object, the Form. By contrast, where the emphasis is on logos and διάνοια, thinking and the soul in which it happens must be different. Observe Socrates' description of thinking, διανοεῖσθαι, at *Theaetetus* 189e6–190a6, as:

> A speech which the soul goes through – by itself, before itself – about whatever it is examining. As one who does not know, of course, I'm declaring it to you. Soul thinking looks to me as nothing else than conversing, itself asking and answering itself and affirming and denying. But whenever it has come to a determination, regardless of whether its sally was on the slow or the keen side, and then asserts the same thing and does

---

[9] *Men.* 81c6, *Smp.* 210e4, *R.* VII.519c10–d1, *Phdr.* 247c1. [10] *R.* VI.490b5.
[11] *R.* VII.521c5–8. [12] *R.* VI.511b2–c2. and VII.534b8–d1. Cf. with *Phdr.* 249b6–c5.
[13] See the description of the Idea of the Beautiful as not perspectivally determined in any way at *Smp.* 210e6–211b2. And see *R.* IX.586a4–5 on being "filled with being."

not stand apart in doubt, we set this down as opinion. Consequently, I, for one, call opining speaking, and opinion a stated speech; it is not, however, before someone else any more than it is with sound, but in silence before oneself. [trans. Benardete with emendations][14]

In the exercise of its discursive function, soul cannot be (or cannot *only* be) a self-effacing receptivity, and it certainly cannot be simple, since it involves an active capacity for becoming present to itself (notice the emphasis on πρὸς αὐτὴν and πρὸς αὐτόν – "before itself" at e6 and a6), for inhabiting both poles of the dialogic relation simultaneously. Soul both questions and answers itself.[15]

Which is it then? Is thinking a pure, receptive vision in which the soul assimilates to its object or a reflective, and thus internally differentiated, discursive process through which the soul must pass in order to close again with itself in the act of opining (δοξάζειν)? Obviously, it must somehow be both. In order for our judgments to be knowledgeable, there must be some moment of openness to the structure of the world that judgments are *about*. This is a necessity. Otherwise, our soul when thinking will resemble the driver sitting in his car on a hydraulic lift in the repair shop, engine revving and wheels busily spinning – but going nowhere.

At the same time, however, this receptivity must be an active one. It must be at work understanding and articulating what it has received. And this too is a necessity since while the act of νόησις may be an identification of the soul with its intelligible thought object, the human being taken as a whole is, in the final analysis, *not* identical to intelligible structure but separated from it. Because of this separation, human life is a perpetual, and frequently unsuccessful, effort to understand that structure and act in light of such understanding.

As we can see, to articulate the powers of thought and judgment demands an exceedingly subtle theoretical examination both of the soul itself and of those objects that it thinks and judges. But the theoretical quickly spills over into the practical when we recall that judgment (and the self-presence which it implies) is the medium of action as well – since the

---

[14] λόγον ὃν αὐτὴ πρὸς αὑτὴν ἡ ψυχὴ διεξέρχεται περὶ ὧν ἂν σκοπῇ. ὥς γε μὴ εἰδώς σοι ἀποφαίνομαι. τοῦτο γάρ μοι ἰνδάλλεται διανοουμένη οὐκ ἄλλο τι ἢ διαλέγεσθαι, αὐτὴ ἑαυτὴν ἐρωτῶσα καὶ ἀποκρινομένη, καὶ φάσκουσα καὶ οὐ φάσκουσα. ὅταν δὲ ὁρίσασα, εἴτε βραδύτερον εἴτε καὶ ὀξύτερον ἐπάξασα, τὸ αὐτὸ ἤδη φῇκαὶ μὴ διστάζῃ, δόξαν ταύτην τίθεμεν αὐτῆς. ὥστ' ἔγωγε τὸ δοξάζειν λέγειν καλῶ καὶ τὴν δόξαν λόγον εἰρημένον, οὐ μέντοι πρὸς ἄλλον οὐδὲ φωνῇ, ἀλλὰ σιγῇ πρὸς αὐτόν:

[15] Cf. *Sph.* 263e4 and 264a9–b1.

soul must split in two and discourse with itself about what is good and choice-worthy before choosing.

The Platonic distinction between νοῦς and διάνοια is recondite stuff, no doubt, but it is an irreducible aspect of the ways in which the self relates to its objects, whatever their nature. Note, then, how the attempt to understand it quickly leads to questions that we today would seek to file away neatly under "metaphysical," "epistemological," and "practical" (or ethical). Here, then, is that abovementioned, peculiarly liminal, character of self-knowledge. It is by virtue of the fact that every philosophical examination in the dialogues inescapably encounters ψυχή and its capacities that self-knowledge most resembles an intersection. Through this intersection, the various elements of Platonic thought must pass in order to relate to one another in some comprehensible fashion. This will explain why, though more explicit in certain dialogues than others, self-knowledge constitutes an integral element of Platonic philosophy broadly construed and so appears throughout almost the whole Platonic corpus. It can be found regardless of the individual dialogue's main theme, its date of composition, its dramatic placement, or its position in the reader's preferred paradigm for interpreting Plato – unitarian, developmentalist, or neither of these two alternatives.

Form, for example, is certainly one of the most famous, though obscure, of those Platonic "elements." Now, however its mode of being is finally to be understood, it must be such that we, as beings who are thinkers and also practical agents, can actually know it. After all, our interaction with Forms, and specifically Forms like Good and Beautiful, is the sine qua non for the possibility of deliberate choice, and thus for the whole realm of praxis. Without it, as Aristotle might say, all praxis would be μάταιος, empty.[16] Accordingly, any attempt to work out the philosophical implications of the hypothesis about form will have to do so in a way that successfully relates it to what we know about ourselves as beings who must choose and act.

Another example: Where are we to locate the real, beating heart of a Platonic work, in its argument or its action? After long years of pitched battles between partisans of one interpretative stance or another, the growing consensus is: in both of them. However, this tells us very little since there is markedly less consensus on the operative details. What is clear is that any answer to this question will involve some answer to the question of what the dialogues are meant to do; that is, how they are meant to affect their audience. And this latter question will, before long, involve

---

[16] Aristotle, *EN,* I, ii, 1094a18–21.

us in the nature of self-knowledge. To see why, we can begin from the relatively uncontroversial, even abstract, assertion that the dialogues were presumably written in order to have a pedagogic effect of some kind. But since such a written dialogue, just like a spoken one, is a logos sent from one soul to another (to borrow Socrates' imagery in *Alcibiades* I),[17] we will not understand how argument and action work together without teasing out some sense of Plato's view about what makes the soul educable at all. But to say that the soul is educable is to say that it naturally wants to be educated, is naturally "dissatisfied" with not knowing. And to understand *that*, we will need to study the dialogues' portrayal of our ability to look into ourselves, note our lack of knowledge, and then be motivated by this lack. Any hope of progress in assessing which tools educate best for which ends passes, once again, through the territory of knowledge and ignorance of the self.

One could easily go on multiplying examples here, but the point is clear enough in its essentials. Properly mapping how self-knowledge relates to all the main themes raised by Platonic dialogues – and not only to those puzzles which our contemporary, very different, conceptual paradigms make us assume are salient – is indispensable to making Plato's thought visible in its sharpest resolution and fullest coherence. Each of the contributions in this volume aims to point, in its own way, down various interpretative highways where such fruitful cartographical work is yet to be done. It is work that can forge interpretive links and theoretical alliances between scholars who otherwise pursue seemingly divergent research agendas on the philosophical corpus of a single thinker, but also promises to have a philosophical impact well beyond the confines of Platonic scholarship.

I.2

Despite the centrality of self-knowledge in Plato's thought, there are surprisingly few books dedicated explicitly to the topic, while those that are extant are instructive but also not exhaustive. Ballard's monograph on self-knowledge, for example, exhibits a masterful command of the topic but is outdated and cannot account for scholarship published in the past fifty years.[18] Griswold's now classic meditation on self-knowledge in the *Phaedrus* restricts its principal commentary to one dialogue, as does Tschemplik's provocative work on self-knowledge in the *Theaetetus*.[19]

---

[17] *Alc.* I 130e2–6.   [18] Ballard (1965).   [19] Griswold (1986), Tschemplik (2008).

Moore's very welcome recent study follows the topic of self-knowledge as it appears not just in the Platonic *Charmides*, *Alcibiades*, *Phaedrus*, and *Philebus*, but in other ancient sources well. However, it concentrates on this theme exclusively as it relates to the figure of Socrates himself.[20] In assembling the present volume, the editors have solicited chapters that are informed by these important works but assimilate and expand on their insights.

The motivating principle behind the contents of this volume is not methodological approach – analytic, continental, or historical – but topical diversity. This, we hope, enables the reader to grasp the axial location of self-knowledge in Platonic philosophy regardless of hermeneutical presupposition or exegetical prejudice. Indeed, the links *between* chapters starting from very different interpretative principles demonstrate productive ways in which self-knowledge might play that integrative role in future research on Plato which we mentioned earlier, uniting otherwise fragmented threads of scholarship.

The volume's contributors address themselves to nearly every major Platonic dialogue, ranging from the Socratic or so-called "early" dialogues like the *Apology* through 'middle' dialogues like the *Republic* to dialogues as 'late' as the *Laws*. That self-knowledge is indispensable not just for Plato himself but for Platonic philosophy more broadly is clear from its presence in dialogues of dubious authenticity (such as the *Theages* and *Alcibiades* I), in spurious dialogues of which Plato is likely not the author but that are nonetheless Platonic in their philosophical sensibility (the *Alcibiades* II), and in the work of Plato's philosophical heirs, from the Old Academy through Middle Platonism to Plotinus and into the Neoplatonism of late antiquity. The chapters develop analyses of self-knowledge across this variegated panoply of Platonic material.

The opening group of five chapters center thematically around the theme of self-knowledge and contemplative knowledge (θεωρία). In Chapter 1, "Self-Knowledge and the Good," Lloyd P. Gerson argues that self-knowledge is best understood as knowledge of self, but this means that such knowledge is knowledge of intellect since intellect is the truest human self. Tracking various arguments in the *Republic* and *Phaedo* with insights resonating with Neoplatonic overtones, Gerson argues that self-knowledge in Platonic philosophy cannot be understood without also inquiring into what is good for ourselves and, in the end, the Good as such. Self-knowledge, Gerson claims, is knowledge not merely of our occurrent

---

[20] Moore (2015a).

subjective states but of the ideal self that is most really real, which requires our consorting with the intelligible world and the uppermost principle in that world. However, pursuing this link between self and intelligibility to the utmost reveals an identity relation: the wisdom sought by philosophy as such just *is* self-knowledge, for self-knowledge is ultimately knowledge of the Good.

In Chapter 2, "Two Faces of Platonic Self-Knowledge: *Alcibiades* I and *Charmides*," Thomas Tuozzo subsequently develops this connection between self-knowledge and knowledge of the Good. Tuozzo argues that both dialogues reveal, in different ways, self-knowledge as a kind of knowing possessing two essential elements. First, it is a kind of self-knowing knowledge that, qua reflexive, also entails a knowledge of one's own good. Second, self-knowledge is a kind of knowledge of other "knowledges" (ἐπιστῆμαι) or crafts. This second element is neither an empty knowledge that knows merely *that* other knowledges are in fact knowledge nor a kind of super knowledge that includes all others. Rather, it is a knowing *how* to use the objects of other knowledges in ways that benefit one's soul, which ultimately involves relating one's private good to the Good itself. The picture of self-knowledge in these two dialogues, Tuozzo shows, coincides in ways that are perhaps not immediately obvious but nonetheless prevalent.

Reading the *Charmides* but reaching different conclusions, Chapter 3, "Socratic Self-Knowledge and the Limits of *Epistēmē*," by Drew A. Hyland articulates how, while one definition of self-knowledge ('knowledge of itself and other knowledges and the absence of knowledge') is refuted, another definition, closer to the sort of wisdom we find in the *Apology*, remains unrefuted in the dialogue (self-knowledge as a knowledge of what one knows and does not know). Hyland locates the presence of this notion of self-knowledge in the opening pages of the *Charmides*, only to insist that it promptly vanishes with the emergence of Critias as Socrates' principal interlocutor. For Hyland, contra Gerson and even Tuozzo to some degree, self-knowledge is *not* theoretical knowledge. It is not something achieved once and for all, but the ongoing challenge of the philosophical life itself. It cannot be asserted propositionally but rather must be *lived* by adopting an aporetic stance that never ceases to question.

The *Apology* also provides the starting point for Sara Ahbel-Rappe, who in Chapter 4, "Socratic Wisdom and Platonic Knowledge in the Dialogues of Plato," interprets the oracle's insistence that 'no one is wiser than Socrates' and refigures it into the claim that the character of the Platonic Socrates himself represents the highest kind of wisdom. Self-knowledge is theoretical then, but in a thoroughly unexpected way. The wisdom of self-knowledge is not so much the equivalent of a constructive epistemology, moral philosophy, or psychology as it is their presupposition and medium. Incorporating insights found in diverse dialogues, from the *Laches* to the *Crito* and the *Charmides* to the *Parmenides* and *Theaetetus*, Rappe argues that Socratic wisdom, insofar as it transmits self-knowledge, is the "container" within which Plato himself constructs his own specific philosophical views on metaphysical, epistemological, and moral questions. Self-knowledge here is only accessed through self-inquiry, and only by actually assuming this inquiring stance ourselves can we as readers meet the Socrates in our own minds. Accordingly, Rappe's chapter is an innovative and provocative reading that situates Socratic self-knowledge at the very heart of philosophy itself. This centrality, a profound truth for Plato, must be actively reappropriated by anyone who wants not just to read a Platonic dialogue, but to philosophize actively while reading it.

Following Rappe, James M. Ambury sheds further light on the way self-knowledge and theoretical knowledge are intimately related. In Chapter 5, "Between Ascent and Descent: Self-Knowledge and Plato's Allegory of the Cave," Ambury concludes the opening focus on θεωρία with a close reading of Plato's most famous image. Instead of concentrating solely on the shadow-like objects of the prisoner's perception and cognition, which is the common scholarly focus, Ambury turns our attention to the psychic changes undergone by the prisoner himself and thus detects a crucial, but heretofore unexamined, emphasis on self-knowledge. According to Ambury, there are four distinct types of self-knowledge at work in the allegory, each of which corresponds to a section of the divided line. Following Rappe, Ambury's chapter illuminates the way self-knowledge and knowledge are intimately related in Plato at the same time as it looks forward – by way of considering Socrates' insistence that the philosopher return to the cave – to the practical dimensions of self-knowledge.

The next three chapters take up this applied aspect of self-knowledge more concretely. In Chapter 6, "Self-Knowledge and the Use of the Self in the Platonic *Theages*," Brian Marrin clearly illustrates the shift from theory to practice. The purpose of the *Theages*, he argues, is to identify the question of the knowledge and 'use' of the self as the essential beginning of philosophical education. Following the use of the self as his guiding thread, Marrin demonstrates the way in which the dialogue offers not a discursive account but rather a dramatic *enactment* of the maieutic attitude Socrates thinks we ought to take toward philosophy and philosophical education. In their brief conversation, Marrin insists, Socrates attempts to exhort Theages to recreate within and toward himself the very maieutic relation that obtains between Socrates and his interlocutors. As such, the *Theages* provides its reader with a kind of drama of self-knowledge that is protreptic to the philosophical life.

Picking up the theme of life or βίος, Sara Brill carries forward the practical emphasis on self-knowledge and adds to it a particularly political coloration in Chapter 7, "Between Biography and Biology: *Bios* and Self-Knowledge in Plato's *Phaedrus*." Beginning with the *Republic* before transitioning to the *Phaedrus*, Brill focuses on the role played by the concept of a 'pattern of life' (βίων παραδείγμα). This concept specifies the narrative structure in life and embodies an understanding of βίος that lies between a historical account of a series of events and a claim to a kind of inner necessity at work in those events. For Brill, what we learn about someone when we know their βίος is not a mere chronology of events, but rather their proximity to truth, and the contribution of the *Phaedrus* to our understanding of Platonic self-knowledge lies in its emphasis on the generative power of truth itself. Knowing oneself is knowing that one's being derives from an orientation toward the truth, and while this orientation may be obscured, it is nevertheless present in any life that can be properly called human.

In Chapter 8, "A Toil-Loving Soul," Jeremy Bell articulates how Plato equates the good life with activity of the soul and the bad life with its opposite, an equivalence we may track alongside the tropes of wakefulness and sleep. While wakefulness is indicative of both self-knowledge and the good life – a life involving recognition that the relation to Being (especially the being of the virtues) is constitutive of the human soul – sleep serves as a metonym for the self-forgetful life that Plato regularly likens to death. Bell addresses the way in which Plato appropriates these contrasting themes from the rich Greek heritage of writers before him – including the three great tragedians, along with Homer, Hesiod, Pindar, and Hippocrates – and transfigures them in dialogues ranging from the *Apology* to the *Republic* and the *Laws*, not to mention the *Theaetetus*, *Statesman*, *Timaeus*, *Phaedo*, and *Meno*. His chapter concludes with an analysis of the Platonic tyrant who, haunted by a complete lack of self-knowledge, is the paradigmatic embodiment of sleep and death, never awakening to the profound depth of his own self-ignorance.

Bell's chapter thus points to the relation between self-knowledge and ignorance, which is an organizing focus of the next three chapters. Andy German takes up this theme in Chapter 9, "Mathematical Self-Ignorance and Sophistry: Theodorus and Protagoras." German's reading of the

Theaetetus and *Republic* treats the seemingly opposed, or rather unrelated, endeavors of mathematics and sophistry that Plato juxtaposes in the *Theaetetus* through the characters of Protagoras and Theodorus. By way of this juxtaposition, he argues, Plato illuminates for us a kind of self-ignorance that can be lodged at the heart of his conception of education as περιαγωγή, the whirling psychological revolution that culminates in dialectic. Theodorus is evidence that, while mathematics may lead the soul upward to the realm of intelligible being, this should not obscure the fact that it might just as easily lead the soul downward, with the danger of sophistry lurking as a distinct possibility. The problem, argues German, is that mathematical knowledge, in and of itself, cannot grasp itself as an expression of logos, or rationality more broadly and correctly construed. Only by coming to know itself, that is, knowing its place as part of a more encompassing intelligible whole, will mathematics realize that its peculiar mode of being is not self-explanatory since it is constituted by the activity of a principle that transcends it. Self-knowledge, therefore, is the ingredient that transmutes the mathematical sciences into dialectic.

The productive link between self-knowledge and ignorance is further explored by Marina McCoy in Chapter 10, "Why Is Knowledge of Ignorance Good?" McCoy argues that Socrates advocates knowledge of one's ignorance for two principal reasons. First, it is an epistemic virtue that leads to progress in inquiry. This is the more well-known reason for Socrates' advocacy. However, though certainly epistemic in character, McCoy is quick to point out that the aporia that follows from knowledge of ignorance must be accompanied by an appropriate existential sense of the self as limited, without which no epistemological progress can occur. Second, knowledge of ignorance allows one to act more virtuously in concrete circumstances. Extending her analysis from the *Apology* to the *Meno*, McCoy shows how Socratic wisdom entails a response of care for others, something of which Meno is incapable despite having made some (albeit limited) epistemological progress in his definitions of virtue. McCoy demonstrates how one's own lived understanding of the Delphic imperative necessarily involves recognizing, and cultivating engagement with, the affective and emotional responses of one's refuted interlocutor.

Eric Sanday develops the importance of intersubjectivity in a different way in Chapter 11, "Self-Knowledge in Plato's *Symposium*." Sanday highlights the tension that obtains between the soul in its theoretical activity, qua abstract subject of a purely "object-oriented" cognition of form, and the soul in our embodied life, characterized by an interpersonal awareness of our own finitude. The work of satisfying the demands of both poles of human existence, Sanday argues, constitutes the fundamental ambiguity of the philosophical life and the fundamental task of self-knowledge. Sanday traces the tension as it manifests itself in the speeches of Socrates and Alcibiades and argues that, far from eradicating this tension, the *Symposium* urges us to live it, endure it, and express it. Alcibiades himself serves as a paradigm for one characteristic way in which such a life may be refused and illustrates the disastrous consequences for those who would follow his approach. Sanday also traces this sort of decentering evasion as it emerges in Hesiod's *Theogony*, most notably in Zeus' internalization of the feminine deities. The *Symposium*, Sanday argues, is both a kind of warning for human beings about how not to live a self-ignorant or self-evasive life and a philosophical recapitulation of the Delphic command which reveals just how demanding it is.

Eros also figures prominently in Chapter 12 by Danielle A. Layne, "Double Ignorance and the Perversion of Self-Knowledge," which distinguishes awareness of one's ignorance, or 'simple' ignorance, from ignorance of that ignorance, or 'double' ignorance. Layne illustrates how Plato is careful to show that self-ignorance and its corresponding pretense to knowledge isolates the interlocutor in a world of illusions at the same time as it alienates her from herself and others. Spanning dialogues that include, among others, the *Sophist, Statesman*, and *Philebus*, Layne treats the erotics of both double and simple ignorance. The flight from recognition of ignorance that we find in the former, Layne insists, is not merely epistemological but entails a failure to love oneself and others in their erotic complexity. On the other hand, the embrace of ignorance we find in the latter results in a love of self and other as what they are – erotic and ambiguous souls who could just as easily be typhonic monsters as they could be divine beings.

As noted earlier, while the presence of self-knowledge spans nearly the entire Platonic corpus, Plato's thinking about it was not stagnant. This is the subject of Chapter 13, "*Philebus, Laws* and Self-Ignorance," by Harold Tarrant. In this final chapter, the author addresses the way in which Plato's treatment of self-knowledge in the late dialogues ought to impact our views on the placement and authenticity of the *Alcibiades* I. While this dialogue identifies self-knowledge as knowledge of soul, a dialogue such as the *Philebus* seems far more concerned with self-*ignorance* than it does with knowledge of soul. Indeed, the threefold division of self-ignorance in this later dialogue actually seems to render problematic the exclusive equivalence of self-knowledge with knowledge of soul. Tarrant argues that there is nothing in the *Alcibiades* I that would suggest a theoretical affinity between it and the hiatus-avoiding dialogues such as the *Sophist, States-man, Timaeus, Critias, Philebus, Laws,* and the *Clitophon* (if it is indeed by Plato). These dialogues, he claims, are actually more in tune with the views of the *Alcibiades* II than the *Alcibiades* I. Generally, Tarrant argues, the later dialogues signal a fundamental shift in Plato's thinking on self-knowledge. Whereas earlier dialogues contained a positive doctrine of self-knowledge – which entails a deep awareness of the core of human being that is the ground of virtuous life – the later dialogues give self-knowledge a predominantly negative valence; i.e., it is a condition of freedom from false convictions and their accompanying, mistaken belief that one knows.

No doubt, this volume leaves its readers with a plurality of views about the knowledge and ignorance of self in Platonic philosophy, some of which are directly opposed to one another. For students of Plato's Socrates, however, such oppositions are pure profit. It was Socrates, after all, who assured Glaucon during their mutual search for a definition of justice that when one rubs together different, and seemingly incompat-ible, accounts of a thing fire may result – and with it, light.[21] It is with this aspiration, and in a like spirit, that the present volume was conceived and is now presented to the reading public – specialists and philosophically inclined generalists alike.

[21] *R.* IV.434e3–435a3.

CHAPTER I

Self-Knowledge and the Good

Lloyd P. Gerson

I.I

All human beings desire that which is good for themselves. Nevertheless, the old saying, "he doesn't know what is good for himself," expresses the obvious fact that we are not always, and are never infallible, judges of what our own good is. But the problem or challenge of discovering what my own good is is logically connected to the determination or discovery of that to which "my" refers. Most people do not find this problematic. Plato frequently appeals to the commonplace that human goods are classifiable according to whether they are external possessions, such as wealth, or bodily goods such as health and beauty, or psychical goods such as knowledge or virtue. Yet the fact that we are not infallible judges of our own good is, at least in part, owing to the fact that goods in one of the above "categories" sometimes conflict with goods in another. For example, the attainment of the good of bodily health may not be simultaneously possible with the attainment of the good of virtuous behavior. It is in the face of such conflicts that the question of the identity of the subject seeking the good is most obviously pressing. It is not even clear what method or methods are available for resolving such conflicts. Admittedly, a conflict between the attainment of an external good and the attainment of one of the other goods has a solution that can rely on a purely logical point. This is that the good that is a possession would seem to necessarily cede priority to the good of the possessor. Even here, though, it is arguable that risking the latter for the former is not necessarily an incoherent strategy. Someone who risks his life diving in treacherous waters for sunken treasure is hardly being irrational, even if it turns out he is wrong about the likelihood of his not being harmed or killed. Or at least so we might infer from the science of risk management assessment.

Such conflicts, however, pale in comparison with those concerning bodily goods and psychical goods. For in these cases, it would seem that the subject who pursues and attains a bodily good such as health is the same as the subject who pursues and attains a psychical good. On what possible grounds could one decide to privilege one good over another, especially in those cases where they conflict? Moreover, part of what makes a psychical good, like virtue, good is that it can consist in the good, including the physical good, of another. Resolving one's conflict between the pursuit of a physical good and a psychical good often includes the challenge of "weighing" one's own clear good, such as health, against the good of another. Suppose, for example, that one determines to pursue health over virtue. In the case where the rejection of virtuous behavior entails that something bad occur for someone else, the choice of the bodily over the psychical assumes that what is bad for someone else can be distinguished from what is bad for oneself. For one who chooses the bodily over the psychical does *not* think that this is bad for oneself; he thinks only that the attainment of the bodily good is better than the attainment of the psychical good.

In this chapter, I shall try to show that Plato views the problem of the discovery of one's own good, in the light of the fact that this is what all human beings pursue, as inseparable from the discovery of the subject or self whose good is attained. More specifically, the discovery of the self is a process of separating merely apparent subjects from the true one. And with this discovery, the question of whether it is possible for one to attain one's own true good at the expense of anyone else is answered. In fact, one's own true good is not only objective – meaning only that one's belief about what this is is not infallible – but it is universal as well. Thus, it is not possible to attain it at the expense of anyone else, no more than it is possible to attain the correct answer to a mathematical question that is not the true answer for everyone else. The objectivity of good would be adequately accounted for – in Platonic terms – by a Form of Good, but the universality of good can only be accounted for by a superordinate Idea of the Good, a principle not only of goodness but of being as well.[1] So, it turns out that the pursuit of self-knowledge is only achieved with the awareness of a metaphysical truth, namely, that the first principle of all is the Idea of the Good. An indication that one has not achieved self-knowledge would be the presence of any residual doubt about this metaphysical truth.

---

[1] See my "Ideas of Good?" (Gerson, 2015) where I explain Proclus' interpretation of the texts where Plato posits a Form of the Good coordinated with other Forms and distinct from a superordinate Idea of the Good. Independently of Proclus, I provide supporting philosophical considerations for this interpretation as well.

Suppose that one is faced with a choice among goods. Desiring that which is one's true good from among these, one has to discover one's true self. Whereas one can pretend to try to adjudicate among goods, the unique, absolutely simple Idea of the Good is, among other things, the true good. Hence, it cannot be opposed by *another* good. Understanding this amounts to understanding that there is, logically, no sense in trying to adjudicate between the achievement of this and the achievement of any other good. But as it will turn out, the achievement of the Good consists in comprehensive knowledge of intelligible reality. Such knowledge amounts to cognitive identity with intelligible reality. In the self-reflexive knowledge of that, one knows exactly what one's true self is.

1.2

The subject of desires and intellectual acts broadly speaking is generated along with psychical states themselves. For example, one discovers that one is hungry and at that moment the subject who is hungry is generated; one discovers that, in the midst of some practical situation, one has a belief about what to do, and the subject of that belief is generated. By using the word "generated" I mean to emphasize the concreteness of the subject and its distinction from a more abstract or even theoretical subject. There are no desires or beliefs without a subject for these, just as there are no desires or beliefs without intentional objects, a point to which I shall return below. The subject does not exist unless or until the state exists. Both the subject and the intentional object are generated at the moment (or very nearly at the moment) when the state is generated. And when the desire is satisfied or the occurrent belief is no more, then their subjects disappear. Thus, terms for subjects such as "I" and "my" are indexicals. That is, they are purely contextual.

This does not, of course, mean that there are no dispositional desires or beliefs; it means only that if these, too, must have a subject, that subject is not obviously identical with the subject of the occurrent desires and beliefs. For if they were identical, normative appeals would be impossible. That is, if the subject of a dispositional desire were identical with the subject of an occurrent desire, there could be no sense in appealing to someone's *other* desires or beliefs not to satisfy that desire; indeed, there would be no possibility for one to resist one's own desire. For such an appeal would, presumably, be made to what is in one's true interest or what one really desires. But if that subject is just the subject of the occurrent desire, such an appeal could only be to a hypothetical subject of a future occurrent desire, not to the real subject of that which is the dispositional desire. It would not even make sense to appeal to a future subject of an occurrent desire since that subject is functionally related to the state in which it finds itself. To say that one should not have the desire that one has is to assume that such an exhortation is to a subject other than the subject of the desire, assuming, of course, that those putative desires are for one's own good. Similarly, that one believes that one should not satisfy one's own desire is to appeal to a subject other than the subject of that desire. But this subject can only be other than the subject of the occurrent desire. It must also, in some sense, be identical with a subject not unrelated to the subject of the desire; otherwise, the phenomenon of weakness of the will would not exist. If one can desire to take drugs and also desire not to have the desire to take the drugs, then the subject of the original desire cannot be unequivocally identical with the subject.

If self-knowledge were knowledge of the subject of an occurrent desire or belief, then self-knowledge would be the easiest thing in the world to attain. Acquiring self-knowledge would entail nothing more than awareness of occurrent desires. Yet the self-knowledge that is supposed to be particularly valuable and hard to come by must be knowledge of a self that is other than the subject of an occurrent desire or belief. How is such self-knowledge to be attained? In *Republic*, Plato pursues a complex strategy on behalf of his account of how self-knowledge is to be attained. I shall first sketch the strategy and then fill in the details.

The central challenge set for Socrates by Adeimantus is to show that justice is better than injustice not merely "in itself" but also for "what it does" (τι ποιοῦσα) to the one who is just.[2] The first part of the response to this challenge is completed by the end of Book IV; justice is psychical health and, like physical health, justice is, therefore, intrinsically desirable, all other things being equal. But at this point we are not even halfway through *Republic*. In fact, the entirety of the remainder of the work is devoted to showing the effects of justice and injustice on those so characterized. The words "what it does" are clearly extremely broad in scope, and even include, in Book X, effects in the afterlife. As it turns out, however, by the time an answer to the second part of the challenge is given, in Books IX and X, the one who is just or unjust is a philosopher, not an ordinary person. Thus, being psychically healthy, where each part of the soul does its own job, is not a state restricted to philosophers. Indeed, the nature of philosophy and philosophers is not even introduced into the discussion

---

[2] *R.* II.367e1–4.

until Book V. So, it appears that a philosopher is the one who is led to believe that there is no circumstance in which being unjust could ever have effects superior to the effects of being just. And this is because the philosopher is one who has identified his good with the good of the "inner human being" (ὁ ἐντὸς ἄνθρωπος).³ And this is as much as to say that he has identified *himself* with the "inner human being."

Clearly, the inner human being cannot be the soul in its embodied entirety since the only other component of the ordinary human being would be the body, which, without a psychical subject, could be in charge of nothing; such a soulless lump would be a corpse. The inner human being must be the rational faculty or intellect. But if what is meant by the rational faculty (τὸ λογιστικόν) is what is meant in Book IV, namely, the faculty that rules over the whole human being for the sake of the whole human being, then it is not at all clear how one would have a basis for identification with *that*. For this rational faculty is explicitly introduced as instrumental to human happiness, which is, therefore, different from the faculty's own good. If, on the other hand, what is meant by the "inner human being" is the theoretical intellect engaged in non-instrumental activity, then a seemingly insurmountable problem arises. For on the assumption that the real identity of the person is the theoretical intellect, someone being exhorted to pursue philosophy and so to discover this identity is being exhorted to become something other than he manifestly is. For the appeal to the philosophical life is being made to one who is not a philosopher and therefore will, presumably, view theoretical activity as, at best, instrumental to his happiness. That is, if one is exhorted to abandon material possessions or physical goods or at least to disvalue them in favor of purely psychical goods – specifically the good of theoretical activity – the appeal is being made to someone who can only view this putative good alongside others. And *his* choice from among them will necessarily be a choice of what is good for the subject that is other than the subject of intellectual or theoretical activity.

It is perhaps legitimate to object that Plato does not assume that philosophy is for everyone and that, indeed, philosophers are made out of those with philosophical natures. Yet it is highly implausible, I think, that a "philosophical temperament" – whatever exactly that amounts to – is sufficient to enable one to adjudicate among proposals regarding personal identity from a standpoint other than that which is distinct from the present proposal, namely, that one's true identity is nothing but that of an

---

³ *R.* IX.589a7–b1.

intellect. The proposal to see one's own identity as "identity with my intellect" could only result in this possibility being considered alongside others as candidates for the subject whose happiness is being sought. But then that subject will be the subject of a nonoccurrent or dispositional state, not of the occurrent state of the assessor. How one can opt for a good of a subject that is, by definition, different from the subject who is considering the matter remains a mystery.

The process of identification of the philosophically disposed nature begins to be hinted at in Book VI. Socrates describes the nature of these persons in this way:

> For surely, Adeimantus, someone who has truly directed his thinking to the things that really are does not have the leisure to look down at human affairs and be filled with grudging and hatred as a result of entering into their disputes. Instead, looking at things that are orderly and eternally identical, things that neither do injustice to, nor suffer injustice from, each other, being eternally in order and existing according to reason, he imitates them, and tries to assimilate himself to them as much as is possible. Or do you think there is some device whereby one who desires to associate with these does not imitate them? (Reeve trans. slightly modified)[4]

This passage makes an extraordinary claim when taken at face value. The philosopher longs to assimilate himself to Forms. This assimilation consists in, or at least involves, imitation of Forms. Perhaps the most common way to take this passage is to interpret it to mean that the philosopher assimilates himself to Forms by instantiating them. So, he assimilates himself to the Form of Justice by becoming just. And, indeed, one might well take the famous passage in *Theaetetus* in this way.[5] But even if the practice of the virtues assists one in assimilation to the Forms, it cannot be what the assimilation here consists in. For it has already been established in Book IV that a just person is one in whom reason rules for the sake of the entire soul, and there is nothing in such a person that indicates that he has any interest in philosophy or in contemplation. Second, being just in one's soul may well amount to an imitation of the Form of Justice, but it cannot be what being assimilated to (or "being made the same as") this Form is. For although an instance is the same as Justice insofar as it does not admit of its opposite, the *bearer* of that instance is not thereby made the same as the Form.[6] In no sense is the human being made the same as the eternal Form of Justice by being just. Even the qualifying words "as much as is

---

[4] *R.* VI.500b8–c7.   [5] See *Tht.* 176b1–2: φυγὴ δὲ ὁμοίωσις θεῷ κατὰ τὸ δυνατόν.
[6] See *Phd.* 102d6–8.

possible" do not suggest this. For the practice of justice in this world has no implications whatsoever for longevity, much less for eternity. Indeed, assimilation to the divine by the practice of justice is problematic since the divine is not where the practice of the virtues is to be found. The immortal gods, for example, do not *need* courage. Nevertheless, this fact does not require us to reject the idea that the practice of the virtues does contribute to the desired assimilation. They are at best instrumental, however not constitutive of it.

The correct interpretation of this passage, I believe, is this. In knowing the Form of Justice or any other Form, one becomes "informed" with the object of knowledge. If we recall the *Phaedo*, it is shown in the so-called Affinity Argument that, given that we do have knowledge of Forms, we could not have this knowledge unless we were, like Forms, immaterial entities.[7] The immaterial entity, of course, is not the human being, but the soul, and in particular, the "immortal part" of the soul. The assimilation to the Form is a literal making of something to be the same as something else because the intellect or rational part of the soul is already made of the same "stuff" as the Forms, but in knowing them is made to be identical with them, that is, cognitively identical. The concept of cognitive identity has three components: (1) identity with the nature or essence cognized, (2) awareness of this identity, and (3) identification of the subject of (1) with the subject of (2). The philosopher discovers his true identity when he discovers that he is the subject engaged in contemplation. The "content" of that identity just is the array of intelligible entities that he knows.

Given the above, we are now in a better position to appreciate the decisive turn in the argument in Book VI, which consists in the "longer road" of metaphysical exposition. Socrates says:

> You have often heard it said that the Idea of the Good is the most important study, and that it is by their relation to it that just things and the rest become useful or beneficial. And now you must be pretty certain that that is what I am going to say, and, in addition, that we have no adequate knowledge of it. And if we do not know it, you know that even the fullest possible knowledge of other things is of no benefit to us, any more than if we acquire any possession without the Good. Or do you think there is any benefit in possessing everything but the Good? Or to know everything without knowing the Good, thereby knowing nothing beautiful or good? (Reeve trans. slightly modified)[8]

---

[7] See *Phd.* 78b4–84b4.   [8] *R.* VI.504e6–505b3.

There are two points in this passage in particular, on which we need to focus. First, it is by relation to the Idea of the Good that just things are useful or beneficial. Here is an explicit link between the central principle of Plato's metaphysics and the solution to the problem of how it can be shown that being just has beneficial effects. Second, without knowing this Idea, the knowledge of other things is of no benefit. We recall that in Book IV, justice is defined as each part of the soul performing its own job and wisdom as the rational faculty of the soul knowing what is good for the whole soul.[9] So, it turns out that knowing what is good for the whole soul is not a matter of practical knowledge but of the theoretical knowledge of the Idea of the Good. Does Socrates mean to insist that unless you know that "Justice is good" then there is no benefit in possessing justice? On the face of it, this seems absurd, since it has already been shown in Book IV that justice is a psychical good analogous to the good that is physical health. What more than this do you need to know? Apparently, quite a bit more if, as it turns out, the knowledge of the Good is attained only after a fifty-year-long educational program. As I have already indicated, to know that justice is an intrinsically desirable psychical good still leaves us with the problem of why we should not put this good alongside others and then make a personal utilitarian judgment about the relative merits of attaining one good or another. The irrelevance of such a judgment rests on the discovery of one's true identity as an intellectual subject. In the above passage, it looks as if the knowledge that consists in this discovery is converging on the knowledge of the Good.

This interpretation is reinforced one page later. Socrates adds:

> Isn't it also clear that many people would choose things that are believed to be just or beautiful, even if they are not, and would act, acquire things, and form beliefs accordingly? Yet no one is satisfied to acquire things that merely seem to be good. On the contrary, everyone seeks the things that are good. In this area, everyone disdains appearance. (Reeve trans. slightly modified)[10]

In this passage, the words "beliefs" (τὰ δοκοῦντα), "seem to be" (τὰ δοκοῦντα), and "appearance" (δόξα) have the same root meaning. Reinforcing the previous discussion of the philosophers and the lovers of sights and sounds who are enamored of "belief," the point of the present passage is that most people are content with apparent justice and beauty. But this is so because they suppose that apparent justice and beauty are

---

[9] R. IV.441d8–10, e4–6. Cf. IV.428d11.   [10] R. VI.505d5–9.

really good, not because they believe that they are apparently good while not being really good. They suppose that these are psychical and physical goods like other goods. In fact, though, they would not be satisfied with justice unless it were really, not merely apparently, good. Why, then, should we suppose that what is a psychical good is not really good? After all, whether or not we know that the Form of Justice participates in the Good, it does in fact do so. So, participating in Justice means participating in something that is really good. Why should someone worry that being just could ever be anything other than really good? Once again, in light of the above, what is one's real or true good will depend on one's identity. What is only apparently good may be preferred to what is really good since the apparently good always appears to the subject as really good. And, once again, adjudicating among goods, one might well make the utilitarian judgment that the apparent good that is not really good is to be preferred over the apparent good that is really good. The justice described in Book IV may be really good for a human being, but if it turns out that we are not really human beings, but rather intellects, our real good will be other than the life of the virtues of the embodied soul.

1.3

It must be insisted at this point that the introduction of the Idea of the Good is not the introduction of a Form that stands alongside the rest. This needs to be emphasized given the widespread tendency in discussions of Plato's ethics and psychology, particularly in *Republic*, to treat the Idea of the Good as on a par with other Forms.[11] Even if, as Proclus thought, there are two Goods, one coordinate with other Forms and one superordinate, it is only the latter that is relevant here. Here is why. Suppose that there is a Form of the Good which is the genus of all goods. So, all possessions, – bodily goods and psychical goods – are good because when things possessing these participate in the relevant Forms, they thereby participate in their genus. So, as Book IV of *Republic* argues, justice is a psychical state that is, all other things being equal, good. But even so, it is

---

[11] Indeed, there are many places in the dialogues that seem to support this view. See *Phd.* 65d4–7, 75c10–d2, 76d7–9; *Tht.* 186a8; *Prm.* 130b7–9; *R.* 507b4–6, 608e6–609a4; *Phlb.* 15a4–7. Cf. *Epin.* 978b3–4. Proclus argued that Plato posits two Goods, one coordinate with other Forms and one superordinate. The former is the genus of perfections (τελειώσεις), the latter the source of being and the first principle of all. See *In Remp.* I 278.22–279.2. Cf. his *Platonic Theology*, II 7, 46.13–20. Cf. *Ennead* VI 7, 25.1–16, on the two Goods. See my "Ideas of Good?" for more on this distinction.

open to anyone, say, Thrasymachus, to ask whether the possession of this good is really good for him, that is, whether this good, in comparison with other goods, is always to be chosen. For example, as noted above, the pursuit of a bodily good may, on balance, be preferable to the pursuit of the psychical good that is justice. Such a person can only be answered – and the very structure of *Republic* from Book V to the end emphasizes this – if we posit not just an objective Good, the genus of various sorts of perfection, but a superordinate Good that is unqualifiedly universal. The unqualified universality means that the question of the resilient Thrasymachus can be definitively answered by showing that it is impossible for his real good to be achieved at the cost of a deed that is other than a good for anyone else. This is an exceedingly implausible position to take *unless* one's own good is the good of an intellect. For only if this is so is one's good, that of the intellect, never commensurable with others. One's own true good can never be trumped by the good of the subject that is not really one's self.

As Plato tells us, knowledge of Forms is not possible without "ascending" to the Idea of the Good, the first principle (ἀρχή) of all.[12] In addition, the Idea is to be "seen" by "the best thing in our soul."[13] Without a superordinate Idea of the Good, it would perhaps be possible to maintain that an intellectual life among the Forms is the best life for a human being. But it would also be possible to pose the identical question posed above by our hypothetical Thrasymachus, namely, why is this sort of life unqualifiedly the best life for me? Such a question may be posed by one who concedes that one's own good is never attainable by actions that are not good for anyone else. But in that case, there still remains the question of why an intellectual life is superior to a practical life. There is no doubt that Plato believes that this is the case, but why?

The superordinate Idea of the Good is, I maintain, virtually all of the Forms, roughly analogous to the way that "white" light is virtually all the colors of the spectrum. For intellects, their good is attained in knowing all that is knowable. But nothing is truly knowable except as an expression or manifestation of the first principle of all. That the first principle of all is also that at which all things aim follows from the principle that the effect is contained in the cause. That is, a desire for a good is, ultimately, a desire for the recovery of one's self. It is the intelligible world – Forms and the Idea of the Good – that determines what one is. As Plotinus puts it, one must know where one comes from in order to know who one is.[14] So, in a

---

[12] *R.* VII.511b–c, VII.533b–c.　　　[13] *R.* VII.532c6–7.　　　[14] See *Ennead* V 1, 1.

way, self-knowledge is knowledge of one's own true or real good. For human beings, one's true good consists in eternally knowing all that is knowable. But this is not possible unless one knows that which is the principle of the existence and the essence of all that is knowable.

1.4

According to the above interpretation, self-knowledge is an achievement. But since it is an achievement of knowledge of Forms, and since knowledge of Forms is an endowment for the incarnate soul, self-knowledge is perhaps better termed a recovery or recollection of the self. And, as Socrates argues in *Phaedo*, we could not make the judgments about the defective instances in the sensible world that we do unless we already had knowledge of their exemplars. So, we may suppose that we could not engage in defective embodied intellection unless the subject of such intellection were the defective image of our real selves. Thus, the akratic Leontius in Book IV of *Republic* is able to make a normative judgment about his desire to gaze on the naked corpses outside the walls of the city. His judgment about his own desires is, or could have been, the occasion for a step in the direction of self-knowledge. For the subject that judges that corpse-gazing is, say, ignoble is closer to Leontius' real self than is the self that desires to gaze. Here is why.

All desire is for a good. So, Leontius' desire to gaze on the corpse is a desire to achieve a good.[15] At the same time, he desires not to have that desire be satisfied. That is, he desires the good of not gazing. Both of these desires are desires for apparent goods, quite independent of whether one or the other of them is also for the real good. We may state this another way by saying that, phenomenologically speaking, all desire is for what appears to be good, whereas the question of whether or not what appears to be good is really good is external to or logically independent of what appears to be so. So much seems to be incontestable. But the normative judgment about the desire to gaze on the corpse is a *judgment about* an apparent

---

[15] See *R.* IV.439a4–7. Cf. IV.438a1–5. The frequent claim that the desire discussed in these passages is in fact a "good-independent desire" is misleading. Once we distinguish between apparent goods and the real good, we can see that a desire, by a subject, for a drink that is neither a desire for good (or bad) drink only means that the desire is not for what is in fact really good. It is a desire, like all desires, for the apparent good taken by the subject to be really good. The acratic moment occurs when one realizes that *another* subject judges the apparent good to be not really good. And the drama arises from the consideration of the question: With which of these subjects am I to be identified?

good; it is not merely a desire for an apparent good in the above sense. In other words, it is not merely one desire for an apparent good in conflict with another desire for an apparent good that just happens to be opposed to the first. It is a desire for the really good, as is evident by its rejection of the desire to gaze as merely apparent. It is true that the desire to have the desire to gaze not be effective is also a desire for an apparent good. Yet the ability to make normative judgments in regard to one's own desires is evidence for a claim about what knowledge of the self means.

Nonnormative reasoning occurs in any proposed action. Minimally, the agent must conceptualize the object desired, along with the steps to take in order to satisfy that desire. Leontius' desire to gaze on the naked corpses is a desire situated within a framework of nonnormative reasoning or judgment.[16] But his judgment that that desire ought not to be satisfied is a normative judgment, this despite the fact that what he judges to be the really good is still a good only apparent to him. The capacity for such normative judgments is startlingly revelatory of the nature of the subject capable of making such judgments. But it is a subject from which we are typically detached or alienated. This is clearly so in the case of the vicious person who, unlike the encratic or akratic, does not even have the normative judgment of the wrongness of his actions.

The normative judgment presumes the universal Good as the basis for the judgment. A practical judgment that an apparent good is to be dropped in favor of a different apparent good is not a normative judgment. Such a judgment presumes only objectivity but not universality. Stated otherwise, preferential or utilitarian reasoning is not normative reasoning. If this is so, one's real good is always and only found in knowing the Good, since that good sought in an apparent good is always open to rejection by a normative judgment that it is *only* apparent. But as we have seen, knowing the Good is equivalent to knowing the Forms. There is no other access to the universal Good, no "trans-rational" embrace of goodness. And so, the acratic who is perhaps struggling to become an encratic, even if not a virtuous person, has rudimentary evidence about his true self. The subject

---

[16] The term used at IV.439D7 is ἀλόγιστον. Many English translators (e.g., Shorey, Cornford, Bloom, Sterling and Scott, Grube, Reeve) succumb to the temptation to translate ἀλόγιστον as "irrational." Rowe has "unreasoning," which is slightly better. An exception is Allen, who, more accurately in my view, translates it as "unreflective." The temptation is owing to a contextual ambiguity in the term with which it is contrasted, λογιστικόν, which is most frequently translated as "rational" or "calculative." To be noncalculative is not necessarily to be irrational or nonrational. Hence the ambiguity. When the terms "rational" and "calculative" are treated as synonymous, the tendency is to take their opposite as indicating an absence of rationality. The term ἄνους ("mindless") can conceal a similar ambiguity. Cf. *Phdr.* 257a2.

that makes the normative judgment is the only subject that is oriented toward the universal Good. And only in knowing that Good can it fully know itself.

For this reason, self-knowledge according to Plato is knowledge of an ideal self, not of the empirically endowed self. But for Plato, of course, the ideal is the most really real. Accordingly, there is no other means of attaining this self-knowledge than by consorting with the ideal world. Such a claim will make evident why Plato explicitly associates knowledge of the Good with philosophical activity.[17] In a way, self-knowledge is the mediating idea between the metaphysics of the Good and the way of life that is philosophy. The wisdom that philosophy seeks is, first and foremost, self-knowledge, and self-knowledge is, ultimately, knowledge of the Good which is virtually all of intelligible reality.

Of course, the obvious objection to Plato's account of the true self is that it extirpates – systematically, one might be tempted to say – individuality. If the true self is "achieved" in contemplation of the intelligible realm, how could one self differ at all from another? This is a question to which Plato does not offer an answer. All individuality seems to be attached to defective or failed achievements. So, "punishments" in the afterlife, whatever these might be, are indexed to an embodied self. The "rewards" are entirely related to the separation from embodied desire to the fullest extent possible. It is evident that early Christian theologians, steeped in Platonism, thought of their competing doctrine of resurrection as "good news" precisely because it enabled them to avoid the seeming paradox of eternal reward seen as the extirpation of individuality.

1.5

The virtuous person defined in Book IV of *Republic* is not the philosopher. This is clear from the story of the virtuous person in Book X who, when given the choice of another embodied life, opts for the life of a tyrant because, as Plato says, he was virtuous "by habit without philosophy."[18] Philosophy transforms embodied virtue because it transforms the self. More precisely, it transforms one's self-conception. It does this by eliciting one's identification with an ideal self.[19] I use the word "identification" in the sense according to which one might "identify" with a social or religious or political cause. One recognizes that the good of this cause is identical

---

[17] In *Symposium* as much as in *Republic*.   [18] *R.* X.619c6–d1.
[19] Very helpful reflections along these lines may be found in Hadot (1995), esp. part III.

with one's own good. I think it is important to insist that this is recognition and not a decision. One might decide to study philosophy, but that decision is not a recognition that one's own good is the good of an intellectual subject. The recognition is the transformation.

What I have been arguing is that this transformation is a cognitive identification with the intelligible world. As Aristotle puts it, in intellection one thinks oneself.[20] The activity of intellection is both a discovery of intelligible objects and, since we are cognitively identical with these, a discovery of one's self. To this, Plato adds the metaphysical claim that this is a discovery of one's own good because the Idea of the Good is virtually what all intelligible objects are. Self-knowledge, for Plato, is nothing other than the knowledge of intelligible being. There is no bare self to know. One knows one's self either as the subject of embodied desires and beliefs or as the subject of cognitive identification with intelligible reality. Human embodied existence is poised between the two.

Given the above framework – specifically, the claim that the ideal or true self is cognitively identical with eternal intelligibles – it is hardly surprising that anyone who rejects the metaphysical foundation for this conception of the self will inevitably reject the conception itself. Thus, a commitment to naturalism or anti-Platonism is constrained from going beyond a conception of the self as the subject of occurrent desires and beliefs. In that case, normativity must be construed other than as does Plato. Broadly speaking, the construal is usually utilitarian. But as I have indicated above, for Plato preferential reasoning is not normative reasoning, neither for the individual person nor interpersonally. For the person, preferential reasoning can only be subjective and ordinal evaluation. So, at any time one can say or think that one prefers the satisfaction of one desire over another and act accordingly. If, indeed, such valuation is subjective and ordinal, then it is not even logically possible to make *interpersonal* comparisons among subjects of desire. For though both A and B might desire x more than y, A desires z more than x, while B desires x more than z. Since almost all political thought assumes the cogency of at least some interpersonal evaluations ("this is good for some, though not for others"), it seems to me that it is worth reflecting on the implications of the rejection of the metaphysical foundation of normativity that Plato proposes. And it is also worth reflecting on why Plato thought that in a work that is explicitly focused on justice in the

---

[20] See *de An.* III 4, 429b9, where I accept the reading of the mss. δὲ αὐτόν over the conjecture of Bywater and Ross, δι' αὐτοῦ.

individual, it was illuminating to introduce a political analogy alongside the analysis of the true self.

Even one who discovers that the "inner human being" is the real self needs to pay some attention to the "outer human being," the endowed self. A life in pursuit of what Plato calls disparagingly "popular and political virtue" is most decidedly not the life of vice or what we might term the dissolution of the true self.[21] As mentioned above, a life lived "by habit without philosophy" is not a bad life. But it is, for Plato, an unstable life. The decent, unphilosophical person inhabiting the embodied realm between endowment and ideal can of course appear successful where the criterion of success is expressed in non-Platonic terms. The criterion of success for Plato, however, is truth. From the psychological fact that no one can desire anything but his own true good as opposed to his apparent good, Plato argues that it is not even possible to have an inkling of what this is without a recognition of the universality of this good. Mere objectivity alone only allows occurrent and hypothetical preferential reasoning. Any conclusion of such reasoning is always open to the challenge: "Is what appears good to you now really good, all things considered?" I would say that the fundamental divide between the Platonist and his opponent is over whether or not this question makes any sense. The metaphysical superstructure according to which the question does after all make sense is the foundation for Plato's account of self-knowledge. It is not just that self-knowledge is achieved by knowing intelligible reality; it is that there is no knowing what a true self is apart from this knowledge. Without the superordinate Idea of the Good, questions about personal identity itself and the ethical questions that depend on establishing personal identity cannot be answered nonarbitrarily.

---

[21] See *Phd.* 82a11. Cf. 69b6–7 where such virtue is labeled a σκιαγραφία ("shadow") of real virtue. There is no space to pursue this point here, but in the light of the explanation of virtue at the end of *Republic* as possessed by the philosopher alone, it seems clear that the virtue in Book IV is of the same sort as that which is disdained in *Phaedo*.

Two Faces of Platonic Self-Knowledge
Alcibiades *I and* Charmides

Thomas Tuozzo

While self-knowledge figures in many Platonic dialogues, it is subjected to dialectical investigation in only two of them: *Charmides* and *Alcibiades* I.[1] These dialogues are also linked by a number of other shared features. Socrates' main interlocutors – Alcibiades in the *Alcibiades*, Critias in the *Charmides* – are figures notorious for their roles in the catastrophic political events in Athens in the later fifth century and whose association with Socrates, according to Xenophon, contributed to the public hostility toward him. There is also a strong erotic dimension to both dialogues.[2] In the *Charmides*, the adolescent Charmides, scion of a rich and prominent family and the beauty of his generation, is at the height of his physical attractiveness and the center of erotic attention among the Athenian elite. In the *Alcibiades*, Alcibiades – though destined to be of much greater historical importance than Charmides – nonetheless is in some respects strikingly similar to him. He is a beautiful young man from a politically prominent and wealthy family. In the dialogue he is a little past his erotic prime, so that the flock of lovers that once attended him (as they do Charmides in the other dialogue) has moved on. And in both dialogues, Socrates is concerned, in the first instance, to assess the state of the young man's soul. In the *Charmides*, he does so in order to see whether Charmides' soul is as beautiful as his body, so that he could qualify as truly blessed (μακάριος); in the *Alcibiades*, he does so in order to show Alcibiades that he does not yet have the knowledge needed to achieve the grand political ambitions Socrates suspects he cherishes. In the *Charmides*, despite Socrates' dramatic report of his own erotic susceptibility to

---

[1] Hereafter referred to simply as "*Alcibiades*." In this chapter, I make the methodological assumption that the *Alcibiades* was written by Plato or by someone who shared his philosophical and literary aims sufficiently to justify using the two dialogues to shed light on one other.

[2] The *Phaedrus* is another erotic dialogue in which self-knowledge is an important theme, though not the topic of dialectical inquiry. Gordon (2012, chapter 5) discusses some parallels between the erotic dimensions of self-knowledge in *Alcibiades* and *Phaedrus*.

Charmides' beauty, Socrates does not approach the boy as a lover. Rather, he seizes on the occasion of Charmides' having a headache to adopt the role of a doctor; indeed, as it turns out, a soul-doctor, prepared to diagnose Charmides' soul and, if it lacks the psychic health of sound-mindedness (σωφροσύνη), to treat it with the "beautiful λόγοι" that are the proper remedy for producing that virtue. In the *Alcibiades*, on the other hand, Socrates presents himself as Alcibiades' one true lover, the lover not of his fading looks but of his soul, ready to perform the lover's traditional pedagogical function of preparing him for his political career.

In both dialogues the young man comes to recognize his need for Socrates' help and vows at the end of the dialogue to attend him from that day forward (in both cases with dramatic foreshadowing of their not keeping this promise for long). Perhaps the most significant difference between the two dialogues, from a dramatic point of view, is the fact that in the *Alcibiades* Socrates has only one interlocutor, Alcibiades, and, as befits a seduction speech, talks to him with no one else present. In the *Charmides* Socrates talks with Charmides in a wrestling school crowded with Charmides' admirers (men and boys of all ages), and, after Charmides' first attempts at a definition of sound-mindedness prove unsatisfactory, his guardian Critias takes over as Socrates' interlocutor. Critias, in addition to having a notorious later political career, was also an intellectual renowned for his poetry and prose writings (his activity as a playwright is alluded to in the dialogue). When he takes over as interlocutor, the discussion attains levels of abstraction and sophistication that it does not reach in the *Alcibiades*.

The similarities between the two dialogues invite a comparison of their treatments of self-knowledge. As I shall argue here, the two dialogues take different dialectical routes to structurally similar analyses of self-knowledge. One way to characterize the difference in their procedures is to say that they can be associated with two different ways of parsing the notion of self-knowledge. One may take the notion "self" to be the logically prior notion: the self is one among many things in the world that we may inquire into and come to know. This is the route that the *Alcibiades* takes. On the other hand, perhaps counterintuitively, we may think of self-knowledge as a kind of knowing that, unlike other kinds of knowing, takes itself as its own object. This is the route that the second half of the *Charmides* explores. Now it is not obvious that these two ways of understanding self-knowledge will pick out the very same thing. Indeed, it is a frequent criticism of the argument in the *Charmides* that in moving from the knowledge of oneself to an investigation of the knowledge of itself, the dialogue changes the subject and pursues the analysis of an abstract and ultimately empty notion that has little relevance to the project of knowing ourselves.[3] Whether in fact self-knowledge understood in these different ways does or does not pick out the same thing depends on the outcomes of the investigations into them. Still, it may seem that there is little chance that they would come to the same thing: while knowing is one of the things that we can do (and indeed must be able to do if we are to have knowledge of ourselves), there are many other aspects of ourselves that (it would seem) self-knowledge should be concerned to know and that a self-knowing knowledge would fail to encompass. But if knowledge of a thing consists in knowing its essence, and if knowing is in some sense the essence of the Platonic self, then prospects improve for these two under-standings of self-knowledge to converge. In what follows, I shall argue that in fact the analysis of self-knowledge (as knowledge of oneself) in the *Alcibiades* comes to a conclusion that is very much like the analysis of self-knowledge (as knowledge of knowing) in the *Charmides*.

Neither of our two dialogues starts off as an inquiry into self-knowledge. The initial concern of the *Charmides* is whether Charmides possesses sound-mindedness (σωφροσύνη), and the subsequent philosophical inquiry (begun by Charmides, continued by Critias) is directed toward an account of that virtue. The concern of the *Alcibiades* is Alcibiades' readiness for engaging in politics. But at a deeper level both dialogues are concerned with the human good. In the *Charmides*, Socrates is interested in whether Charmides' physical beauty, wealth, and social distinction are complemented by a beautiful, that is, sound-minded, soul. If so, he would be as well off as it is possible for a human being to be (μακάριος). Already in Socrates' discussion of Zalmoxian medicine, before the dialectical discussion starts, Socrates sketches a hierarchical relation among human goods: the soul is the source of "all good and bad things for the body and the whole person" (156e). In the *Alcibiades*, in order to determine whether Alcibiades is ready to enter politics, Socrates questions him about what the statesman is concerned to produce, that is, what good he is trying to effect for the city. Furthermore, while the *Charmides* starts with an investigation into sound-mindedness as the good of the individual soul, it frequently turns to the level of the city, to examine whether sound-mindedness as they have defined it would benefit a city.[4] The move is all the more natural in that sound-mindedness and justice (δικαιοσύνη) are elsewhere paired as

---

[3] See Drew Hyland's Chapter 3 in this book as an example of this interpretation.
[4] On this feature of the argument of the *Charmides*, see Tuozzo (2001).

the primary virtues of a city.[5] In the *Alcibiades* the move is in the other direction: from examining the good of the city, which is what the statesman needs to know, the discussion moves to examining how Socrates and Alcibiades themselves might as individual persons acquire the virtue they lack. In both cases, this concern with the human good prompts the turn toward self-knowledge.

Furthermore, in both dialogues the dialectical progression involves contrasting knowledge of what is strictly speaking good for a human being, a kind of knowledge bound up with self-knowledge, with the knowledge we have of other things that are in a lesser sense good for human beings. In each case, the knowledge of these other things proves to be different from, yet importantly dependent on, the knowledge that is the main concern of the investigation. Following out how these dialogues treat the contrast between a central kind of knowledge and other kinds of knowledge will help bring out the important structural similarity between the conceptions of self-knowledge the two dialogues ultimately produce.

In what follows I shall first give a brief analysis of the relevant parts of the argument in the *Charmides*[6] and then show how interpreting the argument in the *Alcibiades* with an eye on the *Charmides* highlights aspects of the *Alcibiades* that are frequently overlooked and reveals the similarity in the two dialogues' accounts of self-knowledge.

2.1

The topic of self-knowledge emerges in the *Charmides* after Socrates' refutation of "doing one's own things" (τὰ ἑαυτοῦ πράττειν) as a definition of sound-mindedness. When Charmides proposes that definition, Socrates perversely – for pedagogical reasons – interprets it as entailing that sound-mindedness consists in making for oneself everything that one needs – clothes, shoes, and everything else that is the product of a craft. A city run along such lines, Socrates points out, would hardly be soundly run (σωφρόνως, 162a4). Though such a city would be inefficient at supplying its citizens with the goods Socrates mentions, that is not its most important fault. The more serious fault is that it is concerned with such goods to the exclusion of the real good of the citizens. Critias, who takes over the defense of the definition that (as Socrates gives us to understand) was originally his to begin with, sees this deeper point. He

---

[5] See *Prt.* 323a1–2, *Smp.* 209a5–8.
[6] For more detail and defense of this interpretation of the *Charmides*, see Tuozzo (2011).

argues that the sound-minded person is not, as such, concerned with such petty concerns at all; rather, such a person is concerned with doing things that can be accomplished nobly (καλῶς). These are the only things that really belong to one (163b–c). The view that doing noble and good things is what counts as doing one's own things, and that providing for one's bodily needs does not, reflects a specific (if inchoate) conception of what sort of thing one most centrally is. It should come as no surprise, then, either that Socrates' subsequent examination of Critias' view focuses on the sound-minded man's knowledge of himself and what is good for him or that Critias responds to this line of questioning by offering, in a long speech that makes appeal to the inscription at Delphi, "knowing oneself" as a new definition of sound-mindedness (164c–165b).

In the discussion that immediately follows his speech, Socrates asks Critias to identify the "noble work" (καλὸν ἔργον, 165d1–2) that self-knowledge produces for us. In doing so, he is picking up Critias' point that doing one's own things should be doing noble things, as distinct from being concerned with items needed for our physical well-being. Critias insists that self-knowledge does not have a product or work *in the way that* crafts such as house-building do, but is unable to specify what qualitatively different sort of thing it does produce. In his questioning, Socrates continues to compare self-knowledge with the crafts that deal with the lesser goods, not so much to get Critias to assimilate self-knowledge to a craft model as to get him to articulate the relation between self-knowledge and these other crafts. Socrates points out that these crafts take something other than themselves for their objects and emphasizes that they do *not* take themselves for their object. This point prompts Critias to reformulate self-knowledge as having precisely these other kinds of knowledge, as well as itself, as its objects (166b–c). It is as though Socrates has revealed a certain deficiency in normal crafts, namely that, while they know their objects, they fail to know themselves. Self-knowledge is a knowing that not only does not have this deficiency but, in addition, makes good the deficiency in other kinds of knowledge by knowing them.

The formula that Critias comes up with, "knowledge of itself and of other kinds of knowledge," is fairly opaque, and the latter half of the *Charmides* is devoted to exploring its meaning. Taking the two parts of the formula separately, Socrates first investigates the possibility of a reflexive knowledge of itself. He argues that deciding this question requires determining what constitutes the knowability of any object of knowledge and then asking whether knowledge itself has the feature that knowable things as such possess. Socrates situates this question within a larger investigation of reflexivity in general, which he says would take a "great man" (169a) to conduct; the dialogue explicitly decides not take this route. Instead, Socrates turns to the second part of the formulation, the knowledge of other kinds of knowledge. Their investigation of that question stumbles on the issue of whether such a knowledge would know the *objects* of the kinds of knowledge it knows; if not, it would seem merely to know the same thing about all of them, namely, that each is a kind of knowledge. If, on the other hand, it did know their objects, it would seem simply to be identical to all of them put together. Projecting something like the latter onto the civic scale gives us a city in which all activities are performed only by qualified craftsmen (173a–d). Would such a city be well off? No. It would differ from the city considered earlier in the dialogue insofar as it would provide its citizens with the lesser goods in an efficient manner, but it would still, like that earlier city, neglect the distinctively human good. The latter is neither the concern of any of the particular crafts nor all of them together. It is rather the concern of the knowledge of the good. Since sound-mindedness is acknowledged to be beneficial, self-knowledge, understood in this way as the knowledge of other kinds of knowledge, must be rejected as an account of sound-mindedness. The investigation, then, ends in aporia.

The investigation foundered because neither of the interpretations of knowledge of the other kinds of knowledge – an empty knowledge of them simply as knowledge and nothing more, or straight-out identity with them – satisfies the requirement that this sort of knowledge is supposed to be beneficial. The dialogue leaves us, then, with the challenge of finding a third interpretation of the knowledge of other knowledges that *does* render it valuable. One such interpretation readily suggests itself: knowledge precisely of how those kinds of knowledge may be used to truly benefit human beings. This is something that those kinds of expertise themselves do not know about themselves, and may well be considered a kind of deficiency in them. Of course, knowing how they may be employed beneficially requires knowing what is truly good for human beings.[7] Now as we saw, the dialogue earlier left as a topic for further

---

[7] We might also ask if there would there be any methodological differences between a knowledge that knows how other kinds of knowledge can be used beneficially and those other kinds of knowledge. At some points, the dialogue conceives of the knowledge of other kinds of knowledge as involving the dialectical questioning of those who claim to possess such a kind of knowledge (167a). Although Socrates shows that such dialectical questioning is not capable of determining who has what technical expertise (170e–170c), this methodology may well be suited to understanding the respects in which a particular knowledge can be used beneficially. See Tuozzo (2011, 322–331).

inquiry the notion of a reflexive knowledge of itself, which, together with the knowledge of other knowledges, would jointly constitute sound-mindedness as self-knowledge. The question naturally arises whether *that* might in some way involve the needed knowledge of the good. The dialogue, however, offers us no indication of how it might do so.[8]

2.2

As we have seen, in the *Charmides* an initial definition of sound-mindedness as doing one's own things led, via the notion of knowing what is truly valuable for oneself (noble things, τὰ καλά), to a concern with self-knowledge and the ways self-knowledge differs from other kinds of knowledge. We ultimately arrived at an analysis of self-knowledge that has two parts: a reflexive knowledge of itself and a knowledge of other kinds of knowledge, in particular, of how those other kinds of knowledge can be beneficial. In the *Alcibiades*, we arrive at a similar conclusion but through a different route.

In the *Alcibiades* Socrates is concerned first of all to determine whether Alcibiades is prepared to enter politics. Accordingly, his focus is on whether Alcibiades has the knowledge needed to do so, and so he asks him on what issues he proposes to advise the Athenians. Alcibiades answers: "their own affairs" (τὰ ἑαυτῶν πράγματα, 107c6). This strikes the note for the rest of the dialogue, which will ask: What is the proper business of a city, and then, more centrally, what is the proper business of the individual? After an initial investigation at the level of the city reveals Alcibiades' current ignorance of these matters, and a protreptic interlude in which Socrates convinces Alcibiades that he has reason to try to remedy this ignorance,[9] Alcibiades pronounces himself eager to take the care of himself that remedying his ignorance requires.

Socrates now focuses on the respect in which Alcibiades needs to become better, which at first leads them back to the question of what the statesman does. The statesman rules people, but over what particular activity of theirs does he preside? While Socrates pursues the question by

---

[8] For an attempt to work out such a conception of knowledge of knowledge, exploiting the claim Socrates makes in the *Republic* that knowledge is "good-like" (ἀγαθοειδής), see Tuozzo (2011, 310–322).

[9] It is at the close of this protreptic interlude that Socrates first invokes the Delphic inscription "Know thyself" in the dialogue (124a8). Here, on its first occurrence, here the inscription is given what may be called a social interpretation: Alcibiades should know himself in the sense of knowing who his real rivals are (the kings of Persia and Sparta, not his fellow Athenian politicians).

means of examples of several persons united in a joint craft activity directed by a master craftsman (e.g., sailing or harvesting, 125b), Alcibiades counters with answers that, though arguably circular, nevertheless gesture toward an activity that is less technical and less hierarchical than Socrates' examples and less easily thought of as directed by a single craftsperson:[10] "conducting transactions with each other and dealing with one another, in the way we live in cities" or "sharing in a polity and having transactions with each other" (125c–d). But these descriptions give us substantive understanding of neither what citizens as such do nor what sort of knowledge is needed to make sure that this activity goes well. Socrates then changes tack and asks what the knowledge in question enables the statesman to produce in the city, to which Alcibiades answers: friendship. Immediately returning to the craft model, Socrates argues that friendship and lack of faction are found among those who are "of the same mind" (i.e., possess ὁμόνοια, a term used for civic concord[11]) and that agreement about their craft is the hallmark of all possessors of a particular craft.[12] So the question remains: What is the craft that secures this agreement among citizens, and what subject matter is their civic agreement about?

In response, Alcibiades ignores the question of craft and offers a different model for agreement or same-mindedness: that found in a family between parents and child, brother and brother, man and wife (126e). However attractive this familial model of civic concord may be,[13] it does not yet give a substantive account of the shared activity of the citizens or of the subject matter of their agreement. Socrates presses the issue by pointing out that different members of a household have different tasks, which require different kinds of knowledge: the man's activity requires the art of the hoplite, while the woman's requires the art of weaving. Since

---

[10] Denyer (2001, 197) notes that Alcibiades' descriptions of the citizens' activity emphasize a certain symmetry and mutuality in them that is not present in Socrates' examples. I do not think that Socrates encourages Alcibiades to assimilate the knowledge they are trying to specify to the model of ordinary craft knowledge; rather, his aim (as in the *Charmides*) is to encourage reflection on the relation it bears to such crafts. Note that Socrates' later description of Alcibiades' (hypothetical) employment of this knowledge in the city (134d1–e2) lacks the hierarchical structure his examples here have.

[11] On political agreement or concord in the *Republic* and its relation to our passage in the *Alcibiades*, see Kamtekar (2004, 137–138).

[12] In the *Cleitophon* a similar move is made: Cleitophon reports a philosophical conversation between two people, one a Socratic, in which the product that the craft of justice produces is said to be friendship, which is then reduced to same-mindedness, which is in turn said to be precisely what any craft produces in its field (409d–410a).

[13] This familial model may have been a staple of Athenian political thought. It is found in Demosthenes *Against Aristogeiton* 1.87–90, as Kamtekar (2004) points out.

these different crafts are not shared by all the members of the household, they do not ground any concord, or (hence) any friendship, among them. But a family of this sort would seem to be doing something right; Socrates proceeds to describe it as a family in which everyone "does his own things" (τὰ ἑαυτῶν πράττουσιν) and goes on to say that a city run along the same lines would qualify as a just one, if doing one's own things is what justice is (127a–d). This picture of a city where all do their own things is similar to the city where all crafts are expertly performed that Socrates discusses at *Charmides* 173a–d. There, Socrates at first professed to find that city happy, and then only with difficulty persuaded Critias that, as so far described, it was not necessarily happy at all. So, too, here in the *Alcibiades* Socrates professes to find such a city just, but (as so far described) without friendship or concord. As in the case of the *Charmides*, something is missing.

Having reached this *aporia*, Alcibiades realizes that he is in a shameful state and needs to cultivate himself. Socrates now distinguishes between cultivating oneself and cultivating "one's own things," thereby hinting at what was missing in the city they described: the citizens they described were doing their own things in a sense that ignored who they really were. In order to determine what we really are, so as to be able to cultivate it, Socrates starts by distinguishing between the things that belong to or are "of" the body and the body itself. Taking care of such things as shoes, rings, and clothes is not the same thing as taking care of feet, hands, or the body as a whole. There is a distinct art for taking care of each of these things, where taking care, as Socrates specifies, involves getting them into good shape and keeping them that way. If we wish to do the same for ourselves, we need to determine what the special art for that would be (128e10). And the best way to determine that, Socrates assumes here, with a reference to the inscription at Delphi, is to identify what we ourselves actually are.

In the discussion of self-knowledge that follows Socrates distinguishes three elements: first, what he calls "the self itself" (or, as it is sometimes translated,[14] "itself itself"); second, what he calls "us ourselves"; and last, our bodies and the things that belong to them (i.e., our possessions). In the course of the discussion, Socrates effectively distinguishes two different paths by which we can approach the question of what we ourselves are. One, which we may call the path "from above," involves understanding first the self itself, and then understanding what we ourselves are on its

---

[14] E.g., by Denyer (2001) and Gill (2007).

basis. This is the first path that Socrates lays out: "Come then, in what way could the self itself be discovered? For in this way perhaps we could discover what we ourselves are, whereas so long as we are in ignorance of that we will, I suppose, be unable to do so" (129b1–3). But immediately after describing this path, Socrates interrupts himself by saying, "Hold on, by Zeus" and enters into what he later tells us is a different approach to understanding the self, one that leaves the question of the self itself aside. We may style this the path "from below": it approaches an understanding of what "we ourselves" are via an understanding of our bodies and what belongs to them, and how we ourselves are related to those things. Pursuing this path of inquiry, Socrates remarks that just as craftsmen use their tools, they also use their bodies, and indeed that we all use our bodies. Adopting the principle that, as in the case of a craftsman and their tools, the user is in every case different from what he uses, Socrates argues that, since we *use* our bodies, we must not *be* our bodies, but rather that which uses them. Since what uses the body can only be the soul, we must be nothing but our souls.

At the end of this argument Socrates remarks that the conclusion has been established not rigorously (ἀκριβῶς) but only in a measured way (μετρίως), since they had not investigated the self itself (130c8–d2); they had omitted that, he says, "because it requires considerable inquiry" (διὰ τὸ πολλῆς εἶναι σκέψεως). Their understanding of what we ourselves are remains provisional, then, until they proceed further upward to the self itself. Socrates will indeed at least sketch this way upward later in the dialogue, but before he does so, he pauses to move back downward to consider those possessing crafts for taking care of the body and its material possessions.[15] The doctor and the trainer, insofar as they know the body, do not know themselves, but only what belongs to them. The farmer and other artisans know neither themselves nor what belongs to them, but only what belongs to what belongs to them (131a2–b2).[16] And just as, in the *Charmides*, Critias thought that practicing the common crafts was too petty to constitute the kind of doing one's own things in which sound-mindedness consists, so, at this stage of the argument, Socrates calls the

---

[15] That which belongs to us, and the things that belong to it, are summarized as "bodies and things" (σώματα καὶ χρήματα) at 132c4.

[16] Note that Socrates construes the doctor's medical knowledge of the body as knowledge of what belongs *to him.* This suggests that the knowledge of the soul that constitutes knowledge of ourselves is a general, impersonal knowledge of soul, and not knowledge of the idiosyncrasies of one's own soul.

common crafts low (βάναυσοι) and unworthy of a gentleman because they are concerned merely with things we use and not with our very selves. After an interlude in which Socrates draws further conclusions from the argument for the two of them (e.g., that only someone who loves another's soul, as Socrates loves Alcibiades' soul, loves that person's self), Alcibiades raises anew the question of *how* we are to care for ourselves. In response, Socrates explicitly refers once again to the notion of the self itself – a reference that English-language commentators generally miss.[17] But this return of the notion of the self itself does not mean that Socrates is here undertaking the "considerable inquiry" that had earlier deterred him. Rather, instead of considering the self itself in its own right, Socrates continues the search upward: having moved from our possessions to our bodies and then to our souls, he continues on, using the mirror analogy, to the divine part of the soul. The Delphic inscription encourages us to know ourselves, Socrates says, the way an eye might see itself. The eye may see itself by looking into a mirror, or something similar: another eye, and, more particularly, the best part of another eye, that in virtue of which it sees: the pupil. Similarly, a soul may come to know itself by looking at another soul, more particularly "into that place of it in which the soul's excellence, wisdom (σοφία), comes to be," and, Socrates adds, "[by looking] into another thing to which this [part of the soul] happens to be similar" (133b). Socrates calls this part of the soul, to which "knowing and thinking (τὸ εἰδέναι καὶ φρονεῖν)" belong, divine, and identifies that to which it is similar as "god" or "the divine."[18] It is by coming to know "all that is divine: god and intelligence (θεόν τε καὶ φρόνησιν)" that a person might come to know himself "most of all" (μάλιστα) (133c6).

Scholars differ on how to take the references to "god" here, and whether to accept as genuine the lines that immediately follow this passage (133c8–17). In these lines, which are absent from our direct manuscript tradition but are quoted as coming from the dialogue by two Christian

---

[17] As Brunschwig (1996, 70) argues, there is a very close relationship between 132c7–9 ("In what way would we know it most clearly? Since when we know this, it seems, we shall also know ourselves") and 129a8–b3 ("In what way could the self itself be discovered? For in this way perhaps we could discover what we ourselves are, whereas so long as we remain in ignorance of that we will, I suppose, be unable to do so"). This relationship strongly suggests that at 132c7–9 Socrates is making a reference to "the self itself," and justifies Schleiermacher's conjecture of αὐτό for mss. αὐτά, a conjecture accepted by most editors (though not by Denyer, whose defense of the mss. reading is not convincing). Finding the bare αὐτό too weak, Brunschwig proposes reading <αὐτὸ τὸ> αὐτό. Olympiodorus (2016, 223.6–7) also sees a reference to the self itself at 132c7. Pradeau (2000, ad loc.) goes further and suggests that a reference to the self itself may also underlie the problematic τοῦτο at 132c2.

[18] Both readings are attested. Denyer (2001, ad loc.) makes a good case for the reading "god."

authors, Socrates seems to suggest that we may look directly to god without the mediation of the soul of another human being.[19] I shall not enter into those questions here, since what is most relevant for my analysis is the fact that our text goes on to identify that which we need to get to know in order to know ourselves as "god and φρόνησις" – translated "god and intelligence" earlier, but just as appropriately translated "god and wisdom" or "god and knowing." It is plausible to take this as a hendiadys, describing a single thing: a knowing that is god or god-like. On this reading, then, the upward path to a specification of self-knowledge in the *Alcibiades* leads to one's coming to know a certain kind of knowing. This knowing of a god-that-is-a-knowing parallels the reflexive knowledge of knowledge that was one-half of the conception of sound-mindedness (σωφροσύνη) as self-knowledge in the *Charmides*. And just as we speculated earlier that the reflexive knowledge of knowledge in the *Charmides* must somehow provide us knowledge of the good, so in the *Alcibiades*, after arguing that self-knowledge comes as a consequence of knowing "god and φρόνησις," Socrates remarks that such self-knowledge is σωφροσύνη and that acquiring it is the only way in which we will be able to "know our own good things and bad things" (133c21–23).[20]

The continuation of the argument in the *Alcibiades* provides a parallel to the other half of the analysis of self-knowledge in the *Charmides*. As we have seen, Socrates had earlier in the *Alcibiades* maintained that, since those possessing arts having to do with our body or its trappings know things that are one or two degrees distant from what we ourselves are, they do not possess knowledge of themselves, but only of what belongs to them (the body) or of what belongs to that (material goods). Now Socrates revisits the issue and denies them even the latter knowledge:

> Then it wasn't quite right to agree, as we did a few minutes ago, that some people know what belongs to them without knowing themselves, while others know what belongs to their belongings. It seems that it's the job of one man, and one craft (μιᾶς τέχνης), to know all these things: himself, his belongings, and his belongings' belongings. (133d–e, trans. Hutchinson, slightly modified)

---

[19] Annas (1985) and Johnson (1999) are good examples of an interpretation that accepts 133c8–17 (found only in Eusebius and Stobaeus) and holds that Socrates here recommends looking directly at some god. Tarrant (2007) considers evidence from non-Christian Neoplatonists that suggests that they had a text in which Socrates only recommends looking at the divine in a soul.

[20] Hutchinson's translation in Cooper (1997) – "would we be able to know which of the things that belong to us were good and which were bad?" – is misleading insofar as it implies that there is some criterion of belonging to ourselves other than being good for one.

Surely, Socrates does not wish here to deny that the doctor in fact possesses the technical knowledge of health, nor, conversely, does he wish to affirm that self-knowledge brings with it the knowledge of medicine and all the other crafts dealing with bodies and material possessions. Indeed, the latter notion, of self-knowledge as somehow identical to the totality of all the ordinary crafts, was an interpretation of the notion of the knowledge of other kinds of knowledge that the *Charmides* rejected as mistaken.[21] Rather, what Socrates has in mind in our *Alcibiades* passage is a knowledge of these things *as* belonging to oneself. And the immediately preceding point, that this knowledge enables us to know the things that are good or bad for ourselves, supports the (in itself plausible) interpretation of this as knowing how these things are good for one. This is a kind of knowledge, then, that does concern the objects that the doctor and other craftsmen know, but it knows something different about them from what the ordinary craftsmen know: namely, their bearing on the welfare of what oneself truly is. This natural reading of the *Alcibiades* passage supports our interpretation of the knowledge of other kinds of knowledge in the *Charmides* as a knowledge of *their* bearing on the human good.[22]

At this point, the discussion in the *Alcibiades* turns from a consideration of self-knowledge at the level of the individual toward its application on the political level. The investigation has uncovered the "single craft" that, grounded in a knowledge of the self itself, enables one to know oneself, what belongs to oneself, and what belongs to that. This craft enables one also to know what belongs to others, and indeed, what belongs to cities, and so qualifies one to be a statesman (ἀνὴρ πολιτικός, 133e4–9). The extension of the knowledge of oneself and one's things to the knowledge of others' things is not, I think, an application of the principle that the knowledge of opposites (here: self and other) is the same. The knowledge of one's own things is the knowledge of how one's body and external things can be used so as to benefit oneself, given what one most truly is. Insofar as this knowledge is general,[23] it is applicable in the same way to all human beings and to the city as a whole. Knowing one's own things is not,

---

[21] See my earlier discussion. Renaud and Tarrant (2015, 76) see the parallel between what is described in this *Alcibiades* passage and the definition of σωφροσύνη as the knowledge of itself and other kinds of knowledge in the *Charmides*. Their calling the version in the *Charmides* "a Socratic super-art" suggests that they may conceive of it as comprising all the arts.

[22] This is also the interpretation of Olympiodorus (225.3–6), who explains that the craftsmen know the objects of their crafts as having their "own nature" (οἰκείαν φύσιν), while the person with self-knowledge knows them as "contributing to that which uses them and as being tools" (συντελοῦντα πρὸς τὸ χρώμενον καὶ ὄργανα ὄντα). The translation of this passage in Griffin (2016) obscures this point.

[23] See above, note 15.

here, a matter of knowing what belongs to me as opposed to what belongs to another. It is knowing what truly benefits a human being, given what a human being most truly is.

Such knowledge will make one capable of directing not only one's own life but also the life of a city or a household, in such a way that the community does well and is happy. The person who possesses it knows himself, and so is sound-minded. His employment of this craft in ruling the city involves his imparting this same knowledge to the community, so that it, too, will be sound-minded – and, Socrates adds, just (134c). The citizens, too, will look at "what is bright and divine" and know themselves and the things that are good for them (134d4–8). With the notion of a "single craft" whereby one knows the self itself and all that follows from it, the dialogue has discovered the craft that Alcibiades could not find earlier: the craft that is to be shared in by all citizens and which will engender mutual concord and friendship. Friendship and justice now prove to be compatible, unlike their apparent opposition at that earlier stage of the discussion (127c). And because the craft that produces this concord and friendship involves some sort of knowledge of the divine, the citizens are not only friends with each other; their civic action in accordance with this knowledge wins the god as their friend, as well (cf. σύ τε καὶ ἡ πόλις θεοφιλῶς πράξετε, 134d1–2).

We have seen, then, that through very different argument paths, the *Alcibiades* and the *Charmides* reach similar conceptions of self-knowledge. Both analyze self-knowledge as a kind of knowing that has two compon-ents (though the *Alcibiades* stresses the way the two components constitute a unified craft more than the *Charmides* does). One element is properly reflexive: it is the knowledge of the self itself in the *Alcibiades*, and the knowledge of itself in the *Charmides*. Insofar as the knowledge of the self itself in the *Alcibiades* is a knowledge of knowing (φρονεῖν), it approaches the self-knowing knowledge of the *Charmides*. Furthermore, this reflexive element entails (explicitly in the *Alcibiades* and implicitly in the *Charmides*) a knowledge of one's own good as well. Both dialogues also emphasize the difficulty of grasping this reflexive knowledge, and both explicitly put off a full treatment of the issue.

The second element of self-knowledge is described in the *Alcibiades* as knowledge of what belongs to one, one's body, and material possessions. While these are all objects of (different) ordinary crafts, they are the objects of self-knowledge in a different way: with respect to how they may benefit or harm oneself. In the *Charmides*, similarly, the second element of self-knowledge is described as the knowledge of other kinds of knowledge. In the dialogue itself, the interlocutors did not find a satisfactory interpretation of this kind of knowledge: the discussion foundered on the false dichotomy that the knowledge of other kinds of knowledge must be either an empty knowledge that only knows that each knowledge counts as knowledge, and nothing more, or a super-knowledge that comprises all the other kinds of knowledge. Here, again, the *Charmides* only hints at what the *Alcibiades* more plainly states: there is another way to understand these other kinds of knowledge, namely, knowing how to use their objects in ways that benefit a person's soul.

CHAPTER 3

Socratic Self-Knowledge and the Limits
of Epistēmē

Drew A. Hyland

In one of the earlier but still widely read English translations of Plato's *Charmides*, that of Benjamin Jowett,[1] this renowned translator makes a most striking and, it must be said, most problematic translation decision. In the early part of the dialogue (up to 169c1), including the three efforts of the young Charmides to say what *sōphrosunē* is, Jowett translates this guiding word of the dialogue by a fairly typical, if itself problematic word, "temperance."[2] But almost as soon as the older Critias takes over the effort from Charmides, Jowett begins to translate the various forms of the same term as "temperately or wisely," "wisdom or temperance," etc.[3] Very soon, however, the reference to "temperance" is dropped,[4] and henceforth in the dialogue, *sōphrosunē*, the very word that is earlier translated as "temperance," is translated as "wisdom." A Greekless reader would very likely get the impression from Jowett that the subject of the dialogue changes at this point from temperance to wisdom. But of course, the terms do not shift; the word used throughout is *sōphrosunē*. Why, then, would a man who knows Greek as well as Jowett, who, it would seem, could not possibly confuse *sōphrosunē* and *sophia* inadvertently, decide to render *sōphrosunē* as "wisdom," the usual translation for *sophia*? I suggest that the answer is that the definitions of *sōphrosunē* offered by Critias depart so radically from the usual characterizations of this Greek word that Jowett is disinclined to render it by one of the usual translations. Indeed, two of Critias' characterizations, "self-knowledge" and especially the development of that formulation into "the science of itself and the other sciences" (and its

---

[1] Still available, for example, in the widely read edition of Hamilton and Cairns (1961, 99–122). My Greek text throughout will be Burnet (1900–1907). Except when otherwise indicated, all translations will be my own. Henceforth, all specific references to Platonic dialogues will name the dialogue followed by relevant Stephanus pages.

[2] The translation is problematic because of the excessive narrowness of the English word in its modern usage. Think "Women's Christian Temperance Union."

[3] E.g. *Chrm.* 164b, 164c, 165d.   [4] *Chrm.* 166b.

expansive variants) sound much more like common understandings of wisdom, and so Jowett rather understandably translates it as such. The translation remains unmistakably a mistranslation. Nevertheless, it is a natural and, at first blush, even a plausible one. For "the science of itself and the other sciences" and "self-knowledge" sounds very much like the two senses of wisdom that Socrates himself distinguishes in the *Apology*. There, the first is the kind of wisdom that others claim for themselves and that he attributes only to the divine, a kind of comprehensive knowledge of the whole (or science of itself and the other sciences), which he denies that he has. The second is his own peculiar kind of "human wisdom" that supposedly distinguishes him from others and is the point of the Delphic oracle's claim that no one is wiser than Socrates; to wit, his recognition that he is not wise (in the divine sense), or more expansively, his knowledge of what he knows and what he does not know.[5] Little wonder, then, that Jowett might be tempted to see in the *Charmides* a shift, despite the consistent use of the same word, from a consideration of *sōphrosunē* to a consideration of wisdom in its various formulations.

I want to suggest, then, that in the vacillation that occurs in the *Charmides* once Critias enters the picture – between *sōphrosunē* as self-knowledge and as a kind of "science" (*epistēmē*) – lies a problem of great importance that hardly goes away after this dialogue: the question of the relationship between Socrates' peculiar version of "self-knowledge" as "knowing what he knows and what he does not know" and the kind of *epistēmē* in terms of which Critias wants to interpret it. For it is most notable that what is *refuted* in this dialogue is the interpretation of self-knowledge as, in its fullest articulation, "the *epistēmē* of itself and the other *epistēmai* and the absence of *epistēmē*" (166eff.) What does *not* get refuted, what stands in the dialogue quietly as unrefuted, is Socratic self-knowledge understood as knowing what one knows and what one does not know. Understanding that possibility requires a sense of knowledge different from *epistēmē*.

3.1

To prepare for this discussion, we need to return to the beginning of the dialogue, where the issue of self-knowledge arises in a dramatic way in the first encounter between Socrates and young Charmides. For there, the

---

[5] *Ap.* 20dff.

sense of self-knowledge – and self-ignorance – that is in play is precisely the Socratic one.

The dialogue begins with Socrates relating to an unnamed companion that he had just returned from the battle at Potidea, the very battle where, as Alcibiades relates in the *Symposium*, Socrates distinguished himself by both his *sōphrosunē* (in the conventional sense of the self-control enabling him to endure uncomfortable conditions) and his courage (saving Alcibiades' life in the battle).[6] Socrates goes to one of his usual gymnasium haunts, and after giving an account of the battle (which we do not hear), he asks about the young people, which ones are distinguished by their wisdom or beauty, or both. In time, the question is answered by the arrival of one who all agree is the most beautiful of the youths of the day, Charmides. Surprisingly, following the suggestion by Critias, Socrates is introduced to Charmides by a ruse. The young boy has a flaw: he is troubled by "headaches in the morning,"[7] and Critias easily persuades Socrates to pretend that he is a doctor who can cure Charmides' morning headaches. Socrates, apparently without qualms, goes along with the ruse, and after a long riff about how he learned from Zalmoxis that one cannot cure the body without curing the soul as well, informs Charmides that he cannot administer the cure until he discovers whether *sōphrosunē* is in him, and suggests that they investigate to see whether it is so (157a–157c).

Now, why would Socrates engage in this ruse, and why in particular would he invoke the need for *sōphrosunē* to be "in Charmides" if he is to be cured? The most plausible answer is that Socrates has immediately perceived what the probable cause of Charmides' headaches is. For they occur, Socrates has been told, "in the morning." What is the most likely cause of specifically morning headaches for a young, beautiful boy in his late teens who comes from a rich and noble family? Hangovers, of course! And what, after we try all the various home remedies for hangovers, do we eventually learn is the only real cure for these hangovers? Moderation, or *sōphrosunē*, in drinking. Socrates immediately puts his finger on the real cure for

---

[6] *Smp.* 219e–220e. Just prior to this (217a–219e), Alcibiades had related another example of Socrates' extraordinary *sōphrosunē* in a different sense: his ability to withstand the temptations of Alcibiades' beauty. This manifestation of *sōphrosunē* is repeated, hilariously, at the beginning of the *Chrm.* (155d), when Socrates gets a glimpse inside the handsome young Charmides' cloak and is "enflamed" (ἐφλεγόμην; a euphemism). In a matter of seconds, he recovers his self-control.

[7] *Chrm.* 155b. ἕωθεν is the Greek for "in the morning."

Charmides' morning headaches; *sōphrosunē* will very much be at stake here.[8] Charmides *lacks sōphrosunē* in this obvious sense, but that is not the only thing he lacks. He lacks the self-knowledge to know what his problem is and what he must do to remedy it.[9] The intimacy of the connection between *sōphrosunē* and self-knowledge has thus already been limned in the dramatic prologue to the actual discussion. Socrates, by contrast, *knows* what ails Charmides, and knows what will cure him, if anything will. And so the effort to articulate what *sōphrosunē* is begins.

The very way the conversation begins supports the intimate relation between self-knowledge and *sōphrosunē*. Socrates could, of course, have simply begun with something like, "Well, then, Charmides, what do you think *sōphrosunē* is?" Instead, he introduces the question in a strikingly elaborate formulation that insistently invokes the issue of self-knowledge. I translate as literally as I can:

> It seems to me, I said, that it would be best to approach the examination in this way. It is clear that if *sōphrosunē* is present in you (πάρεστιν), then you must have an opinion about it. For necessarily, it being in you, if indeed it is in you, it will grant to you the means of perception (ἄισθησιν) out of which you will be able to offer an opinion of what *sōphrosunē* is and of what quality it is. Or do you think not?
> I think so, he said.
> Since you know how to speak Greek, I said, you must be able to say how it appears to you.
> Perhaps, he said.
> In order that we may divine (τοπάσωμεν) whether it is in you or not, tell me, I said, what, in your opinion, do you say *sōphrosunē* is? (158e–159a)

Surely, Plato wanted us to take note of the many complications implicit in this formulation. For our purposes, I want to concentrate on how insistently the issue of self-knowledge is pressed on the young Charmides.[10] Four times in the formulation of the question, reference is made to the question of whether or not *sōphrosunē* is "in" Charmides. Indeed, although the final phrase of the formulation asks straightforwardly what Charmides thinks *sōphrosunē* is, the real force of the question seems rather to be whether or not *sōphrosunē*, whatever it is, really is *in* Charmides. Clearly,

---

[8] Of course, Charmides' subsequent adult conduct as one of the "thirty" during the tyranny is proof enough that Charmides never succeeds in acquiring the virtue.

[9] This scene may contain a hint as to why Charmides never suggests, as a definition of *sōphrosunē*, the common one of "self-control" (as in Alcibiades' examples above). Since this self-control is not "in" Charmides, he does not think of it.

[10] For a discussion of the many other complications, see Hyland (1981), especially chapter 3, "The Meaning of the Question Concerning *Sōphrosynē*: The First Response."

the place where Charmides must look to come up with an opinion about *sōphrosunē* is *within himself*. Only if *sōphrosunē* is in Charmides, only if it is part of who he is, Socrates seems to hold, will he be able to opine about it.

Now, in one sense, this claim seems dubious; does Socrates really believe that only *sōphrōn* people can know what *sōphrosunē* is? Is it entirely impossible to learn what *sōphrosunē* is, for example, by noticing its exhibition in someone else or by being told by a *sōphrōn* person what it is? And can this limitation be generalized to *all* knowledge or at least to all knowledge of virtue? Moreover, does it follow from this that if *sōphrosunē* is in Charmides, then he will certainly know what it is, that its being in Charmides is a necessary *and* sufficient condition for his knowing it?

To be sure, Socrates, strictly speaking, does not ask whether Charmides *knows* what *sōphrosunē* is but only if he has an *opinion* about it – though his subsequent elenchus of the opinions Charmides does come up with testifies that Socrates will hardly be satisfied that Charmides merely has some opinion or other. Or are all these considerations too abstract, missing the real force of what Socrates is asking? Socrates' formulation is consistent, after all, with the various formulations in the dialogues of the teaching regarding "recollection," which also claims that genuine knowledge somehow comes from looking *within* ourselves.[11] And Socrates' own articulation of his philosophical "method" as that of being a midwife who helps others "give birth" to ideas within them also points in the same direction.[12] In any case, such doubts would seem to miss the real force of Socrates' complex formulation, namely, that the real issue here is less a request for a general definition of a particular virtue than whether or not *sōphrosunē* is *in* Charmides. This formulation would thus cast doubt on the view that what Socrates is seeking in this and perhaps other dialogues is simply an abstract formulation of a virtue, a "definition," that can withstand elenchus. The real issue, again, is whether or not *sōphrosunē* is in Charmides and so whether he can articulate an opinion about it. Self-knowledge is inseparable from his effort to say what *sōphrosunē* is.

But what kind of self-knowledge will it be that Charmides will gain if he obeys Socrates' request? Superficially, to be sure, he will learn whether he can come up with an adequate definition of the virtue in question. But in a deeper sense, obeying Socrates' complex request, he might learn much about himself. He may learn whether *sōphrosunē* is in him, and so whether

---

[11] *Men.* 82bff, is perhaps the *locus classicus* of this teaching.   [12] *Tht.* 149aff.

or not he is a *sōphrōn*.[13] Perhaps more to the point, if, as soon happens, he is put in aporia, he will at least begin the project of knowing what he knows and what he does not know. But this is precisely the sense of self-knowledge that Socrates in the *Apology* claims as his own life's goal and what distinguishes him from other people, that is, his own articulation of his philosophical pursuit. By looking within himself to find *sōphrosunē*, Charmides is asked to begin that pursuit of self-knowledge that is Socratic philosophy.

However, the formulation is more complicated still. For Socrates does not strictly say that if *sōphrosunē* is in Charmides he will know what it is, or even that if it is in him he will have an opinion on it. He complicates things immensely by saying that if *sōphrosunē*, *sōphrosunē itself*, is in Charmides, it will offer him "the *means of perception by which he can offer an opinion about it.*" What Charmides will attempt to articulate by looking within himself, then, is not strictly *sōphrosunē itself*, whether or not it is in him, but the "means of perception," which, being present, it would grant him. This raises enormous questions. What are these "means of perception"? And is there not an implication here that an articulation of *sōphrosunē* (or possibly any other virtue) will be not a direct articulation of *sōphrosunē itself* – what will in later writings be called the "form" or "idea" of *sōphrosunē* – but an articulation of these "means of perception" that *sōphrosunē* itself, if it is in Charmides, will offer him? This presses all the more strongly on us the first question above: Just what are these means of perception?

I submit that they most likely would be Charmides' own *sōphrōn actions*, which, if *sōphrosunē* is indeed in him, will be the manifestations of the virtue that Charmides can try to articulate. *Sōphrosunē*, if it is in Charmides, will not be quiescent; it will *manifest* itself in what will be his *sōphrōn* actions. Charmides, in trying to say what he thinks *sōphrosunē* is, will look within himself and examine his own activity, those actions that he may have performed which will be the manifestations, and thus the "means of perception," which the *sōphrosunē* within him has offered and by which he might say what it is. And that is just what Charmides does, at least in his first two definitions of *sōphrosunē*, "a kind of quietness" and "modesty."

---

[13] At the conclusion of the *Charmides*, we see that Charmides has at least an inkling that he lacks *sōphrosunē* and needs the cure (176b), though this is immediately compromised by his expression of willingness to use violence against Socrates (176c).

If the formulation of the first question did not make this plain enough, Socrates' formulation of the second question at 160d–e makes even more striking both the emphasis on Charmides' looking within himself and the emphasis on the difference between *sōphrosunē* itself and its manifestations:

> Then once again, Charmides, I said, pay attention more closely (μᾶλλον προσέχων τὸν νοῦν) and, looking within yourself (ἐμβλέψας), consider (ἐννοήσας; literally "think into") the effect which *sōphrosunē* has on you and what sort of thing would have this effect. Thinking all this together (συλλογισάμενος), tell me well and courageously (ἀνδρείως) what it appears to you to be.
>
> And he, after considering and altogether courageously examining himself (πάνυ ἀνδρικῶς πρὸς ἑαυτὸν διασκεψάμενος), said, it seems to me that *sōphrosunē* makes a man ashamed or bashful, and *sōphrosunē* to be indeed modesty (αἰδώς).

Three things deserve our particular attention in this second formulation. First, we see reiterated the emphasis that Socrates places on Charmides' looking *within himself* to formulate his opinion. Self-knowledge is still very much at issue here. Second, however, Socrates emphasizes that this effort of Charmides, this self-examination, requires *courage*. Now, if all Socrates were asking of Charmides was to try out some definition or other, as happens soon with the third definition, why would this demand courage? Instead, what demands courage is that Charmides examine *himself*. Presumably, the need for courage arises because, as the dramatic introduction in fact intimated, Charmides may discover that he *lacks* the virtue in question. Socratic self-knowledge, the recognition of what we know and do not know, may be painful and demand courage. Third, this time with a somewhat different inflection, our attention is again drawn to the fact that Socrates does not simply ask Charmides to articulate "*sōphrosunē* itself." Instead, he is asked to consider "the effect which *sōphrosunē* has on you and what sort of thing would have this effect," to "think all this together," and to say courageously what the virtue appears to be. Whereas the first formulation also drew the distinction between *sōphrosunē* itself and its manifestations but left opaque the nature of the relation between the two, this second formulation intimates the work that needs to be done by Charmides. He must consider *both* the effects or manifestations that *sōphrosunē* has on him *and* what sort of thing would have this effect, and then to "think all this together" in order to say how *sōphrosunē* appears to him. To say the least, Socrates is challenging Charmides, for he is asking him to do nothing less than consider the relation between *sōphrosunē* and its effects, that is, between the form and its manifestations, and then to

"bind the two together into a whole."[14] Little wonder that the youth will
not be successful.

And fail he does on the first two efforts, though as Socrates says, he does
so "altogether courageously." But just what does this failure amount to?
Socrates had said that if *sōphrosunē* were in Charmides, he would be able to
have an opinion as to what it was. Well, he does have opinions – two so
far. But assuming for the moment that Socrates' two refutations are
adequate, Charmides' opinions do not hold up, at least as comprehensive
definitions of the virtue. Can we conclude from this, as the dramatic
opening has already intimated, that *sōphrosunē* is therefore not really in
Charmides? Possibly. But is the measure of whether someone is *sōphrōn* or
not really to be whether they can give an adequate, comprehensive definition of the virtue that stands up to the Socratic elenchus?[15] Even more
strongly, is the measure of whether or not someone is *sōphrōn* and *knows
what sōphrosunē is* that he or she can give an adequate definition of it? Is
knowledge, all knowledge, reducible to the articulation of relevant definitions? As we shall see, the subsequent discussion with Critias will put this
very much into question.

In any case, Socrates has by the end of the second of Charmides'
attempts refuted those attempts, but he has done so in a gentle, rather
pedagogical way, as would seem to fit the mature philosopher's discussion
with a late teenage young man. That all changes with the third definition,
and the reason why will have everything to do with self-knowledge.

Charmides accepts the second refutation and suggests a third definition
promptly and without the thoughtful hesitation of the first two attempts.
He says:

> It seems to me, Socrates, that this [the just completed refutation by
> Socrates] is correctly spoken. But examine this statement about *sōphrosunē,*
> what it is in your opinion. Just now I recollected what I heard someone say,
> that *sōphrosunē* is doing the things of one's own (τὸ τὰ ἑαυτοῦ πράττειν).
> So examine whether in your opinion the one saying these things speaks
> correctly. (161b)

To this third attempt, Socrates responds so harshly as to seem almost
vicious. "ὦ μιαρέ, you must have heard this from Critias or some other of
the wise." The epithet means literally something like "you vile polluter!" It

---

[14] *Smp.* 202e. As I try to show (Hyland 1981), this involves considering the relationship between
νόησις and διάνοια, surely one of the most complicated issues in the dialogues. See in particular
chapters 3 and 4.
[15] One thinks here of the old adage, "actions speak louder than words."

is sometimes softened in the translations to "you wretch!"[16] The harshness of the epithet clearly signals a change in tone from the gentle pedagogy of the first two refutations. Why is Socrates so angry? It cannot be the specific definition that angers him. After all, it is the very definition that in the *Republic* he gets Glaucon and Adeimantus to agree is an appropriate definition of justice.[17] So it is surely nothing about the intellectual content of the definition that brings on the outburst. Instead, it must be because Charmides with this definition *gives up* the courageous looking into himself that had characterized his first two tries and for which Socrates had praised the youth. Charmides here changes the status of the discussion from the very personal and Socratic examination of himself to a much more abstract and even "academic" situation in which he "tries out" a definition he has heard from someone else to see what Socrates will do with it.

There is thus no small irony in Charmides' third definition: in offering the definition "doing the things of one's own" or "doing one's own business," Charmides *ceases* to do his own business in the philosophic sense at stake here. The dimension of self-knowledge is now dropped, and what is left is an academic contest to see whether a proposed definition can withstand Socrates' elenchus. With this change, any hope of discovering whether *sōphrosunē* is in Charmides, any hope of Charmides discovering further what he knows and what he does not know, is crushed. It is not a question of the examined life that is now at stake, but rather a professional dispute. No wonder that Socrates responds, with anger and heavy irony, that Charmides must have got this definition "from Critias or some other of the wise" (161c).

Predictably, this challenge brings Critias into the discussion in a way that immediately calls into question his integrity. He at first denies that the definition came from him, but soon makes it clear that it was indeed his (161c, 162c–3). Henceforward, then, the discussion is primarily between Socrates and Critias. However, Plato does not allow us to leave behind the question of self-knowledge. For before long, after the formulation "doing the things of one's own" is refuted as a definition of *sōphrosunē*, he has Socrates lead the discussion back to the issue of self-knowledge by wondering at a supposed implication of Critias' definition, namely, that "someone who is *sōphrōn* is ignorant of their *sōphrosunē*" (164c). Critias

---

[16] E.g. by West and West (1986, 28) who nevertheless comment in a footnote on its harshness, and Sprague (1972, 70).

[17] *R.* IV.433aff.

finds this implication utterly unacceptable and, in an elaborate formulation, admits that he may have been wrong in what he said so far. Referring explicitly to the language of the Delphic oracle, Critias asserts a new definition of *sōphrosunē*, that it is nothing less than the Delphic inscription "know thyself," interpreted by him with a flourish as not a command but a greeting (164d–165b). It is important to note that Critias, staying true here to the language of the Delphic inscription, formulates his definition with the Delphic word, τὸ γιγνώσκειν. At both the beginning (164d4) and end (165b4) of his formulation, he uses the phrase τὸ γιγνώσκειν ἑαυτόν and, with some plausibility, closes his formulation by holding out the expectation that Socrates might well accept this definition without further questioning, so close is it to Socrates' own philosophic stance.

We might expect, with Critias, that Socrates would accept at least some version of this formulation, perhaps taking the opportunity to pursue further the question of just what sort of knowledge this γιγνώσκειν implies, in the spirit of the *Apology*. In a certain sense, he does, but in a most strange way; he proceeds by the *via negativa*. After assuring Critias that he doesn't know if this answer will suffice but must examine it, Socrates asks the following most consequential question, which I translate using the Greek for the crucial word change that Socrates makes: "If, then, *sōphrosunē* is a sort of γιγνώσκειν, then it is clear that it would be some sort of ἐπιστήμη, and it must be of something; or no (ἢ οὔ;)" (165c5–6). West and West capture the change by translating the sentence as "For if sound-mindedness is recognizing something, it is clear that it would be a kind of knowledge, and one that is *of* something, or wouldn't it?"[18] Sprague translates, "Well, if knowing is what temperance is, then it clearly must be some sort of science and must be of something, isn't that so?"[19] Both soften Socrates' emphatic "or no," which, taken in its full force, opens the possibility that the answer may indeed be "no, self-knowledge is *not* a kind of *epistēmē*. It is a different mode of knowing." Jowett does not even translate the final "or no," thus hiding from the reader the possibility of doubt that Socrates clearly allows.[20]

This word change on Socrates' part, from γιγνώσκειν to *epistēmē*, largely determines the course of the rest of the dialogue. Critias, like Jowett, pays no attention to the possibility of a negative reply and responds "Yes, of oneself" (165c). So *sōphrosunē* becomes, in this formulation, "the *epistēmē* of oneself." At this point, the dialogue *could* have moved in a number of directions. Socrates might have asked what such an *epistēmē* of

---

[18] West and West (1986, 36). [19] Sprague (1972, 77). [20] Hamilton and Cairns (1961, 111).

oneself would look like. Would it be the kind of personal knowledge, a "knowing what I know and what I do not know," of the sort he claims in the *Apology*? That certainly seems like a mode of knowledge, but it hardly seems like an *epistēmē*. Or would it be some kind of proto-Freudian knowledge of one's personality? Or would an "*epistēmē* of oneself" be a more generalized *epistēmē of the self*, a thorough examination of the nature of selfhood? This *could* be understood as a systematic study of the soul, and while the nature of the soul is very much at issue in many dialogues, it is surely not treated as an object of *epistēmē*; indeed, more often than not it is expressed in terms of various *myths*.[21] In any case, none of these options is pursued. Instead, via a subtle shift, Critias changes the issue from an *epistēmē* of oneself (ἑαυτοῦ: 165c7) to an *epistēmē of itself* (ἑαυτῆς: 166c3), that is, to a "science of itself."

The change occurs at 166c: "It's not like this, but all the others are *epistēmai* of something else, not of themselves, whereas this is the only *epistēmē* which is of the other *epistēmai* and itself of itself." Critias here takes two crucial steps, both of which together will be the downfall of the definition. First, he changes the "object" of the proposed *epistēmē* from *oneself*, that is, from the issue, one way or the other, of self-knowledge, to *itself*, that is, to the *epistēmē* itself. And second, he adds that it is also the *epistēmē* of *all other epistēmai*. In one page, the knowledge in question has moved from the potentially Socratic sense of self-knowledge to something like a comprehensive "science of science" that covers all the other sciences and itself. It only remains for Socrates to wonder whether Critias should not add on to this, "and the absence of science," and we get the full-blown Critian formulation that *sōphrosunē* is "the science of all the other sciences and of itself and of the absence of science" (166e). From the very personal sense of Socratic self-knowledge, we have moved to a curious prefiguration of a Hegelian "encyclopedia of the sciences." It is hardly surprising, then, that Jowett begins at this point to translate *sōphrosunē* as "wisdom."

This change no doubt suits Critias' grandiose and elitist intellectual proclivities, but it will hardly appeal to Socrates. Instead, Socrates tries one more time to bring the sense back to something like his own version of self-knowledge, one that quite accurately captures his own philosophic procedure:

---

[21] Consider the treatment of the soul in, among other dialogues, the *Phaedrus, Symposium, Republic*, or *Phaedo*.

Then only the *sōphrōn* man will know himself (ἑαυτὸν γνώσεται) and will be able to examine what he happens to know and not know, and in the same way he will be able to examine other people to see what someone does in fact know and thinks he knows, and again what he thinks he knows but does not know. No one else will be able to do this. And this is to be *sōphrōn* and *sōphrosunē* and to know oneself (τὸ ἑαυτὸν αὐτὸν γιγνώσκειν): to know what one knows and does not know. Is this what you are saying? Yes, he said. (167a)

In this response Socrates seems almost to be begging Critias to notice the difference between Critias' formulations in terms of a "science" (*epistēmē*) and Socrates' version of his own "human" wisdom as knowing what he knows and does not know, and being able to question others as to what they know and do not know. In fact, in this passage Socrates virtually identifies *sōphrosunē* as self-knowledge in the sense of his own philosophic procedure. But Critias does not notice, and the rest of the dialogue proceeds by Socrates showing Critias that as an *epistēmē*, a "science" of itself and the other sciences and the lack of science, *sōphrosunē* would be neither possible nor desirable. But it is easy to miss the striking fact that what is *not* refuted, one might speculate, what is quietly accepted, is *sōphrosunē* as self-knowledge in the Socratic sense just articulated.

The lesson that one must glean from this subsequent refutation is complicated. On the one hand, self-knowledge in the Socratic sense stands unrefuted: unrefuted as a "definition" of *sōphrosunē*, unrefuted as a *telos* of philosophic living. Second, it at least may be that *sōphrosunē* is precisely that mode of knowing and that way of life. Third, it *is* a form of knowing, but, and emphatically, the knowing that is self-knowledge is not and cannot be an *epistēmē*. For that is what is refuted in the dialogue; self-knowledge *understood as an epistēmē* would be neither possible nor desirable. The guiding question with which the dialogue leaves us, then, is: Just what sort of knowing *is* the knowing that is self-knowledge, the knowing that Socrates always expresses with a form of the Greek γιγνώσκειν, since it cannot be an *epistēmē*? But the very coherence of the question contains an important recognition: to paraphrase Aristotle, "knowledge is spoken in many ways." *Epistēmē* cannot be the only legitimate mode of knowledge, and in at least some cases, paradigmatically that of self-knowledge, it is not even the appropriate mode of knowing. Knowledge is heterogeneous. But surely the chief question that the *Charmides* opens up for us remains: If self-knowledge, understood in the Socratic vein, is at once such a desirable stance, and if it cannot be an *epistēmē*, just what sort of knowledge is it?

We can take at least a few steps toward a response by considering briefly some core passages from the *Apology* and the *Republic*.

3.2

We turn first to the *Apology*, where the Platonic Socrates presents perhaps his most elaborate account of this self-knowledge as at once his "human wisdom" that sets him apart from others, yet at the same time a lifelong *quest* rather than an achieved cognitive state. He begins by distinguishing the sense in which he may have a certain wisdom from the sense in which he clearly does not:

> But I, men of Athens, have acquired this reputation through nothing else but a sort of wisdom. What sort of wisdom is this? It is just that which is perhaps a human wisdom (ἀνθρωπίνη σοφία). I really may be wise in this wisdom. But these men, of whom I was just now speaking, may be wise in some wisdom greater than human wisdom, or else I cannot say. For I do not know it (οὐ ... ἐπίσταμαι), but whoever says I do is lying, and speaks in order to slander me. (*Ap.* 20d–e)

Socrates then begins to elicit the sense of this "human wisdom" that he does have by using it to make sense of what he regards as the enigma of the Delphic oracle's claim, in answer to his friend Chaerephon's leading question, "is anyone wiser than Socrates?" that "no one is wiser." It is an enigma, says Socrates, because one thing that he *does* know is that he is *not* wise in the "greater than human wisdom" sense. Presumably, that means that he is not wise in the sense of having *epistēmē* in some comprehensive sense, the sense, for example, in which the politicians, poets, and artisans that Socrates goes on to examine claim to have it. What sense is this? At very least, he does not have it in the sense in which Critias wants to claim it as the meaning of *sōphrosunē*. He does not have "a science of itself and all the other sciences and the lack of science." *That* would indeed be a "greater than human wisdom."

Socrates, speaking on behalf of Diotima, speaks of this sort of wisdom in the *Symposium*:

> This is the way it is: none of the gods philosophizes nor desires to become wise – because they *are* wise – nor does anyone else who is wise philosophize. Nor on the other hand do those who are ignorant philosophize or desire to become wise. This is just what is difficult about ignorance: the ignorant person thinks himself sufficient in what is noble and good and intelligent. Nor does he desire what he thinks he does not lack or what he believes he is not in need of. (*Smp.* 204a)

Comprehensive wisdom of the sort Critias affirms is for the divine alone. Nevertheless, there *is* a way in which Socrates stands out from the politicians, poets, and artisans he examines. They *think* they know what they do not know, whereas Socrates, knowing that he is not wise, does not think he is. He is thus, he says at *Apology* 21d, "a little bit wiser than [them] in that whatever I do not know, I do not think that I know." But as the passage from the *Symposium* above indicates, this *recognition* that one does not know spurs a desire to know. That is, Socrates' recognition of his lack of wisdom makes him *philosophical* in the literal sense: a lover of wisdom who, recognizing his lack, seeks to become wiser. Socrates' "human wisdom" is *philosophy*. Put differently, Socrates' aporia is *not* ignorance. Ignorance, real ignorance, is "thinking that you know what you do not know." As the *recognition* that he does not know, aporia is a mode of *knowing*. In bringing his interlocutors to aporia, Socrates is not *reducing* them to aporia; he is raising them *up* to the *achievement* of aporia. Aporia is *self*-knowledge, it is Socrates' human wisdom. That human wisdom is *philosophy*. As the passage from the *Symposium* quoted above intimates, and as that dialogue as a whole makes clear, there is a complicated relationship between eros, aporia, and philosophic living.

We can learn something more about this relationship and about the nature of the mode of knowing that is Socratic self-knowledge by noticing how such knowledge gets *exhibited* by Socrates. To begin with the negative way: it is certainly not a knowledge that is static, a once-and-for-all "now I know myself" phenomenon that might parallel, for example, knowledge of a mathematical formula, or perhaps any other genuine *epistēmē*. Self-knowledge is different; it is not the achievement of some sort of closure on something like "who I am" but an *ongoing* challenge. Socrates is wiser than the rest, but he can hardly rest on his wisdom. His wisdom is precisely the challenge of philosophical living, to continue the effort as long as one lives. Socrates would thus seem to agree with Heraclitus: "The soul has a *logos* that increases itself."[22]

Second, self-knowledge is not exhibited, as is epistemic knowing, in the mode of assertion. "This is what I know, and this is what I do not know." If it were so, it would risk farce: two very long lists, one, "what I know," another, presumably much longer, "what I do not know." We hear nothing faintly resembling this from Socrates in any dialogue. And yet his self-knowledge *does* get exhibited. How? Through his philosophic stance of *questioning*. Just as we too easily take aporia to be a mode of

---

[22] Heraclitus, DK (B115).

ignorance, so we too easily take questioning as arising out of simple ignorance: "I don't know, so I question." But for Socrates, questioning, like aporia, is also a mode of *knowing*. I question out of the *knowledge* that I do not know and, more fully, of what I know and do not know. Those who are ignorant, who think they know what they do not know, do not question. They assert, or at very least, rest content with their supposed knowledge. Socratic self-knowledge, by contrast, is exhibited by his questioning stance of philosophy. It is a knowledge that is lived, not merely asserted.

I want to close this chapter with a brief discussion of a contrasting but striking example in the dialogues of self-*ignorance*. Like Socratic self-knowledge, self-ignorance is also not simply asserted, but exhibited. We saw this in the case of Charmides in the dramatic introduction of that dialogue. This happens as well in the *Republic*, for example, in a most strange way. In the famous interlude that constitutes Books V–VII, we see developed a conception of "philosopher-rulers," who have climbed out of the "cave" of ignorance to see the "real" world of forms and even the sun, the "offspring" of the idea of the good. These rulers would seem to be less *philosophers* in the Socratic sense of living a life of questioning than *wise* people, with precisely the kind of comprehensive wisdom that Critias entertains, a "science of itself and the other sciences and the lack of science," including knowledge of the good.[23] In the light of this knowledge, it is suggested, they will "come back down" into the cave and rule the city with perfect justice – similar to the fantasy in which Socrates engages briefly at *Charmides* 171d–172a.

Is such a city even possible, and does Plato intend us to take it as such? That is of course a subject of long debate. But if we think about the preparation of these philosopher-rulers, particularly their early education, we see that this vision of wise rulers gets radically destabilized. For we are told as early as Book III that in order to guarantee the loyalty and obedience of the guardians, some of whom are to become the philosopher-rulers, they must, while children, be deeply imbued with two "noble lies." First, the lie of autocthony, that they were not really born from human parents but from the earth of the city, and second, the lie of metals, that each person is by nature either gold-souled, silver-souled, or bronze-souled, that is, destined by nature to be either a ruler, a soldier,

---

[23] An issue that is broached, but only broached, by Critias in the final refutation of the *Chrm.* (174b–175a), where he tries to define the meaning of "the science of itself and the other sciences and the lack of science" as "knowledge of good and evil" (174b). I cannot address this enormous issue in this chapter. For my take on the larger issue of "the good," see Hyland (2011).

or a worker.[24] It is crucial to notice that Plato has Socrates call these "noble *lies.*" It would certainly have been open to him to call them from the beginning noble *myths.* If they had been, we could have taken them to conform to the understanding of myth that Socrates himself presents in Book II: that myths are "as a whole, false, though there are true things in them too."[25] We then could have interpreted the "truth" of the two "noble myths" to be, first, that we owe a *natural* allegiance to our city that should never be broken and, second, that we are *by nature* suited to membership in one segment of the society, and therefore should have no qualms about the station we are given.

But they are *not* "noble myths"; they are noble *lies.* The difference must surely be that "a lie is a lie is a lie." A lie, unlike a myth, holds no interpretive truths. Therefore, as noble *lies*, it must be *false* that we owe a natural allegiance to the city, and it must be *false* that we are born by nature to a given station in life. The philosopher-rulers, these supposed wise men and women who will rule in the light of their comprehensive wisdom, will be raised and educated on the basis of two massive lies.

As usual, however, complications abound. Two in particular turn the whole notion of the noble lie into more of a problem than the solution to a problem that it is asserted to be.[26] The first complication is that, although Socrates does indeed introduce the lie as just that, a noble lie and not a myth, a short time later, at III.415a, as he elaborates the second noble lie of metals, he explicitly refers to at least *that* lie as *also* a "myth":

> All the same, hear out the rest of the myth (τοῦ μύθου). All of you in the city are certainly brothers, we shall say to them in telling the myth (μυθολογοῦντες), but the god, in fashioning those of you who are competent to rule, mixed gold in at their birth.

What is going on here? Is the autocthony story a lie and the metals story a myth? Are they both lies, as the first formulation certainly indicates? Are they both really myths, as this second version could be taken to indicate? Is Plato here perhaps using "*mythos*" in the loose sense of "story," and referring only to the general "story" being told? Is he perhaps not writing carefully here, and taking "lie" and "myth" to be synonymous? If so, synonymous in which sense? Are they both lies or both myths?

The second complication occurs as Socrates is introducing the two lies at III.414b. Perhaps anticipating the difficulties I have already pointed to, Socrates hedges:

[24] *R.* 414d–415d.   [25] *R.* 377a.
[26] I wish to thank James Ambury for reminding me of both these complications.

Could we, I said, somehow contrive one of those lies that come into being in case of need, of which we were just now speaking, some one noble lie to persuade, *in the best case, even the rulers, but if not them, the rest of the city?* (emphasis added)

The emphasized words open a flood of questions and complications. These lies are to be told very early in the education of the guardian class. Will the few who are to become rulers not be told these lies even as youths? But then how will their loyalty be assured, and in any case how will their futures be identified at such a young age? Will the sign of their future ruling ability be that they don't believe the lie told to them from the beginning? If so, we face the same problem: how will their loyalty be assured? Will they be told much later in their more mature education that these are lies? How will they respond to the recognition that they have been raised on massive lies? Are they proto-Straussians, who will accept this recognition with a wry smile?

In any case, nowhere in the ensuing discussion are we informed of a point in their later educations where these lies are revealed to them as lies. And yet, on the extremely problematic hypothesis entertained, that these rulers will eventually become comprehensively wise, it would seem that they simply must discover at some point the untruthful foundation of their education. Is it obvious how they will respond? We are faced, then, with a formidable set of ambiguities.

Despite all these ambiguities, I am inclined to take seriously the implications of what is explicitly said in the dialogue, that the future rulers will (in the best case) be convinced of these lies and apparently will continue to believe them throughout their lives. But this means that these supposedly "wise" philosopher-rulers, who know the forms, know the good, and rule in the light of that wisdom, will be massively ignorant of the fact that their nurture and education is based on foundational lies. They will be massively self-ignorant. They will, in the precise Socratic sense, think they know what they do not know. We are left to speculate as to what the dialogue would have looked like if we suppose them to have suddenly discovered that the foundations of their educations were lies.[27]

To conclude: for Plato, knowledge is not homogeneous but heterogeneous. There cannot be an *epistēmē* of *epistēmē*, a "science of itself and all

---

[27] The impetus for these comments on the *Republic* arose from my reflections on how I would want to respond to the thought-provoking paper of James Ambury, "Self-Knowledge in Plato's Allegory of the Cave," at the annual conference of the Ancient Philosophy Society in Portland, ME, on April 29, 2016. I thank him for this provocation. A revised version of his paper is included as Chapter 5 in this volume.

sciences and the absence of science," because *epistēmē* does not capture all the knowledge that humans have and need. Perhaps the most striking example in the dialogues of the heterogeneity of knowledge, that is, of the irreducibility of knowledge to *epistēmē*, is Socratic self-knowledge. There are no doubt others.[28] This makes self-knowledge neither inferior nor superior to *epistēmē*. It is simply different. Plato's dialogues, in their astonishingly complex use of *epistēmē*, of drama, of art, of irony, of myth, imitate the heterogeneous character of human knowledge. The heterogeneity of the dialogues is Plato's imitation of the heterogeneous whole.

[28] Eros, for example, or the human soul, of neither of which is there a form, and so of neither of which can there be an *episteme*.

CHAPTER 4

Socratic Wisdom and Platonic Knowledge in the Dialogues of Plato

Sara Ahbel-Rappe

4.1

This chapter constitutes a reading of the figure of Socrates in Plato's dialogues, starting from what I take to be a promise to the reader embedded in the *Apology*'s revelation that "no one is wiser than Socrates" (21a4). The promise is that this revelation will bear fruit in the reading of the dialogues; Socratic wisdom will prove in some way worthy of this distinction as the highest wisdom. Specifically, in this chapter I argue that the Socratic persona represents wisdom, and as such wisdom is the larger container within which Plato constructs his philosophy, which operates as a form of knowledge. Socratic wisdom contains Platonic knowledge. But how do we get at the meaning and contents of Socratic wisdom, especially in light of Socrates' infamous disavowal of both wisdom and knowledge? What is Socratic wisdom and how does it differ from Platonic knowledge?

Socratic wisdom is not exactly a constructive epistemology, moral philosophy, or psychology. By virtue of its relationship to Platonic knowledge, it has applications in these areas, but in itself, Socratic wisdom remains prior to all such constructs. Socratic wisdom is not concerned with transmitting knowledge to another, just because it attempts to foster self-knowledge. The Socratic persona accordingly is associated with a philosophical technique that involves introspection – the reader's own introspection – or self-inquiry. Only by assuming this stance of self-inquiry can the reader meet Socrates, as one who appears in her own mind, and not primarily in the streets of Athens. So to say that "no one is wiser than Socrates" is to say that this highest wisdom can only be accessed as self-knowledge, is only available through self-inquiry.

For late antique authors such as Olympiodorus and Proclus, Socrates represents the intellect, the most divine aspect of the human being.[1] For

---

[1] Ambury (2014, 111).

example, Proclus says in his *Commentary on the Alcibiades* that Socrates "has established himself as corresponding to the intellect of the soul" (*in Alc.* 43.7–9). Ambury points out that if so, Alcibiades also occupies an allegorical role in Proclus' reading of the dialogue and so corresponds to the soul.[2] Proclus writes: "According to the analogy of the extremes we must relate Alcibiades to the rational soul, to which are still attached the emotions and the irrational powers" (in *Alc.* 43.20).

In my view, this late antique reading of *Alcibiades* I can help us make sense of the Socratic persona and its connection to self-knowledge throughout the dialogues. When we encounter this persona, it operates within the dialogues as that presence of mind that is not yet committed to a specific view or doxa. We might say that in the *Crito*, Crito represents the appetitive part of the soul (he is a businessman). Again, in the *Republic*, Cephalus represents the appetites and Polemarchus represents thumos. Or, finally in the *Laches*, Nicias stands in for the honor-loving part of the soul by virtue of his military profession. So in the Socratic dialogues, Socrates converses with the other parts of the soul. The conversation as a whole can be said to represent a complete human soul, in which Socrates tries to bring about agreement and like-mindedness, as well as to instill the motivation uniquely belonging to the philosophical element, that is, the love for wisdom. These inner conversations, in which we look inside the conflicted soul, reveal a Socratic presence that uncovers the desires, ambitions, and opinions of the soul. Socrates is the inner mirror; he represents that knowing self who can become aware of all that the mind harbors and bring it into the light of inquiry.

Because this dimension of the Socratic persona, its power to hold open space for the reader's own inquiry, is in a sense common ground for anyone reading Plato's dialogues, reading them through the figure of Socrates might seem to offer at most a banal starting point. Nevertheless, in what follows, I rely on the obviousness of this invocation of Socrates as an invitation to the reader to enter the dialogues herself. While my reading is grounded in this Socratic invitation, I explore how Plato approaches the nature of the self that is invited along, and how Plato uses this Socratic persona to facilitate self-knowledge. The Socratic self, the one that is invited into the picture through the awe of the Socratic presence, does not so much occupy a theoretical space, but instead involves the real presence of the reader's own awareness, the reader called to (self) attention.

---

[2] Ibid., 110.

Plato's dialogues present a contemplative orientation by means of the figure of Socrates. As in other contemplative traditions (i.e., certain forms of yoga or of Buddhist meditation), there is a technique in the Platonic dialogues whereby the raw ingredients of wisdom are furnished by the mind itself, considered as field of study and exploration. I will draw attention to the way in which the Socratic aspect of Plato's dialogues purports to teach the student how to investigate the mind and its objects directly.

Intellectually, the Socratic encounter takes place as the person becomes aware of the primacy of her knowing, "epistemic" self over the objects of thought, the priority of the knowing self over the opinions harbored by this same self. As Socrates puts it in *Alcibiades* I, to care for the self is not the same as caring for what belongs to the self. What then is the self, apart from all of its accoutrements? The true person, according to Socrates in *Alcibiades* I, is the self itself, the ὀφθαλμὸς (133a5) or "pilot" of the soul, that is, the aspect of the soul that is the subject or seat of knowledge (133c2) and as such it is not identical with any of the things known.[3] But how is the priority of the knower over any of its objects to be discerned? And what does this priority entail?

4.2

Plato introduces us to Socrates in the *Apology* by engaging the reader with a question: "One of you might interrupt and ask, 'Well, Socrates, just what is your enterprise?'" (*Ap.* 20c3–4). To this hypothetical question, Socrates says that he will answer with "the entire truth" (*Ap.* 20d5). The answer that Socrates discloses should be momentous, though on first hearing it reeks of dissimulation, as Plato acknowledges when he narrates Socrates as pleading with his audience not to raise an uproar (*Ap.* 21a5).

The *Apology* tells the story of Socrates' enterprise in his own words. This enterprise is associated with Delphi; it comes to birth after Socrates has been divinely revealed to possess "the highest wisdom" (*Ap.* 21a7: "The Oracle replied that no one was wiser"), and Socrates' query into the meaning of this divine revelation functions as its catalyst. Apollo's pronouncement is the spur, goading Socrates to undertake a new assignment, not to teach but to produce aporia (21b8–9: "And then I scarcely hit upon the following method of investigation. I went to one of those who had the reputation for wisdom"), to create around himself a veritable city of those

---

[3] Cf. *Phdr.* 247c–d for the "pilot" of the soul.

who will come to share this aporia, evidently, a sharing of the highest wisdom, a wisdom that is, nevertheless, no wisdom at all.

Socrates strives to reveal the complete truth behind his enterprise, yet all he can reveal is a puzzle. The god's meaning cannot be made obvious, as it is obvious not even to Socrates: "Whatever does the god mean; what is he hinting at? For I am fully aware that I am wise, neither in great nor small measure" (*Ap.* 21b3–5).

From these two premises, that Socrates is the wisest and that Socrates has no wisdom, he can only infer that "He among you, human beings, is wisest, who knows, like Socrates, that he has no worth with respect to wisdom, in very truth" (*Ap.* 23b2–3). This, then, is first parameter of Socratic wisdom, namely, that it is at once the highest and that it is no wisdom at all. We first meet Socrates at the end of his life, disclosing the nature of the highest wisdom with the enigma that "he who realizes, like Socrates, that he has no worth with respect to wisdom" can be declared to "have the highest wisdom."

We are encountering an idea that suggests that the highest wisdom is not knowledge about anything – in other words, as Socrates puts it, "it is not great or small" (*Ap.* 21b4–5). What then can this wisdom be about? And where in particular can we seek within Plato's texts themselves for clues as to the nature of this highest wisdom, the wisdom that is no wisdom? Starting with this very fact, that the highest wisdom is Socratic wisdom, we might turn to the beginning of Socrates' philosophical life, to the literary encounter that Plato invents, when Parmenides visits Athens and initiates the young Socrates into the nature of what he calls, simply, the "One," via a mysterious exercise.[4]

There is a glaring similarity between those (dramatically) earlier gymnastics Parmenides put a youthful Socrates through and the later Socratic elenchus, the exercise through which he puts his fellow citizens: their aporetic conclusions. It is here that the life-blood of Socratic wisdom most resides, in aporia, in irresolution and the failure to grasp an answer. The Socratic encounter, with which we are so familiar through the elenctic dialogues, starts out with a search for definition and a program of constraints on the formulation of definition. The Socratic elenchus reaches a place that reason and logic cannot attain; it constantly reverts to the failure

---

[4] On the *Parmenides* as the dramatic representation of Socrates at his youngest, see Zuckert (2009, 8–9). Indeed, for Zuckert, the dramatic dates follow a Socratic trajectory, in the sense that these dates shape the narrative progression of the dialogues, what Zuckert calls "Plato's dramaturgy" in terms that tell the story of intellectual biography of Socrates.

of logic to define the nature of virtue or any specific virtue. In a similar way, the paradoxes generated through the survey of problems with the forms, together with the irresolution generated by the eight (or nine) hypotheses in the second half of the *Parmenides*,[5] suggest that there is something in the nature of the reality under discussion that eludes the grasp of the logical mind.

Now in the *Apology*, Socrates describes his response to the declaration that he is wisest in the following words: ἐγὼ γὰρ δὴ οὔτε μέγα οὔτε σμικρὸν σύνοιδα ἐμαυτῷ σοφὸς ὤν ("I indeed am aware that I am wise, neither in great or small measure"). Crucial to this formula are the words "neither great nor small," as they play an important role in the first half of the *Parmenides*, which is precisely a discussion of the "great and small." The defining problem of the first half of the dialogue concerns participation between form and particular. How can the one form be distributed in its participants, either as a part or as a whole? Gill labels this part of the argument, from 130e4 to 131e7, "the Whole-Part dilemma," which she calls the "second movement of the first half."[6] Significant, in my view, is that Plato uses the language of "great and small" throughout this section of the dialogue. This echo between the *Apology*'s "great or small" and the first half of the *Parmenides* is a deliberate link between the beginning and end points of the Socratic intellectual trajectory. In this sense, Socratic wisdom, the highest wisdom, contains the world of the dialogues:

> "Then are you willing to say, Socrates, that our one form is really divided? Will it still be one?"
> "Not at all," he replied.
> "No," said Parmenides. "For suppose you are going to divide largeness itself. If each of the many large things is to be large by a part of largeness smaller than largeness itself, won't that appear unreasonable?"
> "It certainly will," he replied.
> "What about this? Will each thing that has received a small part of the equal have something by which to be equal to anything, when its portion is less than the equal itself?"
> "That's impossible."
> "Well, suppose one of us is going to have a part of the small. The small will be larger than that part of it, since the part is a part of it: so the small itself will be larger! And that to which the part subtracted is added will be smaller, not larger, than it was before."
> "That surely couldn't happen, he said." (131c8–131e3)[7]

---

[5] Or perhaps nine hypotheses, following the sage analysis of Gill in Gill and Ryan (1996, 55).
[6] Gill and Ryan (1996, 32).   [7] Translation of Gill and Ryan (1996).

The problems here concern treating the Form as a physical object existing separately from another such object. It is an absurd attempt to spatialize and quantify a kind of reality that does not have that solid, concrete, objective existence. Yet if the Form is treated not as a physical object but as a thought, a mental object, then other difficulties arise in turn. For example, the thought will constantly proliferate, giving rise to what Gill calls "the largeness regress" that begins at 132a1:[8]

> "I suppose you think each form is one on the following ground: whenever some number of things seem to you to be large, perhaps there seems to be some one character the same as you look at them all, and from that you conclude that the large is one thing."
> "That's true," he said.
> "What about the large itself and the other large things? If you look at them all in the same way with the mind's eye, again won't some one thing appear large, by which all these appear large?"
> "It seems so."
> "So another form of largeness will make its appearance."

In response to the largeness regress, Socrates proposes that forms are thoughts in the mind. Yet, as Parmenides shows, thoughts should refer to extra-mental objects, so that either the extra-mental objects will determine the forms and, in that case, the forms won't be causes, or the extra-mental objects will turn out themselves to be thoughts, since forms are thoughts, in order to retain their explanatory powers. That is, the participants will themselves only be thoughts and the objective world will dissolve.

Following on these problems, the "worst difficulty" argument (133a8–134e8) arises because of the incommensurability between the individual's particular intelligence and the objects of that intelligence which are putatively absolute. What to do in the face of these puzzles? How can the form be known? How can it be conceived? How can the individual knower grasp an object that inherently transcends all individuals? As Gill puts it, "in this final movement Parmenides and Socrates agree that forms are not in us (133c3–5)."[9]

In the dialogue's second half, Socrates is forced to move beyond the physical, beyond the mental and conceptual realm, into a deeper wisdom, the wisdom that is no wisdom, in other words, the highest wisdom. The first hypothesis (137c3–142b1) denies that the One is anywhere, of any size, at any time. It is completely without number. It is not an object. It is neither great nor small. It cannot be measured. It is neither here nor there;

---

[8] Gill and Ryan (1996, 35).   [9] Gill (2012, 41).

it has no determinate nature and so it cannot be thought (142a5–6: "nor is it the object of opinion or knowledge"). Thus in the first half of the dialogue, Socrates confronts the difficulties inherent in his own mind. What he is to study cannot be an object of thought. What ensues is an insight into a reality that is unconditioned by the particular mind. This insight is facilitated by the antecedent dialectical process concerning the nature of the real in the first half: its purpose is to take away any imagination or thought about the One.

The *Parmenides* is notorious not least because contemporary Plato scholars have a difficult time understanding how the second half of the dialogue constitutes a reply to difficulties Parmenides raises about the logic of participation in the first half.[10] Centuries ago, however, Neoplatonists thought that the second half of the dialogue referenced a transcendent principle that eschewed any kind of participation relationships. For late antique readers of the dialogue, this grounding element, the One that is not restricted to a determinate essence, is the subject of the first hypothesis that begins at 137c4 with the words of Parmenides, "If the One is, [surely] the One could not be many?" (137c4–5).[11] The first deduction goes on to show that what follows from positing that the One is, (or that the One is One) is that the One is not: 141e7–10:

> "Therefore, in no way does the One participate in being."
> "It seems not."
> "The One, therefore, by no means is in any way at all."
> "Apparently not."

So far, we have been talking about what Plato calls in the *Parmenides* "The One" that "does not participate in being" (*ousia* – perhaps, here, "essence"). At least it has no determinate nature: it is *apeiron*, without limit, not circumscribed. Its very nature is radically perplexing; it can only be approached via the path of aporia, of paradox, and of negation. Thus Plato tells us only what the One is not: it is not here or there; it is not now

---

[10] Gill has an interpretation that successfully relates the two halves. Cf. Gill (2012, chapter 2, "A Philosophical Exercise"). Gill's brilliant rendering of the connection between the two halves of the dialogues suggests that the first half presents difficulties with the theory of forms that cannot be solved "without proper exercise," supplied by the second half of the dialogue. Gill suggests that the second half demonstrates that without the One, there would be no world at all and, hence, that the world itself cannot exist without Forms. The second half presents solutions to the first half, again according to Gill, by denying the premise, assumed in the first half, that Forms do not participate in their opposites. For a concise survey of what other scholars have taken to be the relationship between parts I and II of the dialogue, see Gill (2012, 50ff.).

[11] Gill (2012, 62) translates as follows: "If it (the one) is one, the one would not be many, would it?" In Greek: εἰ ἕν ἐστιν, ἄλλο τι οὐκ ἂν εἴη πολλὰ τὸ ἕν.

or then; it is not inside or outside; it has no nature; in fact, the One is not. Now we are coming to understand why, when the mind undergoes this training, as it struggles to encounter the truth, the only wisdom it attains is no wisdom: nothing can be said about the One. Plato says that this One can't even be known, so that the highest wisdom is no wisdom.

From this apparent absurdity, that to assume the existence of the One entails that the One does not exist, the Neoplatonists posited the One that does not participate in being as the subject of the first hypothesis.[12] Now, if we are able to entertain at least notionally the idea of a One that is not, then it is possible that here, in the first hypothesis of second half of the dialogue, after being led through a series of puzzles designed to show how inadequately he conceptualizes the relationship between the transcendent form and the particular, Socrates glimpses the One for the first time. He has an insight into the One-that-is-not, thus becoming initiated into the highest wisdom, the wisdom that is no wisdom.

The *Parmenides* and the *Apology*, then, are bookends. The important phrase "great or small" flashes as a signal to register and then negates the possibility of any wisdom at all, and it references the great aporia of the One that is neither great nor small.[13] The former marks the initiation of Socrates into the heart of wisdom and forms the dramatic incipit wherein his philosophical journey begins. The latter marks the completion of Socrates' life in wisdom as well as the dramatic date that signals the approach of Socrates' death. Again, it is the *Apology* that proclaims Socratic wisdom, the wisdom that is no wisdom, as the highest wisdom. By inserting the philosophical trajectory of Socrates in between these two plateaus or perhaps even nadirs of negativity, Plato reveals that Socratic wisdom is the not quite empty space that somehow contains Platonic knowledge, in other words, whatever else unfolds within the span of the dialogues.[14] If Socratic wisdom is the highest wisdom, then all other forms of knowing, including the metaphysical theories that we understand under the banner of Platonism, are subsumed within it.

---

[12] Gerson (2016).

[13] According to a report of Aristotle, Plato actually used "the large and small" to denote an ontological principle. Twice at *Metaphysics*, M 987b, Aristotle mentions "the large and small" as a principle that Plato employs to explain phenomenal change or the existence of the empirical world.

[14] Excepting of course the *Laws*, the one dialogue that escapes past the borders of Socratic wisdom, containing no appearance of Socrates. It is also the dialogue wherein the person who disagrees with the state-mandated religion, or has his "own" religion or altars, will be put to death by a board of bureaucrats who by their selection criteria are admittedly not philosophers.

By associating this wisdom with Delphi, Plato also links Socratic wisdom to the precept γνῶθι σαυτόν (know thyself) and in this way intimates from the very outset that Socratic wisdom is, at its core, derived from or identical to self-knowledge.[15] The teaching of Socrates via the avenue of self-knowledge remains vital within Plato's corpus. All subsequent forms of philosophical discovery are permeated with the Socratic reminder that the true ground of knowledge is just this highest wisdom that is without measure, that is to say, neither great nor small. Hence, Socrates lingers in the dialogues, sometimes in the background, but always representing Plato's own self-interrogations.

4.3

How then, is this highest wisdom, Socratic wisdom, simultaneously a form of self-knowledge? In fact, the key to understanding how "no wisdom" equates with self-knowledge is to be found in several dialogues. Here I will cite the *Charmides*. At *Charmides* 167c5, Socrates is discussing the meaning of the Delphic injunction in company with Critias, future leader of the military coup d'etat of 404:[16] to know oneself is to know knowledge. But Socrates does not think there can be knowledge of knowledge. At least, he asks if there is a vision that is not a vision of anything, but that sees itself and all other seeing; a hearing that hears itself and all other hearings, but is not the hearing of anything; a love that loves itself and all other loves, but is not the love of any good; a knowledge that knows itself and all other knowledges, but is not the knowledge of anything.

Socrates describes this putative knowledge at 167b10 as "a single knowledge which is no other than knowledge of itself as well as of the other knowledges." When Socrates proceeds to examine the structure of this kind of knowledge, he turns, for the purpose of comparison, to a list of other human faculties. He begins by discussing vision, hearing, and sensation in general, as in, e.g., is there any perception of sense perceptions and of the faculty of sense perception, which does not perceive the objects of sense perception?

The negative answer to this query should not be taken for the end of the matter. Indeed the same sequence is repeated three times before Socrates turns to the other items on his list: appetite, wish, sexual desire, fear, and opinion. Included on the list are virtually all of the possible states that

---

[15] On the connections between the Delphic precept and Socrates, see Moore (2015a).
[16] On Critias and the Thirty, see Nails (2002, 111).

comprise human experience, at least on a Platonic view: *epithumia, thumos, doxa,* and *aisthēsis.*

If we regard them as faculties, then sensation, appetite, etc. are always associated with their several unique objects. But considered as states of experience, there is a sense in which they in turn may be seen as objects for the Socratic self. One way of viewing the elenchus in relation to self-knowledge is as a method whereby the interlocutor comes to be aware that he has the desires, opinions, fears, and appetites that he in fact has. But once aware that he has them, he can begin to exercise his autonomy as an epistemic self, to scrutinize their value, and to begin to free himself of those he deems false.

When Socrates questions whether or not there can be self-reflexive instances of *epithumia, thumos, doxa,* and *aisthesis,* he implicitly underwrites a psychology that the Stoics attribute to Socrates, that there is only the rational soul; all irrational states can be treated as functions of the same part of the soul, the ἡγεμονικόν, that governs rational activity.[17] This interrogation in the *Charmides* is also consistent with the Socratic denial of akrasia and with Aristotle's reports about Socrates' cognitive theory of desire and emotion generally.[18]

In the *Charmides,* we are left to imagine (that is, the question is implicitly raised) in what sense states of the mind are objects of knowledge. But the knower, the mind itself, is not such a state; the knower is never an object. Then how can the self be known? What exactly is self-knowledge? The paradox that Socrates demonstrates is that self-knowledge does not even constitute knowledge, as it does not yield an object.

Socrates and Charmides in fact play out the drama of this paradox, as Socrates repeatedly asks Charmides to "perform" self-knowledge on himself: πάλιν τοίνυν, ἦν δ᾽ ἐγώ, ὦ Χαρμίδη, μᾶλλον προσέχων τὸν νοῦν καὶ εἰς σεαυτὸν ἐμβλέψας ("Once more," said I, "now, Charmides, pay closer attention and look into yourself"). Socrates continues: ἐννοήσας ὁποῖόν τινά σε ποιεῖ ἡ σωφροσύνη παροῦσα ("Can you discern what effect the presence of temperance has on you?") (*Chrm.* 160d5–7).

Later in the dialogue, as Socrates contemplates self-knowledge, he asks Critias whether or not it is possible τὸ ἃ οἶδεν καὶ ἃ μὴ οἶδεν εἰδέναι ὅτι οἶδε καὶ ὅτι οὐκ οἶδεν ("to know that one knows or does not know")

---

[17] Graver (2008, 30–31). Graver discusses the early Stoic theory of emotion in the terms of a basic awareness that ἡγεμονικόν has of its own states.

[18] Aristotle criticizes Socrates for identifying virtue with knowledge (*EN.* 1144b17–21). Cf. Irwin (1995, 242). On Socrates' denial of *akrasia* in the *Protagoras* and its association with rational control, see Cooper (1999, 63 n. 54).

(*Chrm.* 167b2–3). Indeed, what could be more obvious than that one knows? How could one fail to "know that one knows"? What we have here, in my view, is perhaps the earliest literary argument for the immediacy or self-certifying fact of self-awareness. The initial question, "Is it possible to know that one knows?" gets derailed in the dialogue because focus shifts from the knower to the array of objects known and becomes a thesis about the self-sufficiency of expert knowledge. Nevertheless, that initial question might be taken as an adumbration of a viewpoint, according to which "that one knows" is developed as a line of inquiry and its implications are studied.

So far, then, there are two components to Socratic wisdom: on the one hand, it is "not wisdom," and on the other hand, it consists in self-knowledge. But how do these two components function in tandem? Precisely because the knower is not any of the things known, therefore self-knowledge cannot be the knowledge of anything. It, on the contrary, as the highest wisdom, is exactly no wisdom, great or small.

4.4

One of the dialogues that illustrate the relationship between Socratic wisdom and knowledge as such is the *Theaetetus*.[19] The Socratic question of the earlier dialogues, "what is virtue?" now appears in a different guise as "what is knowledge?"[20] Socrates tells Theaetetus at the beginning of the dialogue: "I am in a state of aporia with regard to this very point, and I am not able in myself to grasp it adequately, namely, what is the essence of knowledge?"[21] Even before this declaration, that knowledge is something that Socrates cannot grasp, Socrates poses an important question, one that I take to call attention to this distinction between knowledge and Socratic wisdom, when he asks, "Are wisdom and knowledge the same thing?" (ταὐτὸν ἄρα ἐπιστήμη καὶ σοφία; 145e5). Various scholars have debated the question about whether or not Socrates sincerely wants to distinguish between knowledge and wisdom, but what I would suggest is that here, Plato is asking about what knowledge looks like from within the viewpoint of Socratic wisdom.

---

[19] In this chapter, I rely principally on Burnyeat (1990), Blondell (2002), Sedley (2004), Gill (2012), and Kahn (2013). All translations are taken from Burnyeat unless otherwise indicated.

[20] 145e7: τοῦτ᾽ αὐτὸ τοίνυν ἐστὶν ὃ ἀπορῶ καὶ οὐ δύναμαι λαβεῖν ἱκανῶς παρ᾽ ἐμαυτῷ, ἐπιστήμη ὅτι ποτὲ τυγχάνει ὄν.

[21] 145e7 (my translation).

The opening frame of the dialogue is an overt meditation on Socratic wisdom, whereas the main body of the dialogue constitutes an inquiry into the foundations of knowledge. Socrates engages in an exchange with a variety of interlocutors, employing such illocutionary categories of speech as hortatory, admonitory, maieutic, and purgative. The various treatise-like elaborations of ontology, including the physical elements that constitute material reality, mental constructs, or ideation, constitute the world of knowledge. In fact, the entire dialogue will go on to interrogate the relationship between the object of knowledge and the knower. As Burnyeat has written, "What is at stake in the discussion of false judgment is nothing less than the mind's relation to its objects."[22]

The *Theaetetus* analyzes knowledge no longer according to metaphysical constructs, but in terms that are primarily conceptual, analytical, linguistic, or, in other words, concerned with mental objects, as opposed to the explicitly extra-mental objects that the *Parmenides* investigated.[23] In fact, Kahn posits that Plato references the *Parmenides* within the *Theaetetus* because Plato wants the reader to recall the demise of the metaphysics of the Forms, that is to say, the extra-mental absolutes of the *Republic* and *Phaedo*. The references to the *Parmenides* are a pointer to the "death" of the forms in their other-worldly sense. Here, all of these levels of knowledge – empirical, conceptual, formal, absolute – are reduced to the same status. They remain objects for the mind. They are within the purview of the knower but are not the knower.

The first half of the dialogue investigates the realm of the senses. In it, the objects under investigation are sensations, conceptions, and empirical phenomena more generally. The mind knows the world through the senses but the mind itself stays outside the picture. These objects skate across the field of awareness and break apart under the scrutiny of Heraclitean-inspired ontology. Under the guise of Protagorean truth, Socrates investigates the thesis that knowledge is perception but discovers that this realm of experience in itself is radically unstable. There is no direct experience of being, there. The senses are empty of stable, permanent, fixed reality. The conclusion of the first half of the *Theaetetus*, an investigation of empirical experience as the basis for knowledge, is that, in the words of Socrates: οὐδὲν ἄρα ἐπιστήμην μᾶλλον ἢ μὴ ἐπιστήμην ἀπεκρινάμεθα ἐρωτώμενοι ὅτι ἐστὶν ἐπιστήμη – "When we were asked, 'what is knowledge,' our answer turned out to be no more knowledge than the lack thereof" (182e9).

---

[22] Burnyeat (1990, 69).   [23] Gill (2012, 137), Kahn (2013, 19).

The second part of the dialogue offers several models for the mind (Trojan horse, wax tablet, aviary, jury) and so looks at the more refined realms of experience involving judgment, memory, opinion, and truth and falsehood. Here in the later parts of the dialogue, there is a greater intimacy between knower and known. The mind and its thoughts are represented as container and contained. The knower has direct access to the contents of the mind. In fact, some of these mental contents themselves proclaim the truth or falsity of other such contents. There is also a question of objective truth that exists outside the mind, where it is the role of certain components within the mind to ascertain how things are in the world outside it. In the second half of the dialogue, Socrates undertakes to study what happens when this ascertainment fails to capture just how things are in the world outside the mind; in other words, he discusses a theory according to which knowledge is true judgment. What happens in cases of false judgment?

> Then in what way is false judgment still possible? There is evidently no possibility of judgment outside the cases we have mentioned since everything is either a thing we know or a thing we don't know; and within these limits there appears to be no place for false judgment to be possible. (185c5)

At this impasse, Socrates introduces a number of analogies for the mind and its objects, beginning with a block of wax, onto which are imprinted mental contents (191d5). Memory will be a function of the impression's durability (191e1). This model of the mind is ruled out because it does not accommodate the possibility that someone thinks that one thing he knows is another thing he knows (196b8). Socrates rules out this circumstance as a source for false judgment since in that case, "the same man must, at one and the same time, both know and not know the same objects" (196c2).

Next Socrates introduces the analogy of an aviary, wherein the mind is a birdcage and its objects are the birds one keeps inside the aviary. "Now let us make in each soul a sort of aviary of all kinds of birds" (197d6–8). "By the birds we must understand pieces of knowledge" (197e3). Ultimately, this model of the mind ends in an infinite regress. How can a person who has both states of mind, knowledge and ignorance, mistake the one for the other, given that knowledge implies being aware of an object and being correct about it, whereas ignorance implies that one does not have this awareness? Socrates suggests a regress at this point to solve the puzzle:

> Or are you going to start all over again and tell me that there's another set of pieces of knowledge concerning pieces of knowledge and ignorance, which a man may possess shut up in some other ridiculous aviaries or waxen devices?" (200c3)

False judgment is something that Socrates' analogies cannot yet accommodate, and so Socrates turns to ask what must be added to true judgment to give us a complete definition of knowledge. Theaetetus proceeds to formulate another definition of knowledge as "true judgment with an account" (201d1).

The philosophical picture here, of a unified consciousness that is able to scrutinize any of its contents, is an accomplishment in itself.[24] Yet this unified consciousness, whether articulated here for the first time in Plato's thought or not, is now itself the subject of scrutiny. Here the Socratic investigation shines a light on that knowing self, in this way imitating the Socrates of the earlier dialogues. This scrutiny of the knower is both familiar and repeated, and yet disarming because we understand the element under scrutiny as that whereby the knower does its judging, examining, and pronouncing.

Judgments, concepts, perceptions, accounts – all of these are the objects of awareness. They are the elements that function within the enumerative psychology of the *Theaetetus*. So in treating all of these elements on a par, that is, as objects of mind, Plato pursues a unified Socratic psychology that mentions neither the tripartite soul of *Republic* nor the Forms of the *Republic*. We also see the Socratic capacity to observe the entire field of the mind, from "raw feels" ("the wind feels hot to me") to sophisticated models of the mind. The mirror of Socrates here reflects the contents of mind, and in so doing finds that all of the models fall short of capturing that mind. It is this failure to grasp the mind, despite the precise delineation of its elements, which brings us back to the Socratic within the Platonic, even within the natural philosophy that Plato now begins to investigate, according to some commentators.[25]

Socratic barrenness, *atokia*, his lack of mental productivity, points to the knower, that epistemic self, which cannot be listed as an ingredient among any of the things known. On the other hand, after Socrates discloses the fact that he is incapable of production (at 149b10 he says, recall, that Artemis grants the power of midwifery to those who are *atokos*: ταῖς δὲ δι' ἡλικίαν ἀτόκοις προσέταξε τιμῶσα τὴν αὐτῆς ὁμοιότητα), he then turns precisely to the entire range of psychic or mental productions, including to a survey of just what cognition is. At *Theaetetus* 207c, Socrates offers an

[24] Sedley (2004, chapter 6, 113): "The Unity of Consciousness."
[25] Kahn (2013) announces this theme in the title of his work, *Plato and the Post-Socratic Dialogue: The Return to the Philosophy of Nature*. Gill (2012, 240) discusses the object of the philosopher as "Being [which] is inside the nature of every being as its structural core enabling it to fit together with other things outside its specific nature."

exposition in terms of elements is equivalent to a rational account of knowledge. But what are these στοιχεῖα, the elements of the last sections of the *Theaetetus*?

The στοιχεῖα, the elements, are just the discrete moments of, on the one hand, any given thought process and, on the other hand, the discrete constituents of any phenomenal thing. For example, color is in this sense an element. So is shape. But also, a sensory apprehension is an element, and so is a concept. It is anything that can be described as "this" or "that"; it is any of the discrete realities that form a part of whatever it is that comprises, altogether, the total possibilities of experience. At 201e1 and following, Socrates recalls a dream:

> According to this dream, I thought I was listening to people saying that the primary elements, as it were, of which we and everything else are composed, have no account. Each of them, in itself, can only be named; it is not possible to say anything else of it, either that it is or that it is not. That would mean that we were adding being or not-being to it; whereas we must not attach anything, if we are to speak of that thing itself alone.[26] (201e2–202a2)

In the dream, the elements consist of transitory states that follow in succession on other such states. Nevertheless, although each element manifests itself under one or another of various categories of experience (it is, e.g., either a visual datum or a mental image or the shape or form of a material entity), the experience as such is not subject to analysis. It is primary. The flow of these elements in quick succession gives rise to extended experience, to the world with which we are conventionally familiar.

Socrates says, "It is impossible that any of the primaries should be expressed in an account; it can only be named, for a name is all that it has" (202b1). Yet again, these "bare elements" comprise or are "woven into" the more complex objects of consciousness that can then become the subjects of "accounts," "judgments," and "knowledge." Socrates continues, "But with the other things composed of [the elements] it is another matter. Here, just in the same way as the elements themselves are woven together, so their names may be woven together and become an account of something – an account being essentially a complex of names." It is a matter of interpretive controversy as to what these elements are, as well as to what the complexes they comprise are. Are the complexes individuals or types? If

---

[26] Cf. Burnyeat (1990, 338–339).

the elements are a matrix of the components of experience that underlie conventional reality, then the answer to this interpretive crux might be that, on the one hand, some of these elements come under the rubric of conceptual thought; others come under the rubric of perception or sensation. Likewise, some of the complexes will turn out to be abstractions or ideations; others will turn out to be physical or material entities.

The *Theaetetus* is Plato's attempt, so to say, to offer an ontology of experience, of realities that are not encountered outside the mind, insofar as they are analyzed very much as contents of the mind. Uniquely of all the Platonic works, the *Theaetetus* focuses on the psychology of cognition; the elements to which Socrates refers in the dream are taken from a direct analysis of experience. What has happened, according to Sedley, is that "the attempt to diagnose false judgments has ended up taking them to be internal mental processes which are themselves about further mental items, namely bits of knowledge."[27] Sedley continues, "What is missing, then, in the arithmetical example is a metaphysical separation of numbers from the cognitive states by which they are known."[28] Thus even in the earlier discussion, when Socrates attempts to present various models of mind, one aspect of the dream theory is implied, namely, that all phenomena can be understood as elements of experience and that our conventional world view, which sees a mind grasping some entity (e.g., a number), can be reenvisioned as the search for an item in the mental world, that is, the catching of a soul-bird. This aviary world, a flattened world, arises when all forms of experience are seen as not outside the mind and is in many ways a continuation of the Protagorean construct explored earlier in the dialogue, according to which knowledge is perception.[29]

At 197e2 Socrates continues:

> Then we must say that when we are children this receptacle is empty; and by the birds we must understand pieces of knowledge. When anyone takes possession of a piece of knowledge and shuts it up in the pen, we should say that he has learned or has found out the thing of which this is the knowledge; and knowing, we should say, is this.

For Sedley, the problems with Socrates' analysis of knowledge in the *Theaetetus* are deliberately underscored by Plato: Socrates approaches the entire project of discerning the nature of knowledge in terms of cognitive psychology. According to Sedley, Socrates fails to "investigate the ontology

[27] Sedley (2004, 148).   [28] Ibid.
[29] See ibid., 169, for the way that the dream theory draws on the first part of the *Theaetetus*.

of the entities which the mind interrelates."[30] And Plato, in presenting a Socrates who simply has no access to metaphysics, is deliberate in showing the limits of this approach. Plato will make the fine ontological and metaphysical distinctions between mental phenomena and the ontology that underlies those mental states, a distinction not possible without recourse to metaphysics to classify those same items of experience.

What exactly is missing from the aviary or, indeed, from the element theory explored at 201? One question might be, if the aviary is the mind, consciousness, then who is it that does the catching of the birds, whether they are knowledge birds, opinion birds, or even ignorance birds? Who is the subject who searches for a state of mind to get hold of in the first place? The wax model suggests that there is no subject, but merely a passive material that is involuntarily imprinted with the results of experience. Now unless there is a category of experience that is different in kind from the objects that it searches for, and not simply another one of those objects, then of course, knowledge cannot be accounted for. It is not only metaphysics that is missing from these theories but a conscious subject. Although the knower is different from its productions and the knower cannot be known in the same way as one of its productions, the *Theaetetus* does not provide, in its models of the mind for the knower, the person who searches. We can say that the knower is missing. The knower goes unobserved, since it is not any of the things known.

Of course, the mind is always pointed toward or occupied with something. We only notice the mind, as Aristotle puts it, as a "*parergon.*"[31] The mind thus seems to be nothing other than a series of states of mind. And yet to say this surely begs the question, to what or to whom do the mind-states belong? If we specify something or someone who possesses these states, then this too will fall into one of the categories of experience, one of the elements.

In shining the light of Socratic inquiry into the contents of the mind, into the birdcage, so to say, Plato opens up a Socratic inquiry into every phenomenal moment. No longer does this Socrates stay within the pristine silence of not knowing, or barrenness. Instead, he attends to all that the pregnant mind can bring forth. He switches out Apollo (the patron of "know thyself") for his twin sister, Artemis. He finds his way into the

---

[30] Sedley (2004, 152).
[31] This almost seems to fall out from the very idea of awareness or perception, which for Aristotle, is "not of itself but of something else that is necessarily prior to the perception" (*Metaph.* 4.5 1010b35–6).

marketplace of awareness, where objects are traded, one for the other. Or rather, perhaps it would be better to say that young Theaetetus, Socrates' lookalike, venturing into the world of perception, conveys that vantage point to his partner, past the age of childbirth. The Socratic stillness never wavers; those bulging eyes (143e9) stare into or even past the proliferation of objects, into the source of their arising.

4.5

The maxim at Delphi is the gateway to the temple of Apollonian wisdom (which, as we saw, was actually no wisdom, great or small), as that maxim becomes the occasion for aporia and thus issues an invitation to study the self qua knower. It hints at or invites attention toward the self, which, prior to this invitation, was hidden behind the closed door of a thought, tightly grasped, as either true or false. A state of mind can be opaque, while a thought or opinion closes in on itself, with no visible means of egress for the one who, so to say, occupies a given thought position. Such a thought comes to function as a tyrant within the politics of awareness. The mind in this state is also guilty of the double ignorance of not knowing and yet thinking that it does know. The sage, Socrates, i.e., one's own capacity to be aware of every and any object, meets that tyrant, that ignorant inter-locutor in conversation, thus determining the question and ultimate fate of one's own self-knowledge.

CHAPTER 5

Between Ascent and Descent*
Self-Knowledge and Plato's Allegory of the Cave

James M. Ambury

> The phrase γνῶθι σεαυτόν is a stock phrase,
> And in it has been perceived to be the goal of all
> Of a person's striving. And this is entirely proper,
> But yet it is just as certain that it cannot be the goal
> If it is not also the beginning.
>
> Kierkegaard, *Either/Or, A Fragment of Life, The Papers of B*

In this chapter, I argue that Plato's famous allegory of the cave is as much about what it is to know oneself as it is about knowing the objects of philosophical cognition. I divide the chapter in accordance with the four principal types of self-knowledge I identify in the passage: eikastic, aporetic, dianoetic, and intellective. Each of these types of self-knowledge corresponds to a distinct level of the divided line. I argue that the final model of self-knowledge is best understood as self-knowing, an active psychic condition in which the soul is disclosed to itself in the performance of its essential activity. I conclude with some remarks about the nature of philosophical education and Socrates' insistence that the philosopher return to the cave. This injunction is based on the Platonic view that, despite his ascent out of the cave, the prisoner who does not return does not know himself and cannot truly love wisdom.

5.1

Just before the beginning of Book VII, Socrates and Glaucon have finished articulating the divisions of the divided line (VI.509d6–511e5). After some

* Different versions of this chapter were presented at the Ancient Philosophy Society conference in Portland, Maine, and the Society for Ancient Greek Philosophy conference at Fordham University in New York, both in 2016. I am grateful to those audiences for their cordial reception of my general thesis and their insightful questions and criticisms. Particular thanks are due to my commentator in Portland, Claas Lattmann, for his careful attention to my paper and thorough analysis of its principal points.

81

initial confusion, Glaucon clarifies the difference within the intelligible realm between thought (διάνοια) and understanding (νόησις). The language in the passage, however, is not strictly cognitive but also the language of affect. Glaucon claims that the state (ἕξις) of the geometers is thought but not understanding (VI.511d4). Socrates adds that, just as there are four subsections of the divided line, there are four correspondent conditions (παθήματα) of the soul. Socrates tells the allegory in order to develop an account of the soul's condition and awareness of itself at each level of the line.

Socrates instructs Glaucon to compare human nature and its education or absence thereof with a specific experience (πάθος) (VII.514a1). At first it might seem that the allegory is merely about the human condition, which need not necessarily be a story about self-knoweldge. Indeed, Socrates seems to strengthen this suspicion by itemizing a set of criteria that describe that condition: the prisoner has been trapped since childhood, fixed in the same place, with legs and neck chained, unable to turn around, and hence only able to look forward. There is a fire behind him and a small wall in front of that, along which puppeteers move all kinds of different objects (VII.514a2–515a3). Thus told, we might think that the allegory is not about self-knowledge or at least not the kind of self-knowledge that requires self-awareness. We might think self-knowledge is just knowledge of a set of propositions that precisely articulate an account of human nature.

The exchange between Socrates and Glaucon that follows the intial description of the cave proves that this is not the case:

> GLAUCON (515a4): It's a strange (ἄτοπος) image (εἰκόνα) you're describing, and strange (ἀτόπους) prisoners.
>
> SOCRATES (515a5–8): They're like us (ὁμοίους ἡμῖν). Do you suppose, first of all, that these prisoners see anything of themselves (ἑαυτῶν) and one another besides the shadows that the fire casts on the wall in front of them?[1]

Glaucon twice uses the word ἄτοπος, "out of place." The word appears elsewhere in the Platonic corpus to indicate an interlocutor's confusion with something Socrates says to him or even with Socrates himself.[2] Whatever is out of place deviates from the expected, the typical, the

---

[1] All translations are from Cooper (1997).

[2] *Grg.* 473a1, 494d1; *Phdr.* 230c6; *Smp.* 215a2, 221d2; *Alc.* I 106a3, 116e4. I have argued elsewhere that the goal of the elenchus is to "displace" the interlocutor, that is, to move him from seeing Socrates and philosophy generally as out of place to seeing himself, from a philosophical perspective, as out of place. See Ambury (2011).

normal, the everyday. That Glaucon uses this word to describe not only the example but the people in the example indicates that he is unfamiliar with the phenomenon Socrates is describing. This unfamiliarity indicates that he does not know himself. Socrates immediately replies that the prisoners are like us in order to stress this point. Someone with self-knowledge would indeed be struck by the image, but not because it is out of place or strange. Rather, he would be struck by how appropriate or "in place" the description is. Glaucon himself is like the prisoner in the allegory. He is unaware of his psychic nature; he does not know himself.

There is no explicit argument in the allegory that the self is the soul and that, consequently, self-knowledge is knowing one's soul.[3] Nonetheless, Socrates' claim that the prisoners are "like us" points the way toward such an identification. He emphasizes not that we resemble them but that they resemble us. The condition of the prisoner is an image (εἰκόνα) of our own condition – while their bodies are enchained, our souls are enchained. Our condition is similar in that it is an imprisonment; it is dissimilar in that it is not an imprisonment of the body. The imprisonment of human beings is a psychic imprisonment. It is the soul's inability to know not just the forms, but also itself.

The emphasis on self-knowledge is clear from the moment Socrates develops this image. The first thing we learn about the prisoners is that they see shadows not just of the puppets but also of themselves. Commentators have typically either missed this point entirely or acknowledged it before moving quickly past it without developing its significance.[4] It signals, first, the most basic and naïve kind of self-knowledge, familiarity with a shadow-like image of the self. This image, like all images, is by definition incomplete. Let us call this *eikastic self-knowledge*. It corresponds to the bottom portion of the divided line. As the prisoner's shadow is nothing but a reflection of his body caused by the light behind him, so the eikastic version of the soul is a reflection caused by the varying influences of the prisoner's education and upbringing.

---

[3] Indeed, while we frequently hear that the soul is more important than the body – *Ap.* 29d7–30c1, *Grg.* 465c7–d6, *Phd.* 79c2ff, *Lg.* XII.959a5–6 – we rarely find a strict argument that the self is the soul. Cf. *La.* 185e1–6 and *Chrm.* 154e1–7. This is perhaps because Plato uses "self" not as a substantive but as a pronoun. The one explicit argument that the human being is soul is found in *Alc.* I 129b5–130c7, a dialogue of dubious authenticity.

[4] The former group includes Morrison (1977, 227), Annas (1981, 252), and Kraut (1992, 317); the latter includes Robinson (1953, 149), Cross and Woozley (1964, 206), and Murdoch (1977, 4). For a useful summary of the debate surrounding the prisoners' own shadows that includes these and other secondary references, see Brunschwig (1999).

The second purpose served by beginning with an emphasis on the shadow of the self is that it introduces the difficult problem of self-reflexivity. Socrates' ἑαυτῶν, "of" themselves, shows us this. Any discussion of self-knowledge must account for this reflexivity, but eikastic self-knowledge cannot. In this primary phase of self-knowledge, the prisoners see shadows of themselves but do not recognize that these shadows are indeed shawdows "of" themselves. This does not mean that they cannot identify their particular shadow; after all, they can communicate with each other and move their arms and so may reasonably be expected to know which shadow is theirs.[5] What they do not recognize is that the shadow is in fact a shadow "of" the body. Their imprisonment renders it impossible for them to reflexively experience their own appearance *as* appearance.[6] They think they can see themselves but they cannot.[7] This is why Socrates does not merely describe the human condition. He seeks an account of the soul's experience of itself, and this requires the soul's awakening to the nature of intelligible reality and the role it plays in apprehending that reality.[8]

Socrates next claims that the prisoners would suppose that the names they use in their everyday language apply to what is passing in front of them and believe that truth is nothing other than the shadows of those artifacts (VII.515a5–c3). It is here that one might wonder what has happened to shadows of self, and even suspect that they have disappeared from the allegory.[9] What we find, however, is not that the distinction is dropped but that the prisoners themselves do not consider it. That it is not explicitly mentioned is not evidence that it has disappeared entirely. The

---

[5] Contra Burnyeat (1997, 238–243) – one of the few commentators who analyzes the possibility of drawing a distinction between the prisoner's shadows and the shadows of the puppets. Burnyeat argues that it is difficult to see how the prisoners could identify with these shadows, since they are immobile and the shadows they see are moving. Instead, he claims that the human shadows that the prisoners see are just shadows of human statutes behind them. His interpretation is strengthened by Socrates' claim (VII.515c1–2) that the only things the prisoners consider real are the shadows of the puppets (τὰς τῶν σκευαστῶν σκιάς). I shall have something to say about this passage below. For a full treatment of Burnyeat, see Brunschwig (1999, 164–168).

[6] Smith (1997, 202) puts the point this way: "The prisoners' experience of reality is not merely one in which they perceive images, but fail to recognize that they are images ... by saying that the prisoners in the cave are 'like us,' Plato puts 'us' at the cognitive level of εἰκασία."

[7] Cf. *Alc.* I 132d5–8 – Socrates amends the Delphic imperative from know thyself to see thyself.

[8] Cf. Bosanquet (1895, 264): "[The prisoners] have never observed the genuine facts of human nature in themselves or in others." The point in the passage is less about facts than it is about reflexive experience.

[9] Even Brunschwig, otherwise so attentive to the distinction between the types of shadows, downplays the importance of the very issue to which he calls our attention – the presence of self-knowledge in the allegory – arguing that reference to the prisoners' shadows is isolated and that there is no echo of it in the context or allusion to it in the earlier passage on the divided line.

prisoner takes no substantial account of his own condition because, in his view, there is nothing wrong with his condition. Strictly speaking, he does not even recognize himself as conditioned.[10] He is not aware of his own imprisonment because to be so aware is to recognize the possibilities of the body that has for his entire life been restrained. The self shadows disappear from the text, not because they are not present, but as an indication that the prisoner is completely oblivious to them. His release from this oblivion marks the transition to the second phase of self-knoweldge.

5.2

The prisoner's oblivion is what makes the experience of his release so incredibly painful and perplexing. Socrates claims that if the prisoner was freed and compelled to stand up and look at the light, he would be pained. On account of being dazzled (διὰ τὰς μαρμαρυγὰς) he would be unable to see the real objects that cast shadows (VII.515c6–d1). Τὰς μαρμαρυγὰς here bears a double meaning. On the one hand, the prisoner's eyes are dazzled by the light he has never seen. On the other hand, the word also indicates quickness of movement. It is not just seeing the light that hinders the prisoner's vision – he is in great pain because of the quick movement of his body. Socrates indicates as much by claiming that the prisoner stands up, turns his head, walks, and looks up, all physical movements that he never previously executed. The prisoner's release has compelled him not just to see the objects surrounding him but to self-reflexively experience himself in relation to those objects.

The passage of the prisoner from his original condition to this new condition is marked by his first substantial instance of self-awareness. At this point, the next kind of self-knowledge in the allegory becomes explicit. If compelled to answer questions about the objects passing by the fire, the prisoner would be in a state of ἀπορία (VII.515d6). His confusion is as much about himself as it is about the puppets casting the shadows. Socrates claims that he would believe the things he saw earlier were truer than what he is seeing now. The text here does not read τὰς τῶν σκευαστῶν σκιάς, as at VII.515c1–2, but rather τὰ τότε ὁρώμενα: the things he saw then. This more generic construction is open enough to refer

---

[10] I here agree with Burnyeat's point (1997, 240–241) that the prisoners see images of human beings conditioned by their culture; I do not think, however, that this means that "it is the generic characterisations that matter to their conception of themselves and each other, not the actual details of each individual life." Rather, their imprisonment is so dangerous, and their subsequent release so jarring, precisely because they have each individually been so poorly educated.

not just to shadows of the puppets but to the prisoner's own shadow as well. To be sure, Socrates is referring to the puppets. But the prisoner is as confused over his own inability to see as he is about the things he sees. He is experiencing his own body and its relation to the world differently from how he ever has. Indeed, he is slowly discovering that what he sees or does not see depends very much on the orientation of his body.[11]

The freed prisoner progresses to the phase of *aporetic self-knowledge*. His experiencing his body for the first time is an analogy for the soul's experiencing itself for the first time. One thinks of the painful experience of undergoing a Socratic elenchus that leads to ἀπορία. The soul that undergoes philosophical interrogation for the first time experiences itself in a way that it has not previously. In its confusion, it is self-reflexively aware of itself as lost or confused. This confusion, while achieved by examining one's own opinions and getting rid of one's ignorance, cannot be reduced solely to an awareness of those opinions and their logical interrelation.[12] What is at stake is not whether my opinions about justice, for example, are or are not consistent and whether I should change them. This would be akin to exchanging one set of shadows for another. What is at stake is my very self, the orientation of which affects whether or not I recognize that the shadows are in fact shadows, and nothing more.[13] Only then do I recognize that a change in conception of self entails a change in conception of the knowable.

A person experiencing aporetic self-knowledge recognizes that his whole self is different from what he previously assumed. On the divided line, the soul is no longer at the level of image but at the level of belief (πίστις).[14] This does not indicate that the prisoner is wholly concerned with a particular belief about X or Y but that he is aware of himself in the condition of δόξα, that confused or wandering realm between not being

---

[11] Cf. note 6. Part of Burnyeat's argument that the prisoners are seeing shadows of human statues behind them is his claim that "if the shadows of themselves are cast by their own immobilized bodies ... they will get no closer to the truth about themselves when they are forced to turn round towards the wall and look at 'the things whose shadows they saw before'" (1997, 239). The experience of aporetic self-knowledge, I think, shows how the prisoner, merely by being freed, comes to learn about himself.

[12] Contra Sichel (1985), who draws the distinction between enchained and freed prisoners solely in these terms: "For enchained prisoners, self-knowledge is based on their society's ideology and their own limited cognitive development. Freed prisoners possess a higher degree of self-knowledge since they recognize their beliefs and have consistent, coherent belief systems" (436).

[13] On the elenchus and its refutation of not just opinions but of the whole self, see *Sph.* 230b4–d4. On ἀπορία, see *Ap.* 23d4, *Men.* 80a2, and *Tht.* 149a9.

[14] *R.* VI.510a5–6.

and being.[15] He is aware that the shadows are shadows of objects but cannot comprehend these new objects.[16] More importantly, he is reflexively aware that there is a completely unexamined dimension of himself that must have always been there but of which he was previously ignorant. His shadow, what he believed about himself, is now seen as nothing more than an illusion. The freed soul realizes: "whatever I was, I was mistaken; I am no longer that, nor, strictly speaking, was I ever truly that." The eikastic self is experienced as an illusion at the same time as there is nothing to replace it. Ἀπορία is frightening in this respect: the soul has no idea what it is.[17]

5.3

When the prisoner feels the pain of ἀπορία he flees toward the things he is able to see. He seeks the comforts of the familiar, of what he is used to; he seeks refuge in the place from which he came (VII.515e1–4). The soul longs to return to its previous condition. The desire is so intense that the prisoner has to be dragged away from it by force (ἐντεῦθεν ἕλκοι τις αὐτὸν βίᾳ), pained all the way through, still unable to see (VII.515e5–516a3). ἐντεῦθεν indicates what is happening to the soul: it is being pulled *from* one affective condition *into* another; it does not want to ascend out of the cave. Once this transition has taken place, the prisoner will achieve the third level of self-knowledge.

Once out of the cave, Socrates claims the prisoner would need time to "get habituated" before he could properly see the world around him

---

[15] At *R.* VII.533e7–534a5 Socrates calls both of the lower portions of the divided line, taken together, δόξα. On δόξα as the wandering intermediate, see *R.* V.476a9–b8, 479d3–10, 477a9–b9, 478d1–12, and VI.484b3–7.

[16] In her work on this passage, Annas (1981, 255) argues that it is difficult to fit the line and cave together on the grounds that πίστις on the divided line is the normal state of seeing objects, while in the cave it is a painful state of bewilderment. I suggest, however, that we should understand the line from an outside, neutral, third-person perspective, whereas the cave is primarily about the prisoner's reflexive experience of his own condition. The domain of the text surely recognizes that we spend very little time looking at images when compared with real objects, but it is this very distinction that the prisoner himself fails to make. The domain of εἰκασία is greater in the cave because Socrates' point is that the prisoner's failure to recognize a shadow as a shadow renders the whole of his experience false.

[17] Cf. *Phdr.* 229e5–230a7. Moore (2014, 19) interprets the passage this way: "[Socrates'] concern with himself is not a concern for the nature of a self as such, as some entity distinct from the person engaged in knowing, except to the extent that knowing about selves … gives one confidence that self-knowledge is even possible, and provides the ideal to which one might be committed." The highest phase of self-knowledge in the allegory, which I articulate below, accords with this interpretation of the *Phaedrus* passage insofar as the soul actively grasps itself not as separate from itself but in the performance of its most essential activity.

(VII.516a5). "Get habituated" here is συνήθεια, to become acquainted with through repeated action. The prisoner's vision improves when he exercises it. Slowly, his eyes become accustomed to seeing the world around him, images at first, then the objects in the sky, and finally the sun itself (VII.516a5–b3). He can see objects correctly only when he has conditioned himself to see them. His first vision of the sun, for instance, is only in an alien setting (ἐν ἀλλοτρίᾳ ἕδρᾳ); he can only see the sun in its own place (ἐν τῇ αὑτοῦ χώρᾳ) after learning to see properly. Only when the prisoner becomes accustomed to his new condition can he conclude that the sun governs the visible world and is cause of all he used to see (VII.516b4–7).

The language of place remains relevant here and indicates the dialectical relation between the prisoner and what he sees. Only after accustoming himself to his new place, his new psychic condition, can what seemed to be the proper "place" of knowledge, the visible realm, be recognized as dependent and derivative. The proper "place" of knowledge – the intelligible realm – is only disclosed when the soul is in the right condition. Accustoming oneself to a new place is an analogy to psychic conversion.[18] By beginning to orient itself to the condition most appropriate to its nature, the soul takes the first step in approaching the objects of philosophical cognition. This reorientation requires the exercise of the intellectual capacity of the soul in a way that is first experienced as foreign and only later as natural. The aporetic soul, uncomfortable in its confusion, must accustom itself to the world around it by exercising its most essential capacity.

Once accustomed to his new condition, Socrates indicates that the prisoner would have a unique experience of himself:

> What about when he reminds himself (ἀναμιμνῃσκόμενον αὑτὸν) of his first dwelling place (τῆς πρώτης οἰκήσεως), his fellow prisoners, and what passed for wisdom (σοφίας) there? Don't you think he'd count himself happy for the change (οἴει αὑτὸν μὲν εὐδαιμονίζειν τῆς μεταβολῆς) and pity (ἐλεεῖν) the others? (VII.516c4–6)

This is the first mention in the whole of the allegory of the prisoner's reflection on himself (αὑτὸν) as a concrete, knowable object of his own thinking. While the aporetic soul recognized itself as more than its shadow, it remained unsure of itself. It is only at this point in the text that the soul

---

[18] See R. VII.518d3–7: dialectic converts (μεταστραφήσεται) the soul and turns it around (περιαγωγή). Cf. VII.514b2: the prisoners in the cave are incapable of turning around (περιάγειν).

beholds itself as a fixed epistemic entity. The dwelling place (οἰκήσεως), the condition in which it once felt most comfortable, and its purported wisdom (σοφίας), what it thought it knew, are now seen as illusory. The illusion, moreover, can only be understood as illusory to the soul that has truly freed itself from that condition. Its new condition makes it possible for the soul to grasp itself as changed, as different from a previous version of itself.

We thus find a third kind of self-knowledge in the allegory, that is, *dianoetic self-knowledge*. By comparing its present condition with its previous condition, the soul is reflexively aware of itself as both the soul that was imprisoned and subsequently confused. This corresponds precisely to the third level of the divided line, at which Socrates says the soul uses as image what was imitated before.[19] The soul beholds the previous aporetic version of itself (which cast the shadow version of self we called eikastic) as an image of thought. While the aporetic soul was confused about its condition, here the freed soul recognizes its difference from its previous version and deems itself happy for the change. Whereas the prisoner in ἀπορία was miserable and wanted to return to his previous condition, he now pities those in that condition. He recognizes his complete psychic change and believes himself better than he was.[20]

The prisoner's eros has also significantly changed when moving from aporetic to dianoetic self-knowldge. He no longer desires anything that is held honorable by the prisoners and is so happy with his new condition that he would rather go through any suffering than live as they do (VII.516d4–7). This growth shows the effect of a properly philosophical education on the soul.[21] Growth is indicated not only by a change in what we know but also by a change in our affective condition. At the same time, this means an increasing reflexive awareness of what satisfies the soul and a

---

[19] *R.* VI.510b4–5.

[20] Howland (2004, 137) makes the insightful observation that when Socrates quotes Homer's Achilles in this passage – distinguishing the better life of the serf from the glory he achieved with his death (*Odyssey* xi.489–90) – we see that the freed prisoner considers those in the cave to be living the life of shadows, akin to the shades of Hades. We thus find another reference to the shadows of the prisoners. Cf. VII.521c1–3.

[21] *R.* VI.485d10–e1: when someone's desires incline strongly for one thing, they are thereby weakened for others. See Gill (1985, 18–21) for the education of desire. Reeve (2006, 49–58) interprets the change of the prisoner's desires as he ascends out of the cave in light of the changes undergone by the soul in Books VIII and IX. At the level of dianoetic self-knowledge, Reeve places the honor-loving timocrat, governed by his spirited desires. Reeve's thesis makes explicit the point that the prisoner's development of self-knowledge must not be understood merely in terms of his object of cognition but also in terms of his psychic condition, an integral dimension of which is his conative focus.

commitment to cultivating the sort of life that leads to pursuing appropriate psychic nourishment.[22]

It might seem at this point that the allegory should finish. The prisoner has escaped and is happy in his condition. But Socrates proceeds to ask what would happen if the prisoner were to return to the cave. At this point in the text there is no apparent reason for him to do so, for it is only later that he responds to Glaucon's claim about the injustice of the prisoner's return. I will argue that Socrates raises the issue here because despite the prisoner's ascent, he does not yet truly know himself. The final type of self-knowledge, the most complete, can only be achieved when he returns to the cave.

5.4

When Socrates describes the prisoner's hypothetical return, he claims the man's eyes would be filled with darkness if he returned to the same seat (τὸν αὐτὸν θᾶκον), and his habituation (τῆς συνηθείας) would not be quick (VII.516e3–517a2). Just as he needed time to habituate himself after coming out of the cave, he would now need time to habituate himself after returning. There is, however, a crucial difference. The reaction of the other prisoners indicates that his adjustment is not a readjustment. Having passed through the aporetic and dianoetic phases of self-knowledge, the prisoner can never truly reacquire his previous condition. If he tried to do so by competing with the others, they would ridicule him and claim his eyesight is ruined, and if he tried to help them escape, they might try to kill him (VII.517a2–6). The freed prisoner and those in the cave now appear to each other as out of place, incapable of understanding each other. The difference is that the freed prisoner knows himself in ways that are impossible for the others.

Before Socrates develops this relationship further, he tells Glaucon that the entirety of the allegory must be fitted together with the divided line (VII.517a8–c5). Socrates describes the soul as taking a journey from the visible realm (ἕδραν) to the intelligible realm (τόπον).[23] The language of place reflects the relationship between the changing condition of the soul and the possibility of philosophical cognition. The prisoner's ascent out of the cave and knowledge of himself is in direct proportion with his ability to understand. As soul becomes more knowable, formal reality becomes more intelligible. However, soul is not eternally self-identical like form. It

---

[22] *Phdr.* 247c3–e6, *Ti.* 90b1–e1.   [23] Cf. *Phdr.* 246e4–248b5.

cannot consistently grasp itself as the intentional object of its own cognition. There is for this reason no form of Soul anywhere in Plato.[24] As such, soul cannot be the object of νόησις strictly speaking. The closest approximation the prisoner can achieve is to remember the previous psychic conditions with which he no longer identifies. If the soul is to know itself, therefore, it must do so in a way that is qualitatively different from the way it knows forms. The soul is "akin" to the forms in ontological profile; it is not identical to them.[25]

The "knowledge" of "self" is not cognitive contact with an eternally stable principle of intelligibility. Instead, the highest phase of self-knowledge is a disclosure of self that takes place in the exercise of intellect. I call this *intellective self-knowledge*, following the name for the psychic condition Socrates describes at VI.511d8 and corresponding to the highest level of the divided line. When the soul engages in dialectic and transcends hypotheses, it performs its essential function and is reflexively aware of itself doing so.[26] Intellective self-knowledge is in this sense best described as self-knowing, in two distinct senses. First, it is a self-*knowing*, a soul that is knowing. The knowing soul is engaged in the activity most appropriate to its nature. Only the performance of its essential activity makes it possible for the soul to glimpse intelligible reality. At the same time, it is also a *self*-knowing, a knowing of self. A soul engaged in dialectic reflexively knows itself in the condition of understanding (νόησις). Socrates does not state this explicitly, not because there is no emphasis on self in the passage but because self-knowledge requires a different model of knowing altogether. Self-knowing is not knowledge of oneself as thought-object but presence to oneself as performing subject. Such a soul is neither confused over itself – as in aporetic self-knowledge – nor reflecting on itself as a static thought-object – as in dianoetic self-knowledge – but is reflexively disclosed to itself through the very activity that leads it to knowledge of formal reality.

That soul is similar to but also different from form entails not only that they cannot be known in the same way but also that soul cannot remain forever in the condition of νόησις. This condition is an ideal

---

[24] The lone exception is *Phdr.* 246a3, though I agree with Griswold (1981) that this is a nontechnical usage. Griswold argues that the wholeness of soul eludes episteme but not all conscious experience, and adds that the soul's definition, self-motion, cannot be referred to independently of the experiences it undergoes and tasks it executes. This is consistent with my argument (later) regarding the soul's disclosure to itself.

[25] *Ep. VII.*344a2–4, *Phd.* 79d1–7.

[26] On this definition of dialectic, see *R.* VI.511b3–c2 and VII.533c7–e3. Cf. *Phd.* 101d3–102a1.

toward which soul repeatedly strives but that it cannot permanently maintain, for soul is not wholly intellectual, but thumodic and epithumetic as well. While the freed soul recognizes that contact with forms is its only true nourishment, it also recognzies that it cannot remain forever in contact with them. The first reason that the prisoner must return to the cave is therefore ontological – soul cannot inhabit a place to which it does not exclusively belong, cannot always maintain itself in a condition of intellect.

There is, however, a second reason for the prisoner's return. Though it is impossible for the prisoner to remain outside the cave, Socrates must now answer the question, What if it was not? That is to say, he addresses the question of whether or not, regardless of possibility, the prisoner should want to remain outside the cave. Is the return something merely necessary for the prisoner but to which he begrudgingly agrees, or is it beneficial and hence desirable as well? Socrates makes the latter claim. The second reason for the prisoner's return to the cave is not ontological, but ethical.

Consider what happens next in the allegory. Socrates shifts from considering the prisoner's return as a possibility ("if") to an argument about what is best for the prisoner. He is well aware that soul will be always pressing upward (VII.517c9), eager to remain in the intelligible. The prisoner's desire is no doubt exacerbated by the degree to which he seems out of place among the prisoners in the cave – not sufficiently accustomed (ἱκανῶς συνήθης) to the darkness around him, he behaves awkwardly (ἀσχημονεῖ) and appears completely ridiculous (σφόδρα γελοῖος) when compelled to contend about shadows (VII.517d4–e2). A person of intellect (νοῦς), however, would not judge until he recognizes the reason for the confusion. Just as the eyes need adjustment when they pass from dark to light but also from light to dark, so the soul must habituate itself on the basis of whether it passes from the visible to the intelligible or vice versa. The person of intellect would judge a soul that has returned from the intelligible to the visible happy in its condition and life (εὐδαιμονίσειεν ἂν τοῦ πάθους τε καὶ βίου), and he would pity (ἐλεήσειεν) one that has moved solely from the visible to the intelligible (VII.518a1–b4).

It is not the prisoner who escapes the cave and remains outside who is declared happy; rather, it is the prisoner who escapes and then returns. This is the complete reverse of what one would expect, especially when one considers that at VII.516c4–6 Socrates uses exactly this language to describe the prisoner's own self-judgment during the phase of dianoetic self-knowledge. The escaped prisoner previously judged himself happy and pitied those he left behind in the cave. Socrates now deploys the same language in this later passage in order to indicate that the escaped prisoner's judgment, while appropriate at that specific moment of his psychic development, is mistaken. To escape and not return would render the prisoner miserable and, by analogy, the soul unhappy. Thus, even if the prisoner could remain outside the cave, he should not. His return is something that benefits him, and he should want to go back.

The argument here may strike many as counterintuitive. That it does so speaks to the absence of attention paid to self-knowledge in the allegory. Socrates claims that the soul that returns is happy in its experience or condition, its πάθος. Why? Because the soul's grasp of intelligible reality requires its separation from its objects of cognition. The intellective soul organizes its βίος, its life, so that it can love wisdom, and this love requires that the prisoner not just journey out of the cave but also return to it.[27] The journey is circular, not linear.[28] Initially, the soul will cling to the visible when shown the intelligible, and then want to remain within the intelligible instead of returning to the visible. Neither of these alternatives is ethically satisfactory, because in either case, the soul would not be happy.

The philosopher's return to the cave is an indication that the soul truly knows itself. The repeated practice of dialectic cannot be achieved either completely inside the cave or completely outside it. Within the cave, there is only becoming and change; outside the cave, there is only being and stability. Soul itself is neither but is in between the two.[29] To be sure, philosophical education reorients the soul toward the intelligible (VII.518b6–d7). But this reorientation signals not the soul's complete abdication of the visible for the sake of the intelligible, but its desire to discern the intelligible within the visible. The soul that knows itself understands this and returns to the cave in order to ascend back out again. Put differently, the self-*knowing* soul, insofar as it is also *self*-knowing, recognizes that its most essential activity requires both its separation from and repeated intercourse with the objects of philosophical cognition. The soul that does not know itself as such, that attempts to identify itself entirely with those objects, however akin to them it is, loses the distinction

---

[27] On the relationship between βίος and self-knowledge, see Sara Brill's Chapter 7 in this book.

[28] *Phdr.* 248e3–249a5: a soul that is philosophical returns to the place from which it came. For the view that noetic thinking is always circular, see Lee (1976).

[29] Cf. *Smp.* 203b1–204b8 – Eros is between poverty and plenty. That Eros in Diotima's speech is neither ignorant nor wise but a lover of wisdom is consistent with the view that soul that knows itself returns to the cave so that it can ascend again. For the view that the ascent of the *Symposium* can be mapped onto the descent in the *Republic*, see Principe (2006).

between the two and is therefore incapable of desiring them.[30] For Plato, the soul that does not know itself cannot truly love wisdom.[31]

5.5

I would like to conclude by considering Glaucon's claim that to make the philosopher return to the cave is unjust (VII.519d8–9). It is here that one might object to my account on the grounds Glaucon does. If the entire purpose of philosophical education is to free the soul from the cave, to compel the philosopher to return is completely antithetical to that education, entirely unjust, and would render the soul unhappy. Socrates' reply, that their purpose is to spread happiness throughout the entire city and not just confine it to one of its parts, seems to suggest that the return of the philosopher entails his being less happy than he otherwise would (VII.519e1–520a4). The philosophers, Socrates claims, must be compelled to return to the city because they are indebted to it for their upbringing, which seems to suggest that they do not wish to do so (VII.520a6–d4). The objection, then, may be stated succinctly: (1) the return to the cave reverses the work of philosophical education; (2) the return is completely unjust to the philosophers who have no desire to rule but are forced to do so.

Our perspective on self-knowledge can help us reply to both. I will address the second objection first. If we take the city/soul analogy seriously, Socrates' insistence that the philosopher returns to the cave to harmonize the political classes is analogous to intellect putting the soul in order.[32] Socrates does not say that the philosophers do not wish to

---

[30] It is perhaps in order to overcome this separation that many Platonists from Plotinus onward insisted that self-knowledge is a matter of the soul's reverting or turning back on its true self, intellect (see, e.g., *Enn.* I.6, 6.13–18, cf. I.8, 4.25–28), and that the intelligibles are internal to intellect (*Enn.* V 5). On intellect as the true self, see Lloyd Gerson's Chapter 1 in this book.

[31] Howland (2004, 148): "Socratic philosophizing actually seems to involve *repeated* 'round-trips' of the sort depicted in the Cave, or to consist in a shuttling, up-and-down movement of discourse whereby the examination, through dialogue, of the concrete texture of our experience opens up new approaches to the Ideas, and the exploration of these freshly opened avenues, in turn, sheds new light on the nature of our experience."

[32] It is here that I offer a rather general reply to the incredibly precise article by Brown (2000), whose close analysis argues that the philosopher truly does not want to return to the cave. The majority of my analysis is psychological, his political. Brown insists that it could never be in the philosophers' best interest to rule – neither in the case that their knowledge of forms will create in them a desire to express their knowledge in actions (the expressivist thesis) nor in the case that the philosopher will imitate the forms by participating in well-ordered, harmonious relationships (the imitationist thesis) – on the grounds that these positions ignore the compulsion (ἀνάγκη) said to be necessary to make philosophers rule who otherwise would prefer not to do so (5ff.). In what follows I offer brief remarks about preference and compulsion. Regarding expression, it is indeed in

return, but that they are the least eager (ἥκιστα πρόθυμοι) of anyone in the city to do so (VII.520d2). While they identify themselves with the intellectual dimension of the soul and love wisdom, they also know that they are more than intellect and that in order to ascend to the intelligible, the soul must be in proper order.[33] The philosopher's return, understood as soul organizing itself, is in no way unjust but is rather precisely what justice requires (VII.520a6–9). When Glaucon worries that the philosophers will live a worse life (χεῖρον ζῆν, VII.519d8–9), Socrates replies that the purpose of the law is to ensure that the whole city "does well" (εὖ πράξει, VII.519e2). The philosopher's return to the cave does not violate his sovereign happiness, or soul's functioning well. Given the ontology of soul, it is its condition of possibility. The compulsion of which Socrates speaks is a matter of soul's self-transparency and assent to order itself so that it can exercise intellect.[34]

Socrates insists that a city is poorly governed not only when those who have no experience of truth rule but also when power is held by those who have spent their entire lives being educated. The former have no single goal toward which their actions are oriented, and the latter refuse to act at all (VII.519b7–c6). The point here is similar to what we said earlier: both the prisoner and the escaped philosopher cling to their respective conditions, neither of which can render the soul happy. A truly philosophical education ought to remedy both these defects, such that the soul has a single goal toward which it consistently acts. Moreover, Socrates suggests that the condition for the creation of the ideal city is the philosopher's happiness (VII.520e4–521a8). This happiness is the soul's functioning

---

the philosopher's interest, insofar as he knows himself and loves wisdom, to establish order *within* his soul, the outward manifestation of which is rule. While this does not mean that the philosopher's soul depends on there being order in the city, it does commit him to at least attempt to engender it. My thanks to Andy German for helping me clarify this point. One does not need to look for support for this idea in Diotima's speech in the *Symposium* regarding a lover's desire to express the object of his love, as does, e.g., Irwin (1995, 298–317); one can simply find it in the *Republic* itself in the passage cited above, VII.518a1–b4, in which the philosopher who returns is said to be happy. As far as imitation is concerned, it is in the philosopher's interest to pattern himself after formal reality, and given that Socrates insists much earlier in the text that being (τὰ ὄντα, II.382b2) is nothing other than what is most authoritative (τὰ κυριώτατα, 382a8), ruling would seem to be in the interest of the philosopher who most *is* himself, and knows himself as such.

[33] On the relation between putting the soul in order (ontologically and ethically) and its relation to thinking Forms, see my argument in Ambury (2015).

[34] I therefore interpret Socrates' later comment that ruling for the philosopher is not fine but necessary (VII.540b4–5) to mean that, once they see the Good, philosophers recognize the need to establish order in the soul and, by extension, also in the city.

well, which requires not the separation of inside from outside the cave, but its mixture.[35]

Socrates claims that this is what the education of the philosopher accomplishes. More completely educated than the others, the philosopher is better able to share in both kinds of lives (μᾶλλον δυνατοὺς ἀμφοτέρων μετέχειν). Each philosopher must return to the common dwelling place (συνοίκησιν), and because of their education, they will see much better than everyone else (VII.520b6–c6). We see here the completion of the circle by those who achieve intellective self-knowledge – returning to the cave to discern the intelligible within the visible confirms that they truly know themselves.[36] The reply to the first objection is therefore that the return to the cave is not antithetical to philosophical education, but confirmation of its success.

What, then, is the proper "place" of the soul, its appropriate condition? It is in between the third and fourth levels of the divided line, always prepared to transcend hypotheses and grasp first principles. It desires to exercise itself, to reflexively experience itself in the condition of intellect. Mapped onto the allegory of the cave, soul is neither wholly inside the cave nor outside it, but on the path that connects the visible and the intelligible. Loving wisdom requires that we dialectically traverse this path repeatedly and consistently engage in dialectic. In so doing, we make a journey in which we know not just forms but ourselves.

[35] For explication of this passage and the view that the philosopher's complete happiness depends on his soul functioning properly, which in turn requires harmony between his contemplative activity or ruling activity, see Kurihara (2008).

[36] Kraut (1991, 52–53) articulates this point in terms of imitation. Because the philosopher not only contemplates but imitates form, his refusal to return to the cave to rule would signify his rejection of the Forms as models of human behavior.

CHAPTER 6

Self-Knowledge and the Use of the Self in the Platonic Theages

Brian Marrin

The *Theages*, when it has even been studied, has been a despised work.[1] Since Schleiermacher, its authenticity, along with a number of minor dialogues like the *Hipparchus* and *Minos*, has been continually doubted and its philosophical significance perhaps even more so.[2] In recent years, however, two substantial studies of the *Theages* have appeared that in one way or another challenge that orthodoxy. Joyal, while ultimately upholding the judgment that the dialogue is spurious and lacking in substantial philosophical interest, nonetheless has argued that it deserves careful study "unencumbered by the assumptions and assertions of the past two hundred years."[3] Bailly agrees with Joyal that the dialogue merits unprejudiced study and, while not defending outright its authenticity, does not consider the evidence of its spuriousness to be decisive.[4] I do not intend here to enter into the question of authenticity directly, but to attempt to interpret the dialogue as a philosophical work worthy of Plato or one of Plato's students. The dialogue's central theme, I shall argue, is self-knowledge or, to use slightly paradoxical language, the "use of the self." Its purpose is nothing more than to identify the *question* of the knowledge and use of the self as the essential beginning of philosophical education. The dialogue,

---

[1] To give only one example, Vlastos (1991, 202) dismisses it as nothing but a "monument to the level of credulity to which some of Socrates' superstitious admirers could sink after his death." Further examples are compiled in Cobb (1992, 267). Cobb argues for the authenticity of the dialogue.

[2] Cf. Cobb (1992). A few other scholars, such as Grote (1888), Friedländer (1958, 34), and Pangle (1987, 3–16), have argued generally for the authenticity of the *Theages* and other such dialogues.

[3] Joyal (2000, 7). Joyal finds little or no evidence for spuriousness based on language or stylometry, and suggestive but inconclusive evidence, given its similarity to the "early" dialogues, from its parallels to some "late" dialogues (specifically the parallel Aristides episodes at *Thg.* 130a–e and *Tht.* 150e–151a). He therefore considers decisive the *Theages'* treatment of the *daimonion* or divine sign, which he thinks could not have been written by Plato (ibid., 131). In this chapter, I call into question Joyal's reading of the *daimonion* in the *Theages*. For a more recent, and still inconclusive, examination of the stylometry, cf. Johnson and Tarrant (2012, 233–35).

[4] Bailly (2004, 3f., 70ff.).

then, expands, or at least deepens, our conception of philosophical pro-treptic as understood by the followers of Socrates.

The manuscripts of the *Theages* give it the subtitle *On Wisdom* or *On Philosophy* and it was classed sometimes among the so-called maieutic dialogues.[5] Yet in the dialogue we find no definition of philosophy or any articulation of a philosophical curriculum. What the *Theages* offers instead is not so much an account as a dramatic enactment of the kind of attitude that Socrates thinks we ought to take to philosophy and philo-sophical education, one that could well be called a maieutic attitude.[6] But the *Theages* offers only the briefest example of Socrates' maieutic practice.[7] Instead, it presents Socrates' attempt to explain to Theages the nature and expectations of philosophical education. The characterization of philo-sophical education that can be extracted from the dialogue is that it involves a kind of "use of the self." Philosophy is not about learning from the instruction of a master or teacher, but a new way of relating to oneself and to one's philosophical companions. The intention of the "use of the self" that Socrates attempts to demonstrate to Theages is to recreate within oneself the very maieutic relation entered into by Socrates himself with his companions. The *Theages* presents Socrates as neither a teacher nor a mystic who transmits wisdom by his mere presence, but rather as a catalyst of the philosophical advancement of his companions. The dialogue is not so much an exposition of philosophical doctrine as a drama of philosoph-ical self-knowledge.

The phrase that I have been translating here, with some awkwardness, as the "use of the self" seems to arise from an idiomatic expression found on several occasions in the Platonic corpus, as well as in Xenophon and other authors.[8] It can refer both to the "use" of another person and to a reflexive use of oneself. But in neither case does it seem possible to give the phrase a straightforwardly instrumental sense. Instead it seems to be equivalent to the English "what will you do with yourself?" In the *Theages*, Socrates will ask Theaeges "what would he do with himself" regarding his son

---

[5] For the subtitles, cf. the *apparatus criticus* in Joyal (2000, 175). For the dialogue as maieutic, cf. Diogenes Laertius 3.51. For the various classifications of the Platonic corpus in antiquity, cf. Chroust (1965).

[6] Diogenes Laertius, 3.49–51, classifies the maieutic dialogues as a subspecies of the "gymnastic," in turn a division of the "zetetic" dialogues, that is, those dedicated not to the exposition of doctrine ("hyphegetic") but to the investigation of a problem. For a consideration of the maieutic nature of the *Theages*, cf. Opsomer (1997, 134).

[7] Cobb (1992, 284) argues that "[t]he primary contributions of the dialogue ... lie in the depiction of Socrates' elenctic educational method."

[8] Cf. Liddell et al. (1996), entry on χράω, c.iv.3.

(τί … χρήσαιο σαυτῷ, 126d8) and immediately repeat the question, asking, "what would you do with him?" (αὐτῷ ὅτι χρῷο, 126e6).[9] Yet despite the colloquial register of these phrases, their more literal rendering is necessary in order to bring out their philosophical significance.[10] The connection between the colloquial and the philosophical can be seen in the analysis of art (*technē*) in the *Theages*. If every art or wisdom is the knowledge of the use or rule of something, as the art of charioteering is the knowledge of using or ruling a team of horses (123d), then with the colloquial question "τί χρήσαιο σαυτῷ;" Socrates is implicitly raising the question whether there is a kind of art or wisdom that is a knowledge of the use (or rule) of the self.[11] This idea of the use or rule of the self is hardly alien to Plato's thinking. The *Republic* defines justice in the soul as a harmonious relation that is a kind of self-rule.[12] More suggestively, in the *Clitophon* justice is once defined as the knowledge of how to properly *use* the soul.[13]

The dramatic situation of the *Theages* has some resonances with the *Clitophon*. Clitophon had faulted Socrates for protreptically exhorting his companions to pursue the knowledge of justice while being either unable or unwilling to teach them that same justice,[14] while in the present dialogue, Socrates will respond to Theages' desire to *be made* wise by explaining that he cannot teach anyone to become wise and that the results of association with him are unpredictable. The dialogue begins with the respectable farmer Demodocus asking Socrates if he could have a word in private (ἰδιολογήσασθαι). When Socrates agrees, he suggests that they withdraw into the Stoa of Zeus Eleutherios so that they might be out of the way (121a1ff.). Demodocus' precautions suggest that he is about to broach a very delicate subject, a suspicion that is confirmed by his next address to Socrates. With a rustic metaphor he explains his problem. It is

---

[9] A few lines later, Socrates repeats himself again to Theages: καὶ μέμφῃ εἰ ἀπορεῖ ὅτι σοι χρήσηται, 127a2. Cf. Bailly (2004, 194ff.) for other examples in Plato. All translations from the *Theages* are my own. I have followed the text published in Joyal (2000). For other Platonic texts I have followed Burnet's Oxford edition.

[10] For Plato's tendency to exploit the latent implications of ordinary speech, cf. Von Fritz (1963, 51ff.) and Lisi (2016, 65ff.).

[11] Cf. *Phd.* 89e5–7, where the misanthrope is one who ἄνευ τέχνης τῆς περὶ τἀνθρώπεια … χρῆσθαι ἐπεχείρει τοῖς ἀνθρώποις. The use of the self came to have a quasi-technical sense in the Stoics. Cf. Benatouïl (2006).

[12] Cf. esp. *R.* IV.442c–443b; also VII.540b1, ἑαυτοὺς κοσμεῖν, and IX.592b3, ἑαυτὸν κατοικίζειν.

[13] Cf. *Clit.* 408a5–7: ὅστις ψυχῇ μὴ ἐπίσταται χρῆσθαι, τούτῳ τὸ ἄγειν ἡσυχίαν τῇ ψυχῇ καὶ μὴ ζῆν κρεῖττον ἢ ζῆν πράττοντι καθ' αὑτόν. For an interpretation of the use of the soul in the *Clitophon*, cf. Marrin (2017).

[14] *Clit.* 410b5ff.

the same for all plants, animals, and even human beings: the planting or begetting is the easiest part, while the caring (θεραπεία) for the shoot proves exceptionally difficult (121b). It has been the same with his son Theages. Demodocus' fear has only been increased by the newly-conceived desire of his son, now a young man, "to become wise" (σοφὸς γενέσθαι, 121c8ff.). This "not ignoble, but precipitous" desire was aroused by the recounting, by some of the boy's companions, of certain speeches (λόγους) they had heard in town, and he is now asking Demodocus to engage him with one of the sophists who would be able to "make him wise" (σοφὸν ποιήσει, 121e7–d6).[15] Demodocus thinks it better to obey his son and retain some possibility of supervision than to deny him and risk his going off alone and being corrupted, and so has come to town to set him up with "one of those who seem to be sophists." Socrates has turned up at "just the right time" and Demodocus wishes to ask his advice on the matter (122a2–9).

As will become clear later in the dialogue, Demodocus is not being entirely candid with Socrates. The *logoi* that Theages had heard of turn out to be from his friends who have already associated with Socrates (128c2–5), and it is with him that Theages wishes to associate (συνεῖναι, 127a8–10).[16] Demodocus is "ashamed to say how much" he desires the same thing (127b1–b6). His "happening upon" Socrates was in fact no accident, but a deliberate effort to persuade him to take charge of his son.[17] Demodocus, then, a respectable man who has occupied the "highest offices" in Athens and is highly esteemed in both his deme and the city as a whole (127e), presents an ironic reversal of the common opinion about Socrates. Instead of Socrates seducing a promising youth and turning him against his parents, we are faced with one of the *kaloi kagathoi* (cf. 122e9) attempting to seduce Socrates into associating with his son so that he might not be corrupted by one of the sophists.[18]

---

[15] Cf. 126d5ff.: παραδοῦναι τὴν αὐτοῦ σοφίαν. γενέσθαι can be understood as the passive of ποιεῖν, cf. *Phlb.* 27a1f.

[16] The verb συνεῖναι, and the corresponding συνουσία, becomes almost a term of art in the *Theages*. Perhaps the best, though slightly archaic, translation would be "intercourse," which captures the full range of connotations, from intellectual to sexual, of the original Greek. But I have generally opted for the blander "association." For a discussion of the use of the terms in the Platonic corpus, cf. Tarrant (2005).

[17] Cf. Benardete (1953, 20) and Bailly (2004, 6).

[18] In this respect, the *Theages* can also be compared with Aristophanes' *Clouds*, where the desperate Strepsiades, wishing to learn the "unjust speech" in order to avoid paying his debts, sends his spendthrift son Pheidippides to Socrates, where he is corrupted to the point of beating his own father. Cf. Benardete (1953, 1–3). The complex dynamic between father and son exploited by Socrates, analyzed carefully by Benardete, bears comparison to *Ly.* 210b–d.

Socrates accepts Demodocus' request for advice but insists that before entering into their deliberation they establish just what it is that they are deliberating about, "lest I understand it to be one thing, and you something else, and then far along in the conversation (συνουσίας) we realize how ridiculous we are" (122b8–c2).[19] Socrates here is not looking in the first place to establish a definition of education or wisdom but, as he immediately makes clear, to discover what it is that the boy Theages really wants. Demodocus had said that he desires to become wise, but it has occurred to Socrates that the boy might not "desire what we think he desires, but something else" (122c9ff.). Instead of deliberating with Demodocus about his son, Socrates prefers to speak with the boy himself.

In the *Theages*, then, the themes of self-knowledge and desire are intimately connected. Theages wants to find someone who will *make* him wise. And Socrates' aim will be to explain to Theages that it is impossible for anyone to be *made* wise and to see if Theages' dedication to wisdom or philosophy can survive this initial disappointment. Thus he begins to question him in order to learn more clearly what he wants (122d3ff.). From the beginning, Theages makes it clear that he knows exactly what he wants and that it is his father who has refused to listen to him (123a5–8). Faced with Socrates' initial attempts to clarify what kind of wisdom he desires (e.g., the wisdom of piloting ships or of driving chariots), he stubbornly insists that he simply desires wisdom without qualification (123c–d). But when Socrates postulates that every kind of wisdom is the knowledge of the use or rule of something (123d8ff.), he answers that he desires the wisdom to use or rule over all the inhabitants of the city (124a1, 124c1–4).[20] When pressed to give a name to those who exercise such rule, he can find none more fitting than "tyrants." Theages, then, wishes to learn the art of tyranny (τυραννική) and to be a tyrant (124e4–10). And further pressed by Socrates, he will conclude that "I suppose that I would pray to become a tyrant over all men, and if not, then over as many as possible. And so would you, I think, and all men – and perhaps even more to become a god – but I wasn't saying I desired that" (125e8–126a4).

---

[19] Besides the Platonic parallels mentioned in Joyal (2000, ad loc.), cf. *Cri.* 49d2ff.: οἷς οὖν οὕτω δέδοκται καὶ οἷς μή, τούτοις οὐκ ἔστι κοινὴ βουλή. For the wider significance of this, cf. Cobb (1992, 284).

[20] Cf. Bailly (2004, 158). Gorgias calls such rule the μέγιστον ἀγαθόν (*Grg.* 452d5–8), and Meno defines virtue as being able to rule human beings (*Men.* 73c9–d1).

Theages' words are intended to be dismissive of the idea that he wants to be a tyrant, and he immediately clarifies that he really wants to "rule over the willing, like the other renowned men in the city" (126a7ff.).[21] But even if tyranny is not the serious object of Theages' deliberation, it is still crucial to Socrates' dialectical strategy to bring him to recognize that it is the genuine, if unacknowledged, object of his desire or eros.[22] For only in this way can he pose to Theages most emphatically the question of the end or of the highest good. The promise of tyranny or of total power forces Theages to consider the problem of the final end. For while the less powerful may distract themselves from the problem of the end in the search for ever more powerful means, the omnipotent tyrant or god is liberated from all constraint and so cannot avoid asking himself what it is all for. After mastering everything external to him, he must turn inward – he must ask what he is to do with himself, or in Socrates' words, how to "use himself." Socrates' strategy with Theages, then, by confronting him with the erotic prospect of tyrannical power, is to lead him to recognize the question of the use of the self.

Socrates establishes the connection between tyranny, eros, and wisdom with a playful allusion to a poem of Anacreon. Having established that it is not just any wisdom that Theages needs, but the wisdom of an expert in tyranny, he identifies it with "that which Anacreon said that Kallikrite knew" (125d1off.). Theages, then, who is familiar with the poem in question, must desire "an association (συνουσία) of this kind with a man who happens to practice the same art (ὁμότεχνος) as Kallikrite, daughter of Kyane, and who 'knows the art of tyranny' (ἐπίσταται τυραννικά), as the poet says that she did, so that you might yourself might become a tyrant over us and the city" (125d13–e7).

Theages takes this reference to Anacreon to be a joke at his expense, and Socrates does not explain his intention in quoting a poet famous for his erotic lyrics.[23] Given the reputation of Anacreon it is safe to assume that Kallikrite's knowledge of *tyrannika* was not political expertise but rather her mastery of the art of seduction.[24] Her exercise of tyranny is not political

---

[21] Cf. Joyal (2000, 240).
[22] For a close parallel, cf. Aristotle, *EE*, 1225b32–35 on the distinction between βούλησις and προαίρησις. At *EN*, 1113a23, Aristotle specifies that προαίρησις is the choice of means, while βούλησις is always of the end.
[23] Tarrant (2003,156) calls this "a playful passage concealing much seriousness."
[24] Cf. Joyal (1990, 123). Also, Joyal (2000, 30 and 238) on 125d13, συνουσίας: "it is reasonable to detect a sexual *double entendre*."

but erotic.²⁵ Socrates, then, is saying that aspiring political tyrants must desire the "intercourse" of erotic tyrants – that they ought, so to speak, to become slaves to eros. It is easy to see how Theages could take this as mockery. But Socrates' mockery has serious intent, for he will later claim that while he does not have the ability to teach the art of political tyranny, the only knowledge that he does possess is that of τὰ ἐρωτικά (128b4).²⁶

Socrates, then, seems both to affirm and to deny that he is the kind of wise man with whom Theages as aspiring tyrant must associate. But what can he mean by this? Having induced Theages to at least partially walk back his desire for tyranny to the more moderate desire to rule over the willing "like the other renowned men of the city" (ἐλλόγιμοι ἄνδρες), that is, those who are skilled in politics (126a7ff.), and to pursue wisdom in the art of politics (τὰ πολιτικά, 126c3), Socrates inquires again what teachers Theages might find for this kind of wisdom. If it is not the *politikoi* themselves – for Theages has already heard the Socratic argument that successful politicians seem to be incapable of imparting their wisdom to their sons. Then Socrates suggests that he must study with one of the sophists such as Prodicus or Gorgias or Polus (128a). These men claim to be able to teach the wisdom that Theages desires and to know "these blessed and beautiful sciences" (μαθημάτων, 128b1ff.), of which Socrates himself is quite ignorant. Socrates, on the other hand, "happens to know practically nothing save for one small piece of learning, erotics" (σμικροῦ τινος μαθήματος, τῶν ἐρωτικῶν, 128b4). Theages' reaction to Socrates' claim is the same as to his earlier citation of Anacreon: "You see, father? Socrates does not now seem very willing to associate with me (συνδιατρίβειν) ... but says these things in order to make fun of us" (παίζων πρὸς ἡμᾶς, 128b7ff.).²⁷

What is the connection between the supposed wisdom of the sophists, who claim to teach the art or science of politics, and Socrates' claim to erotic wisdom, which he suggests is the true condition of being a wise tyrant? What links them is the very question of desire and of the use of the self. While tyranny – or, even more, the desire for apotheosis – is the most radical expression of the prereflective desire for infinite power over external

---

²⁵ Bailly (2004, 180 ad loc.) acknowledges that this is an "attractive conjecture" but hesitates, given that "we do not possess Anacreon's full poem." But he does not offer any alternative explanation for Theages' opinion that Socrates is making fun of him.

²⁶ Socrates' claim to erotic knowledge is found in various forms throughout the dialogues as well as in Xenophon. Cf. esp. *Smp.* 177d and *Phd.* 257a.

²⁷ Cf. 125e4: σκώπτεις καὶ παίζεις πρός με. Tarrant (2005, 132) suggests that one reason Socrates might be so elliptical in comparing himself with Kallikrite is the presence of Theages' father.

things, Socrates argues that the desire for tyranny does not fully understand itself, for it does not pose the question of the highest good. The
question of the highest good for a human being is only posed along with
the question of the use of the self, that is, the question "what shall I do
with myself?" or "how must one live?"[28] The question, "how must one
live?" is the fully articulated Socratic development of the question of
human desire. Thus, Socrates contrasts the teaching of the sophists,
which promises a technical mastery of the art of politics and persuasion
in order to satisfy one's given desires, with his own art of erotics, which
puts those very desires in question. This art is nothing more than his
capacity of uncovering for his interlocutors the true nature of their
desires, of their *eros*. It is the art of articulating the inchoate and unreflective desires of his interlocutors, and is to this extent also a maieutic
art. By bringing to light the erotic yearning of Theages, Socrates allows
him the possibility of entering into a more coherent and reflective
relation with these very yearnings, and so to deliberate rationally about
whether and how they are to be satisfied. Socrates' erotic art is the art of
the use of the self.

Socrates had argued that an aspiring tyrant ought to submit himself
to the tutelage of a master of erotic tyranny, and leaves it for Theages to
realize that he was really talking about himself. Socrates' erotic tyranny,
of course, is nothing more than his philosophical companionship. It
does not teach the instrumental use of tools such as other arts, but the
noninstrumental "use" of oneself. With the "art" of the use of the self,
it is a question not of fitting means to ends but of understanding the
end itself and oneself as the end.[29] The art of the use of the self, then,
cannot follow any set of rules or technical instructions, for it is not
concerned with any technical question. The use of the self is essentially
aporetic, or at least has the initial intention of bringing one to a state of
aporia wherein the question of the good life is recognized precisely as a
question. The proper use of the self begins with the posing of the
question of the use of the self. Or, as Socrates suggests in the *Apology*,
the love of wisdom is not only the beginning of wisdom but already a
partial or "human" wisdom.[30]

---

[28] Cf. *Grg.* 492d5: πῶς βιωτέον.
[29] Cf. Aristotle, *EN* 1113a6ff.; also *Physics* 194a35ff.: ἐσμὲν γάρ πως καὶ ἡμεῖς τέλος, διχῶς γὰρ τὸ οὗ
ἔνεκα.
[30] Cf. *Apo.* 23a–b.

Roughly the last third of the *Theages* is devoted to Socrates' account of his *daimonion* or daimonic sign, and any reading of the dialogue must take into account its obvious importance without forgetting to situate this account in the context of the dialogue as a whole.[31] The account of the *daimonion* serves a clearly defined dramatic purpose. It serves to explain to the young Theages what it means to associate with Socrates and what he can expect from this association (συνουσία). Socrates' chief aim is to ensure that Theages has no illusions about what he might learn from him. Theages thinks that the only thing standing between him and becoming like those who have been improved by association with Socrates is Socrates' own willingness to be with him (128c2–8). In order, then, to elicit in Theages a certain minimal self-knowledge or ability to "use" himself properly, Socrates explains his own peculiar "use of the self," one mediated by a daimonic voice not entirely dissimilar to an oracle.

Socrates' *daimonion* was undoubtedly the subject of popular interest and speculation,[32] and the account we find of it in the *Theages* is more in line with popular conceptions than what we find in the rest of the Platonic corpus.[33] This popular presentation of the *daimonion* seems to be particularly appropriate to the pious Demodocus (cf. 122d9ff.) and the young Theages, who even thinks that it could be appeased by prayer and sacrifice (131a6ff.). Socrates' account is in two parts: first, a summary description of the *daimonion* followed by several anecdotes meant to prove its efficacy (128d1–129d8) and, second, an account of "the power of the *daimonion*" in determining the outcome of one's association with Socrates (129e1–130e5).

Theages had said that he knew of some of "my peers and those a little older who were worthless before associating with [Socrates], but when they had been with him, in a very little time were shown to be better than all those than whom before they had been worse" (128c2–5). And if Socrates is "willing," Theages "will also be able to become such as they are" (128c7ff.). But Socrates affirms that Theages has failed to understand the nature of this association and proceeds to explain to him, in terms very similar to the *Apology*, the nature of his divine sign, which sometimes

---

[31] It is important to note, with Bailly (2004, 3), that "in essence, the dialogue is not about Socrates' divine sign. Socrates describes it and cites instances of it as a digressive illustration."
[32] Cf. *Euthphr.* 3b5ff., *Ap.* 31c7ff.; Xenophon, *Mem.* I.i.2.   [33] Cf. Benardete (1953, 28).

prohibits but never positively exhorts (προτρέπει, 128d2–7).[34] Here, however, the *daimonion* prohibits not only Socrates' own actions, but also those of his friends when they are with him.[35]

Socrates proceeds to recount briefly, and sometimes elusively, a series of four anecdotes about those who refused to heed the advice of the *daimonion*. The anecdotes seem to serve no other purpose than generally to impress upon Theages the dire consequences of disobeying the verdict of the *daimonion*. Nevertheless, the second and longest anecdote, involving Timarchus, is important for understanding the operation of Socrates' *daimonion* in the *Theages*. Socrates was at a symposium with Timarchus and Philemon, who were plotting an assassination. Timarchus twice rose to go and each time told Socrates that he was leaving, only for the *daimonion* to forbid his going. But the third time Timarchus got up to leave without telling Socrates, "wishing to go unnoticed" (129c3–6). With Socrates unaware of his departure, the *daimonion* said nothing and Timarchus went off to meet his fate. While some commentators, thinking that the *Theages* presents a heavily personified *daimonion*, have found it strange that it would so easily be duped,[36] the point of the anecdote seems to be rather to reinforce the dependence of the operation of the *daimonion* on Socrates' attention. The *daimonion* only advises him about his own actions or about those who have come to consult him.[37] The *daimonion* is not some guardian spirit or sixth sense that enables Socrates to perceive what he otherwise would not. It is essentially bound up with his own ordinary awareness of things. It can only intervene in the actions of others when they have consulted (that is, made their enterprise "common") with Socrates and are therefore of concern to him.[38]

On the basis of the examples cited above, the voice of the *daimonion* seems to speak to Socrates precisely in those situations which demand with the most urgency an answer to the question "what shall I do with myself?" that is, "how shall I *use* myself?" The *daimonion*, Socrates seems to be suggesting, is somehow a complement to his art of erotics. Its principal and striking difference is that, while eros always urges the lover on toward the desired object, the *daimonion* never encourages but only discourages. In the *Republic*, in a passage that mentions Theages, Socrates claims that it

---

[34] Cf. *Ap.* 31c8–d5.   [35] Xenophon agrees on this detail (*Mem.* I.i.4).
[36] E.g., Heidel, quoted in Joyal (2000, 276 ad loc.). For the correct reading, cf. Bailly (2004, 235 ad loc.).
[37] As Bailly (2004, ad loc.) correctly sees.   [38] Cf. 128d6: ἀνακοινῶται; 128e1ff.: ἀνακοινούμενος.

was his *daimonion* that kept him from entering into politics.[39] Socrates' *daimonion* seems to be the check on his eros that keeps it from becoming tyrannical.[40] It is the intuitive or even mantic expression of his use of the self.[41]

If the first part of Socrates' account of his *daimonion* is meant to impress upon Theages the importance of heeding its negative command, especially if it were to forbid Socrates to associate with Theages himself,[42] then the second part is explicitly intended to explain the "power" of the *daimonion* as far as the association itself. "The power of this *daimonion* is all-powerful (τὸ ἅπαν δύναται) also in the association with those who spend time with me" (129e1–3). But there is nothing in Socrates' words to suggest that the *daimonion* does much more than forbid association with some and tacitly accept it with others.[43] Socrates proceeds to explain to Theages this daimonic power by dividing into four groups those who seek association with him. The first consists of those with whom the *daimonion* forbids him to associate, of whom he says, "it is impossible to be benefitted by conversing with me" (129e4ff.). A second group consists of those with whom the sign does not forbid association, but nonetheless receive no benefit from their time with Socrates. There are many who belong to this group (129e6ff.). The last two groups are those "with whom the power of the *daimonion* collaborates in their association," the same ones that Theages has already noticed and who have motivated his own desire to associate with Socrates (129e7ff.).[44] All those who associate with Socrates under these auspices show immediate improvement, and some (the third group) receive a "stable and lasting benefit." But many show amazing improvement for the period of time that they are with me, but when they

---

[39] *R.* VI.496b6–c5. Theages is said to have been kept from politics, and so to have practiced philosophy by default, because of a serious illness.

[40] Interpreters of the *Theages* often identify the *daimonion* with eros, e.g., Pangle (1987, 170) and Joyal (2000, 97), but for Socrates eros is a universal phenomenon, while the *daimonion* is peculiar to himself. It might be safer to say that the dialogue identifies the *daimonion* with Socrates' *knowledge* of erotics, that is, his ability to use his own eros (cf. Benardete 1953, 32, who notes the parallel of *Thg.* 128b4–6 and *R.* VI.496c3–5, even as he fails to distinguish between eros and knowledge of the use of eros).

[41] The connection between the *daimonion* and the mantic is clear enough, but cf. Plato, *Ap.* 40a4: μαντικὴ ἡ τοῦ δαιμονίου; and Xenophon, *Ap.* 12ff.

[42] For the accusation that Socrates would appeal to his *daimonion* "ironically" as an excuse to avoid conversation, cf. Xenophon, *Symposium* VIII.v.3.

[43] Joyal (2000, 89–92). Cf. Bailly (2004, 242 ad loc.) for a more cautious analysis.

[44] "Collaborates" (συλλάβηται) is taken by Joyal (2000, 283 ad loc., and 89–92) to show the active and mystical role of the *daimonion* in Socratic education.

pull away from me they once again don't distinguish themselves at all from anyone" (130a1–4).

It is the fourth and last group, whose experience Socrates illustrates with the example of Aristides, the son of Lysimachus, that naturally draws the most attention, but it is of decisive importance to note the existence of the third group, those who receive a stable and lasting benefit from the association with Socrates even after they have left that association. For if the benefit can last beyond the term of the association, then the continued, quasi-mystical συνουσία of the *daimonion* cannot be the necessary condition of their lasting improvement.[45] But if this is the case, why does Socrates pass over this third, and evidently superior, group in order to devote the rest of his account to the experience of Aristides? I suggest it is because the example of Aristides is particularly appropriate to Theages' level of understanding. Theages, we have seen, already attributes to Socrates the power to "make" people wise, a claim that the account of the *daimonion* is explicitly meant to refute (130e5–10). The example of Aristides is meant to reduce Theages' expectations by showing that the "gains" made by his peers can be fleeting and do not at all depend on Socrates' efforts.[46]

In a short time, Aristides had made "very great improvement" while associating with Socrates, before he left on a military campaign (130a5–8). On his return, he relates to Socrates his experience. Before leaving on campaign he was able to converse (διαλέγεσθαι) with anyone at all and make a good showing of it, but now he avoids conversation with anyone with an education (130c).[47] He affirms that Socrates never taught him anything directly but that this dialectical power increased when he was in physical proximity to Socrates (and especially when he gazed into his eyes)

---

[45] For Joyal (2000, 92–97), the Aristides episode is decisive for an understanding of the *daimonion*. But as Tarrant (2003, 155) notes, even if we accept (as he does) the account of Aristides as meeting with Socratic approval, it is still "uncharitable to see *Theages* as ascribing all educational advances ... as simply due to the δαιμόνιον." Tarrant (2005, 140) also takes Aristides' description as paradigmatic of Socratic education: "it is through his words that we hear what the effect of Socratic *synousia* is really like."

[46] Bailly (2004, 29) is therefore wrong to claim that "*Socrates offers Aristides as a paradigm*" (emphasis in original), for he is only a paradigm of one kind of (inferior) student. Bailly is too quick to dismiss Joyal's suggestion (2000, 287) that "some irony may be intended in Aristides' misconceived boast," given that apparently the "mediocrity of the descendants of Aristides the Just became a commonplace."

[47] Bailly (2004, 29ff.) argues that this passage "shows Socratic association fostering rhetorical, conversational, and wit-bandying skills," which "would, however, be of little account to the Platonic Socrates." But this seems to be an excessively uncharitable understanding of διαλέγεσθαι, especially as Bailly admits that the "dialogue's first half has instruction worthy of the Platonic Socrates, albeit simple and elementary." Cf. also Bailly (2004, 250 ad loc.).

and that it gradually "dribbled away" after he left him (130d4–e4). This evidently superficial understanding of Socratic education has been taken as decisive proof of the dialogue's spuriousness,[48] but it is crucial to note that these are the words of Aristides, not of Socrates, and that Socrates only recounts it as an example of the experience of one kind of student.[49] While his next words might seem to endorse Aristides' account,[50] they are in fact nothing more than a summary of his entire account of the *daimonion*: "So, Theages, this is what association with me is like (τοιαύτη ἡ ἡμετέρα συνουσία): if it is dear to the god, you will make very great and swift improvement, but if not, you will not" (130e5).[51]

Socrates, then, nowhere affirms that this improvement is essentially dependent on physical proximity to himself or on the positive influence of the *daimonion*.[52] Instead, the point of the anecdote is to underscore the fact that the results of Socratic education do not depend on Socrates at all, but on the nature of the young men who associate with him. While some will receive a "stable and abiding benefit" (130a1), others will not; and since the *daimonion*, while "collaborating" in some undefined way with the prior group, does *not* positively distinguish between the two kinds of people, there is no way of knowing beforehand whether one will obtain this benefit or not. Socrates therefore suggests to Theages that it would be "more secure to be educated in the company of one of those who are themselves in control of (ἐγκρατεῖς) the benefit that they bestow on human beings rather than whatever you might happen to achieve in my company" (130e7–10).

The question, then, that Socrates implicitly poses to Theages is: To which category of student does he belong? He poses to Theages once again

---

[48] Joyal (2000, 99ff., 289). This line of argument is at least as old as Tarrant (1958).

[49] Cf. Pangle (1987, 167ff.). The idea that wisdom can be transmitted by contact is mocked in the *Symposium* (175c–d). But Aristides' account clearly expresses one experience, however partial, of Socrates, and we should not be too quick to dismiss the charismatic or erotic effect that Socrates evidently had on his companions. Friedländer (1958, 130), commenting on this passage, objects to "people today [who], lacking the experience, call this sort of thing un-Platonic and mistake it for 'occult phenomena.'"

[50] Tarrant (2003, 155) does take Socrates to be approving of Aristides' account. He recognizes (157) that "Plato would dismiss this as false educational progress" but not that the *Theages* itself implicitly calls it into question.

[51] Joyal (2000, 291 ad loc.) goes too far in saying that these words draw "attention to the capricious nature" of the *daimonion* and therefore "reflect popular notions of divinity in general rather than the picture … developed elsewhere in the Corpus." Socrates' words are simply a way of saying that the *daimonion* is not under his power, not that it is irrational or capricious.

[52] Cf. Cobb (1992, 283). Neither is it the case, *pace* Bailly (2004, 251), that "Socrates claims here that one problem with Aristides was that he left Socrates' company prematurely." This claim is made at *Tht.* 150e.

the question of self-knowledge, this time not in terms of eros or of what he truly desires but in terms of his own capacity to learn. But the account of the *daimonion* also demonstrates that neither Theages nor Socrates can know what kind of student Theages will be before the association begins. Self-knowledge is only won through experience, through the use of the self. Theages must recognize that association with Socrates is essentially aporetic, not only in the sense that it begins with a recognition of one's own ignorance and the desire for knowledge but also in the sense that it may, in the end, provide no way forward. Aristides recognized how slavish he and others were before associating with Socrates, but the result of his own time with Socrates was nothing but a sense of shame at his own commonness (φαυλότης, 130b6ff., 130c6). Socrates offers the example of Aristides precisely because of his shortcomings, lest Theages think that in Socrates he has found a sure thing.[53]

Socrates' intention in his account of the *daimonion*, then, just like his questioning of Theages in the first part of the dialogue, is to bring him to the position where he can properly deliberate about what he will do about himself. Theages' immediate resolution, to "make trial of this *daimonion*" by associating with Socrates, and even to attempt to propitiate with "prayers and sacrifices, and whatever else the seers declare" (131a1–7), shows both the extent and the limits of his understanding of Socrates' words. He has understood Socrates far enough not to wish to actively resist the *daimonion* or to expect definite results, but he still believes superstitiously that its decision might be swayed by religious offerings, something that Socrates had never suggested.[54] What is important to Socrates is that Theages understand that even if the *daimonion* does not resist their association, there is no guarantee that he will be benefited from this association or be made wise in art of politics as he originally desired.

[53] The evident parallels between the *Theages*' account of Aristides and midwifery passage at *Tht.* 150b–e, which also mentions Aristides, are evidence for Joyal that the latter is a "source" for the former, and the discrepancies between the two passage are further proof of the dialogue's inauthenticity (Joyal 2000, 54). But Bailly (2004, 278–279) notes that the *Theages* could just as well be a source for the *Theaetetus*. It is beyond the scope of this chapter to consider the *Theaetetus* passage, but it should be noted that it is quite possible for the same author to alter an anecdote according to the specific needs of an individual dialogue. One might compare the very different references to Socrates' role in the trial of the Ten Generals after the battle of Arginusae in *Ap.* 32c–e and *Grg.* 473c–474a.

[54] Joyal (2000, 293 ad loc.) underlines that it is Theages, not Socrates, who is speaking here, but thinks that the idea is consistent with the dialogue's characterization of the *daimonion* as "capricious." Cf. note 50 above. Vlastos (1991, 282) is wrong to assert that "Socrates goes along" with the idea of propitiating the *daimonion*. His final words refer to the general resolution that initiates an association between the two.

The ultimate aim of Socrates' practice of erotics, which has been shown to be also a practice of the use of the self, is to pose and seek to answer the question of what one desires, or what kind of life one ought to lead. What the *Theages* only barely suggests is that this Socratic use of the self implies a turning away from politics as usually practiced as well as from the technical or pseudo-technical teachings of the sophists.[55] We cannot, of course, be sure that Theages has understood any more than the merest rudiments of this aspect of Socrates' philosophical practice, and we do not, after all, hear in the dialogue what was the result of his association with Socrates or whether the *daimonion* even permitted it in the first place. From the *Republic* and *Apology* we know that Theages did in fact participate to some extent in the Socratic circle,[56] but the *Republic* suggests that he never was truly dedicated to the life of philosophy. Explaining the various circumstances that lead someone to practice philosophy instead of entering into politics, Socrates mentions that "the 'bridle,' too, of our comrade Theages might be such as to restrain him. For in Theages' case all the other conditions were ready for him to fall away from philosophy, but the sickliness of his body restrains him by keeping him out of politics."[57] We may then conclude that Theages turned out to be one of those whose association with Socrates the *daimonion* did not forbid, but who did not receive any lasting benefit from that association. He was, at best, another Aristides, and perhaps the most he could have learned from Socrates is just this: like Aristides, he may have acquired a form of chastened self-knowledge that would have moderated his political activity had he been able to enter into politics in the first place.

One of the greatest obstacles to an appreciation of the *Theages* has been its apparent lack of philosophical interest.[58] It does not discuss at length the kind of questions that we typically encounter in Plato's early or aporetic dialogues, to which group it would otherwise seem to belong. But I have argued here that the *Theages* is not supposed to be understood in the first instance as an exposition of philosophical doctrine, but as a

[55] For the parody of sophistic teaching at 125b–d, cf. Joyal (2000, 29ff., 236).
[56] Cf. *R.* VI.496b6–c3 and *Ap.* 33e, which implies that Theages was already deceased. Cf. Nails (2002, 278). Joyal (2000, 59) takes the *Republic* as evidence that Theages was one of those who received lasting benefit from Socrates, but the fact that it was only sickness that kept him from leaving philosophy for politics suggests otherwise.
[57] Cf. *R.* ibid. Whether the *Theages* is genuine or not, it can be assumed that its author could count on his readers being aware of the basic facts of Theages' life.
[58] To cite only one recent example, consider Bailly (2004, 71): "The *Theages* adds nothing to the Platonic system, and appears to contradict an important element of it." The apparent contradiction is Bailly's mistaken identification of Socratic education in the *Theages* with rhetorical ability (cf. note 47).

kind of drama of self-knowledge that would fall very broadly into the category of protreptic. Every kind of wisdom (*sophia*) implies the capacity to rule or govern (ἄρχειν, 123d–124c), that is, to use the things that fall within its domain (χρῆσθαι, 126b–c). In asking the question of why one would want to become wise in the first place, and wise in what, there is additionally raised the question of the good life, or the question "what shall I do with (how shall I *use*) myself?" This aporia of the use of the self or the rule of the self could only be answered by a kind of wisdom that had for its object the self or the human soul, and only someone with such wisdom would be able to use or rule himself or others. According to the *Theages*, it is only Socrates' erotic wisdom that can fulfill this function. But it is precisely this erotic wisdom that overturns the commonsense understanding of the rule of human beings, for it seems to be born of the recognition that those who claim to be wise in politics, such as the politicians and sophists, are not so actually (128a–b).

Socrates' erotic wisdom, then, does imply a certain kind of use of, or rule over, himself and those who choose to associate with him, but it is not a wisdom that expresses itself in a body of doctrine or issues any command. Instead, it can be nothing more than the practice of philosophy itself or the pursuit of wisdom. The first and essential task of this erotic art of Socrates is to reveal to his interlocutor or companion the true nature of his desire, so that it might be converted from a potentially tyrannical eros to rule over others to a philosophical eros that is satisfied with ruling over itself. The use of the self that is at work in the desire to become just is equivalent to the Socratic knowledge of ignorance, which not only is the precondition of genuine philosophizing but is itself already an important achievement of philosophical reflection. This is the intention and philosophical significance of the *Theages*: by enacting this drama of self-knowledge and the conversion of eros, to bring the reader to the same point where Theages finds himself, so that he may, unlike Theages, take the final step himself and come to genuinely practice philosophy.

CHAPTER 7

Between Biography and Biology
Bios and Self-Knowledge in Plato's Phaedrus

Sara Brill

There is perhaps no better-known philosophic claim than the one Plato's Socrates makes in defense of his life: the unexamined life is not worth living (ὁ δὲ ἀνεξέταστος βίος οὐ βιωτὸς) (*Ap.* 38a5). Far less frequently observed, however, is the extent of Plato's concern with both the object under question here, βίος (*bios*), and the curious epistemological status of its examination. If we turn to the *Republic* for a moment, it merits emphasis that neither soul nor manner of life is listed among the objects of study recommended to philosophic natures for their ability to turn the soul toward being. And yet, the Socrates who gives a detailed account of the lives of, for instance, democratic and oligarchic souls in *Republic* 8 and 9 seems to have been quite an astute observer of "manner of life," giving us several examples of what an account of βίος, a bio-logy, might look like in the Platonic context.

The importance of such an understanding is emphasized in a crucial moment in the dialogue's final book. Halfway through his recounting of the myth of Er, Socrates draws a distinction between the patterns of life (τῶν βίων παραδείγματα), which souls may choose, and an ordering (τάξιν) of soul, which, due to necessity, becomes different according to the βίος that is chosen (X.618b). As Socrates goes on to describe the variety of lives available for choice (nonhuman animals, tyrannies, the lives of men and women of repute, etc.) and the combination of factors they comprise (wealth and poverty, sickness and health, etc.) "pattern of life" emerges as specifying a kind of narrative structure to living, one which relies on a vision of *bios* that is poised between a historical account of a series of events and a claim to some inner necessity at work in those events. It is knowledge of this inner necessity – of the logic that emerges from an understanding of the interaction between beauty and wealth, for instance, and certain conditions of both city and soul – that enables one to choose a better life from a worse one. And it is this most powerful (κρατίστη)

113

choice that one should devote one's life to making well, letting everything else go (X.618e).

Indeed, the significance of this passage lies, in part, in its presentation in mythic form of the question that animates the entire dialogue, namely, What kind of life is choice-worthy? It thus forms part of a larger preoccupation on Plato's part with βίος as a philosophic object, that is, with what is implied by the possibility that living can have a "manner" or "way."[1] To be sure, in naming the integration of a living being's parts and capacities in response to its particular habitat, βίος delimits an object of analysis well beyond the scope of human life.[2] But within the human context, it serves to mark out the way in which human life is oriented toward ends about which the human being may be more or less aware and to suggest that knowledge of self must include knowledge that one has a "manner of life" directed toward some end. Moreover, because the capacities and parts of this particular living being include the possession of *logos* and its habitat includes the polis, the demarcation of human βίοι must include not only the various ways in which humans take up this capacity but also the political milieu in which they do so. That is, knowledge of one's βίος must include knowledge of the political context in which it unfolds, a context in which one's λογιστικόν is either fostered or hindered and which asserts the collective construction of both self-knowledge and self-deception. As Plato makes clear, one's πολιτεία plays a decisive role in shaping one as a lover or a hater of *logos*, and these two positions have a powerful effect on the kinds of lives that are available to one.

Two aspects of the patterns of life mentioned in the myth of Er are essential in this regard: their status as objects of choice and their narrative structure. Because these lives are chosen, Plato can offer an account of biodiversity as an expression of ethical factors (as he does in the *Timaeus* and the *Phaedrus*). Because these lives follow a narrative pattern, that is, answer to a necessary relation between their parts such that they adhere to a coherent and iterable type that is recognizable to sufficiently trained eyes, they also provide a limit to the operation of choice. While one may choose to perform a just or unjust act, one cannot alter the inexorable effect of such an act on one's character and future choices. Thus, a study of βίος opens on much larger questions, invited especially by the assertion that

---

[1] See Brill (2016).

[2] As Lennox (2010 and 2009) has so effectively demonstrated in the context of Aristotle's zoology. To be sure, we cannot assume βίος operates in the same manner for Plato as it does for Aristotle, but neither are their senses so distinct as to evacuate the sense of integration of parts and capacities, and this is all that is essential for my reading here.

ψυχή will accommodate itself to the chosen βίος: In what sense is one's life one's own? To what or whom does a βίος belong and in what sense of belonging? Is βίος an attribute of the human who has chosen it, or rather, is the individual the effect of a particular instantiation of βίος? And, perhaps most fundamentally, what do we know about someone when we understand their βίος?

As a way of taking up these larger questions, this chapter turns to the *Phaedrus*, the dialogue that explores perhaps most explicitly the relationship between βίος and *logos*, both as it is broached in the character of Socrates and as it is implied in an understanding of what a philosophic βίος must know about itself. I argue that the ruminations about βίος that run throughout the entire dialogue install as most authoritative in human life what is called variously, and at times interchangeably, truth or being. It is this power that generates living beings and determines the shape and manner of human life. In the *Phaedrus*, what we learn about someone when we know their βίος is their degree of proximity to the truth. To know oneself, in this context, is to know that one's being derives from one's orientation toward the truth, an orientation that may become obscured and damaged but that is nonetheless operative in any life that can be called human and whose primary symptom is the possession of *logos*. Thus, the *Phaedrus'* contribution to our understanding of what Plato takes self-knowledge to be lies, in part, in its accounts of the generative power of truth.

But the dialogue is also about *how* one might come to attain knowledge of one's orientation toward the truth, and how the avenue of realization it describes – the erotic relationship[3] – is fraught with the possibility of failure, due in no small part to the political context in which seduction is undertaken and to the vulnerability that attends the human possession of *logos*, a vulnerability that makes a critical philosophic account of rhetoric necessary. Because of its acute awareness of the landscape of power in which the erotic relationship unfolds, the dialogue illuminates the political dimension of self-knowledge (as well as self-ignorance). An investigation into its contribution to our understanding of what Plato takes self-knowledge to be should start there. In making good on these claims, I will thus begin by offering some orienting comments about the particular political tenor of the dialogue. I will then focus on the great image in the palinode, charting the conceptual universe it creates, the form of power it investigates, and the generative force of this power in human life. I will

---

[3] The stages of which, in the context of the *Phaedrus*, are mapped thoroughly in Belfiore (2012).

then turn, briefly, to the shift in focus from the beauty of human beings to the beauty of *logos*, that is, to the account of rhetoric, in order to draw out the significance of this shift to the dialogue's conception of self-knowledge.

7.1

If the mirror serves as a nodal image for the operation of power as well as art, this is due not to its veracity but to its capacity for amplification. It is this capacity for the infinite generation of images that promotes the fantasy, articulated in Racine's title to the painting occupying the center of the Hall of Mirrors, that "the King governs by himself." What the Sun King saw reflected in the 357 material signs of his wealth adorning the Great Gallery was the perpetual reproduction of his sovereignty; that is, he saw himself surrounded by courtiers seeking audience. In his morning stroll from his bedroom to his chapel, the sovereign was given to himself and to others as he wanted to be seen.

The amplifying capacity of the mirror was well known to Plato, whose *Phaedrus* tells us quite clearly that at the heart of every seduction, and constituting the source of its power, resides an image. This is, of course, the image that the lover reflects of the beloved, as it is under the influence of this image that the beloved falls in love, if at all. The source of this love remains a mystery to the beloved, or, as Plato's Socrates puts it, the beloved "does not realize that in his lover he is seeing himself as though in a mirror" (255d). Nevertheless, the success of the lover's efforts at seduction rises or falls with the fate of this image.

Something similar is at work between the conventional rhetorician, who employs "the likely" (272d–e), and his audience. The likely is persuasive because it affirms me and my perspective on the world; it tells me that I am right, that my expectation will be met, and gives me an image of myself as knowledgeable, competent, in control, and in need of nothing. Indeed, it is from the generation of images of self – images that require others for their creation and maintenance and that may either enable or impede self-knowledge – that seduction derives its power. By means of such images, the rhetorician can be said to seduce his audience, and his efficacy is bound entirely to the power of this image and to the fantasies to which it gives rise.

Holding together the dialogue's reflections on eros and on rhetoric, then, is a sustained reflection on the particular and peculiar operation of seduction as a form of power; on its ability to generate, create, shape, and mold, to reproduce others in the image of oneself and to generate oneself following the image of another. The *Phaedrus,* like the *Symposium,* makes an intervention into Greek theorizing about power and the two poles that provide the matrix by means of which Greek intellectuals discerned and described it: the power to take and the power to make.[4] We see the play between the two throughout the dialogue, and the line between them thin in the violence with which one is taken by love (figured in Boreas' seizure of Oreithuia and in the many liquid metaphors of gushing, swelling, streaming, flowing). In these moments, taking threatens to overtake making and to serve the claim that taking *is* making, a claim that presents empire (with its requisite, structural pleonexia) as a creative act, "bringing" Athens to the world, and thus eliding taking with giving.[5] It is against this possibility that Socrates' conception of the mutual respect between philosophic lover and beloved presses. It would seem to do so by affirming human agency against the potentially tyrannizing, despotic power of desire. But throughout, this effort is complicated, fruitfully, by the other possibilities that submission to one's desire can open, possibilities of transformation and ascent. I want to examine the mechanisms and organs of this model of power, the manner in which it works through image-making and fantasy-generating to create orders of desire that, in turn, yield orders of life.

Thus, I aim to challenge the claim of one translator that the *Phaedrus* is the least political of dialogues.[6] To be sure, the eros Socrates describes inspires a rejection of certain ties in favor of others – the soul of one in love "has already forgotten mothers, brothers, and all her companions" (252a) – but we must keep in mind that for Plato political things include not only the matters of one's homeland but also the πολιτεία in one's soul.[7] He is working, then, with a conception of politics that lays heavy emphasis on, to borrow from Judith Butler, the psychic life of power, and which makes

---

[4] I have in mind here the long history, across genres and time periods, connecting κράτος with both various forms of seizure and taking (evident, for instance, in Hesiod's myth of the Hawk and the Nightingale, Aeschylus' many meditations on the power of Zeus, Thucydides' accounts of Athenian attitudes toward its colonies, and Plato's and Aristotle's reflections on the damaging effects of *pleonexia,* to name just a few) and with the efficacy of τέχνη (figured as Promethean wisdom in Hesiod and, as with Sophocles' famous ode to human ingenuity and its limits in his *Antigone,* Plato's many uses of τέχναι as models of the rule of knowledge, etc.) so carefully documented in the work of classicists like J.-P. Vernant, Marcel Detienne, Pierre Vidal-Naquet, and Nicole Loraux and scholars in classical political theory such as Josia Ober, Kurt Raaflaub, and Arlene Saxonhouse.
[5] An elision Vernant (1990) documents in his analysis of Hesiod's Prometheus.
[6] Scully (2003, vii). My argument aligns with a few other commentators who have observed a central political thread to the dialogue (Griswold 1986 and Bentley 2005), although I take the character of this thread a bit differently.
[7] *R.* IX.591e–592a.

clear why a philosophic study of τὰ πολιτικά would have to include a serious engagement with the one arena in which Socrates did claim to have some expertise, τὰ ἐρωτικά (*Smp.* 177d8–9).

Before turning to the investigation of power at work in the central image of the palinode, however, one final point of orientation is necessary. That the image is constructed in order to provide a likeness of the soul is clear. But it is worth being very careful about what the palinode likens the soul to: not the charioteer and horses per se but the innate power (συμφύτῳ δυνάμει) of a winged team of horses and a charioteer (246a). This signals to us that what is being described in this image, what is being likened to soul, is not an object but a capacity. So, while of course it matters what the parts of the image signify (the wing, the horses, the yoke, the reigns, the chariot, the charioteer, etc.), we cannot lose sight of the fact that the parts are there in order to image a certain dynamic, a power that results from their interaction, and not the other way around. What is necessary, then, is a reading of the image that follows its character as marking out a psychodynamic.[8]

This character makes certain demands on the reader. In particular, it requires us to attend to the intertwining of ideational and affective content in the palinode and to view its place within the larger aims of the dialogue as a whole. Indeed, when we focus on the work the palinode is doing in the dialogue, we see that its central myth functions to foster attachment precisely to ideas – infusing them with desire – in a process of fantasy-construction that yields actions as well as images and that invites a comparison with psychoanalysis in which their divergences are as illuminating as their similarities.[9] This is particularly true when it comes to determining the therapeutic value of the image. To characterize its aim as a form of cathexis, for instance – with its Freudian sense of investment for the sake of release – is misleading when applied to what Plato is doing here. The point is not to invest desire in an object in order to release the desire, but rather to transform it or, better, to turn it so that it causes a transformation and, once so turned, to feed it. Similar problems arise with the term "sublimation." As I take it, the point is less to attain stability than to court the right kind of disruption, a kind figured by the Bacchic revelers to whom Plato turns several times in the dialogue (e.g., 228b, 234d, 245a). Whatever therapy the dialogue may aspire to offer, and I believe it does, it is not designed to

---

[8] I take this character to mitigate the concern Burger (1980, 54) raises about the absence of reference to the chariot itself when Socrates introduces the image.

[9] See, e.g., Bersani and Phillips (2008).

reestablish equilibrium so much as to inspire self-overcoming.[10] To the extent that Socratic self-knowledge involves, as Christopher Moore puts it, "the ideal of stabilization and clarification of oneself," this aspect of the *Phaedrus* gestures toward an end higher even than that of self-knowledge, but one that requires such knowledge as a step along the way.[11]

Thus, I take the purpose of the palinode to be the creation of an attachment to a set of ideas, values, and actions that are definitive of a particular way of life. Throughout, I am largely in agreement with a number of scholars on the psychagogic tenor of the dialogue, figured in Socrates' efforts to turn the "dualizing," or "two-wayed," Phaedrus (who is attracted to both logos and wisdom) in one direction and to show him why love of *logos* is best realized in love of wisdom.[12] But I want also to call attention to Plato's observations about what forces are at work in this process. In doing so, I will take a somewhat different approach to the unity question from that of Jessica Moss, for whom the two parts of the dialogue "consider two methods of soul-leading, love and rhetoric," while "the dialogue as a whole asks how either or both can be successful in directing the soul towards truth and the good life."[13] I do not see here two different methods. I am arguing, rather, that ψυχαγωγία operates through seduction[14] and that rhetoric is seduction through *logos*. The enigma, then,

---

[10] In this I differ from Werner's reading of the therapeutic aims of the dialogue. See Werner (2012, 248–251). I take the distinction Rowe draws between the therapy of the academic tutorial and the therapy of the psychotherapist's couch (Rowe 2011, 210), and that Johnson draws between philosophy and psychoanalysis (Johnson 1999, 16) and the model of self-knowledge as thinking about one's past actions that Annas calls attention to and aligns with psychoanalysis (Annas 1985, 121–124) to be addressed to an understanding of therapy that operates outside both a Socratic understanding of philosophy as a way of life and a Platonic understanding of the intermingling of "internal" psychic and "external" political forces. To be sure, there are good reasons to draw such distinctions in light of contemporary alignments of self-knowledge with a kind of neoliberal obsession with the individual. But we certainly cannot accuse Freud of such an alignment, given his insistence on the collective and political nature of self-formation, as Jonathan Lear (1992) observes in his response to Bernard Williams' concerns about the "city–soul" analogy in the *Republic*. The question of whether contemporary practices of psychoanalysis do or do not follow such a conception of self-formation is well beyond the scope of this chapter, and I am working here with Freudian language primarily as a way of observing a few useful points of divergence and convergence between Freudian concepts and claims made in the *Phaedrus*.

[11] Moore (2015a, 6). As Moore notes, this claim is an extension to those made in McCabe (1994) and Gerson (2003).

[12] Asmis (1986), Ferrari (1987), Yunis (2011), Moss (2012), Werner (2012), and Moore (2014 and 2015a).

[13] Moss (2012, 3).

[14] It is easy enough to see the parallel between "ducere" and "ago" in my psuchagoge/seduction equation, but what of the "se," the "astray" or "to the side"? Here too though I think we have a good translation, since, for one who is compelled by conventional forms of value and honor, the call to philosophy, conceived as the ardent pursuit of being, will be a leading astray, a leading to the side, as the Illisus leads Socrates and Phaedrus away from the city walls.

is how *logos* inspires eros, an attachment that is as polymorphous, to borrow again from Freud, as it is intense. Indeed, as Charles Griswold makes clear, it is the very connection between *logos* and eros that allows the dialogue to link the question of self-knowledge to "the themes of what we want and how we talk about ourselves."[15] I will argue that this connection is bound up with the power truth exerts on human life. It is this attachment that the lover of *logos* (among whom both Socrates and Phaedrus number themselves) most vividly presents. The opening of the dialogue displays precisely this intertwining by presenting a *logos* about eros that has touched Phaedrus' erotic attachment to *logos*. The primary shift in the dialogue, then, is less between eros and rhetoric than between an obvious example of erotic attachment – to beautiful people – and a less obvious erotic attachment: to beautiful *logos*.

In this, I am largely in agreement with Andrea Capra that "true rhetoric is erotic and true eros is rhetorical."[16] But I would add that for Plato, more radically, conventional rhetoric is also erotic; the problem is not that one form of rhetoric lacks an erotic dimension and the other does not, but rather that one form of erotics is "better," more noble, more capable of inspiring recollection than another. Just as one can be an ignoble lover of boys, so too one can be an ignoble lover of *logos*, and this love of *logos* – attachment to any words that inspire one's pleasure – is potentially devastating.[17] But more than this, one does not even have to be a lover of *logos* in order to be seduced by it. Thus, the dialogue also calls attention to the vulnerability that attends the human possession of *logos*, a vulnerability whose political repercussions are felt in and emerge as much from the private register as from the public. There is, then, a critical political project at work in the *Phaedrus*, a keen awareness of Athens' vulnerability to fine turns of phrase.

This vulnerability increases the stakes of Socrates' effort to turn Phaedrus and also decisively shapes the forms taken by this effort of turning. This is, after all, not an innocent project, and Socrates' valorization of the philosophic life is hardly an accidental outcome of its "demonstration" of the generative power of truth. As Socrates tells us, seduction operates through images. If Socrates is to succeed, that is, if he is to attract Phaedrus' deepest attachments and orient them toward philosophy, Phaedrus must be able to identify with the portrait of the

---

[15] Griswold (1986, 5).   [16] Capra (2014, 21).

[17] Moss (2012) too notes an ignoble form of love of *logos* as running parallel to the ignoble form of love that Socrates' palinode is intended to correct.

lover of wisdom Socrates creates. And this returns us to the relationship between politics and self-knowledge. For within any but the best political environments, a *logos*-loving life is not on its own sufficient to ensure a philosophic life. Such a life needs a further seduction. Socrates' turning of Phaedrus requires, then, an iconography marshaled in the service of philosophy, a fantasy of a very particular kind, and I hope throughout the following pages to gather together a few aspects of the *Phaedrus'* philosophic imaginary.

7.2

Ostensibly, Socrates' palinode takes as its task the elucidation of a noble and gentle form of love, one that would act as an antidote to the vulgar, envious, and favor-grubbing exchange of pleasure for benefit highlighted in Lysias' speech, and the power structure behind this form of love. That structure is made explicit in Socrates' first speech, where desire rules (δυναστευούσης) and tyrannizes (τυραννεύσασα, 238b), and is itself violently moved (ῥωσθεῖσα) by the force (ῥώμης) of love (238b–c). Both tyrant and tyrannized, the vulgar lover enviously guards against any real benefit to his beloved, seeking a weak beloved to begin with and doing everything in his power to further weaken him and encourage the beloved's dependence. Again, it is against this portrait that the palinode rubs, seeking to provide an alternate image and, in due course, to inspire Phaedrus himself to cease moving in two directions and instead to "devote his life solely to love with wisdom-loving speeches" (ἀλλ' ἁπλῶς πρὸς Ἔρωτα μετὰ φιλοσόφων λόγων τὸν βίον ποιῆται, 257b).

In the course of this effort, Socrates will mutate the emphasis on taking that structures Lysias' speech and Socrates' first speech, shifting focus from taking to being taken and transforming this, in turn, to a form of making. The figure of the divinely inspired (enthused) bacchant serves as an emblem of this transformation, as one whose power derives from having been taken by the god, and is expressed in the ability to make others as like the god as possible (see especially 253b). But this is made possible by, and becomes a praise of the philosophic life through, a provocative claim about the nature of human life and its possession of the very thing with which Phaedrus and Socrates are in love: *logos*. For if devotion to love is best realized by wisdom-loving speeches, this can be so because something else has been installed as the ultimate authority in human life, the authority that makes human life human and that determines, in its proximity or distance, the kind of βίος a human is to have. Socrates calls this authority truth.[18] And thus, the great myth of the palinode serves as a sustained meditation on the power of truth. It is truth that holds the power of generation, it is proximity to truth that determines what is divine, and it is truth that directs which souls are to be sown in human bodies and what kinds of lives those humans will lead.

But if this is so, it is all the more striking that much of the image is concerned with documenting a certain incapacity, a certain weakness that is expressed in two registers, the disembodied and the embodied. First, we encounter a tension surrounding the soul's impulse toward truth. While all souls desire truth because all souls are nourished, sustained, and preserved by it, some souls (presumably because of their actions in previous embodied states, although this is somewhat unclear) are more able to gain access to it than others.[19] Thus, this first conflict is not, most immediately, a conflict between reason and desire or between one desire and another, but rather a matter of weakness with respect to one's ability to pursue the object of one's desire.

Second, we encounter a tension between the impulse toward truth (which, at a crucial juncture in the dialogue, is expressed rather as a standing still, as a form of reverence, 251a) and the impulse toward pleasure. This second conflict is the conflict of embodiment, the conflict that arises once souls with weaker capacities to pursue their desire for truth lose their wings and fall (or are sown) into a body. At this point, their weakness is translated into mortal temporality, as an effect of embodiment perceived from the perspective of its entanglement in time; that is, the weakness is expressed as a forgetting. In becoming embodied, these souls have become mysteries to themselves – they have forgotten what truly nourishes them, and it is this mystery, this forgetting, and the conflict that ensues, that defines their form of life. In the face of the reminder of our attraction to truth, that is, in the presence of the beautiful beloved, we are haunted by truth, and in the void created by forgetting, the draw of pleasure steps in.

[18] Throughout the palinode he describes this power in terms that move somewhat fluidly between "beings" or "things that are" (τὰ ὄντα), or even "what is really real" (τὰ ὄντα ὄντως, 247e, τὸ ὂν ὄντος, 249c) and "truth" (ἀλήθεια) (see, e.g., 248b: the soul is most eager to see the plain of truth; 249b: "the soul that has never seen the truth cannot pass into human form"). However, he casts the entire account of the region beyond the heavens as an account about truth (περὶ ἀληθείας, 247c), and so, in the interest of readability, I will follow White (1993) and Nicholson (1999) in referring to this authority as "truth," while acknowledging the close proximity here between truth and being.
[19] See Ferrari (1987) for a helpful discussion of the ambiguity here and the moral vision it recommends.

But this haunting belongs to the kind of beings humans are, to their very inception as living beings; it is native to them. Because, as it turns out, embodied souls are not equally forgetful, and the life (βίος) one has is determined by the degree of access to truth one's soul attained. All humans are born oriented toward truth, and their possession of *logos* arises from this orientation; how one takes up this orientation, however, varies. And so the myth strives to discern the dominant factors that shape human lives and identify the horizons, the limits, of human choice. For, while truth can grip with powerful force, its most proper mode of expression is that of attraction, and attraction, the myth tells us, is subject to taste (253a–b). The result of this account of embodiment is a topology of lives, an account of human βίος as conceived not by human family but by access to truth, as it is this access that determines the kind of life in which the soul will be "sown": (a) a philosopher or lover of beauty or a musical and erotic nature; (b) lawful king or warlike ruler; (c) politician, businessperson, or financier; (d) gymnast or doctor; (e) prophet; (f) poet or some other imitative artist; (g) craftsman or farmer; (h) a sophist or demagogue; (i) tyrant. The inclusion of the tyrant in the list of human βίοι Socrates offers is instructive not only for its cautionary tone but also for its insight into tyranny. The problem with the tyrant is not that he does not desire to truth, not that he is not attracted to truth, not that he lacks *logos*, but that he is the greatest mystery to himself; he least understands his desire and thus least understands himself.[20]

It is worth lingering over this alignment between truth and life for a moment, with its anticipation of the coming interweaving of *logos* and life in Socrates' claim that a *logos* should be structured like a living being (264a). From its hyperouranian location, truth exerts a profound, intimate, and direct power over the souls that seek its company, souls that will animate the bodies of the living. And while, to be sure, we cannot equate living with embodiment, we also have to notice that the terms by which the power of truth is illuminated are drawn from the most fundamental of bodily facts, the need for nourishment (truth provides our souls with the greatest and most appropriate nourishment; see, e.g., 248b–c) and the germination of life.

That is to say, this ode to the power of truth contains a fantasy of birth. When Socrates speaks of the soul being sown into a man who will become a lover of wisdom or a farmer or a poet, he points toward the inception of

---

[20] See Jeremy Bell's Chapter 8 in this book for a discussion of tyranny as the ultimate form of self-ignorance.

such lives. And while his specification that the soul is sown into the seed (γονή) of such a person/life may evoke the material conditions of childbirth, the seed, as it turns out, belongs not to a parent of the lover of wisdom (or farmer or poet) but the lover of wisdom, farmer, or poet himself: "in the first generation, the soul can never be planted into a wild animal, but the soul which has seen the most shall be planted into the seed of a man who will become a lover of wisdom, or a lover of beauty, or of something musical and erotic (μὴ φυτεῦσαι εἰς μηδεμίαν θήρειον φύσιν ἐν τῇ πρώτῃ γενέσει, ἀλλὰ τὴν μὲν πλεῖστα ἰδοῦσαν εἰς γονὴν ἀνδρὸς γενησομένου φιλοσόφου ἢ φιλοκάλου ἢ μουσικοῦ τινος καὶ ἐρωτικοῦ, 248d).[21] To be sure, this is a process in time – the life will develop – but the seed in question is already in the individual. This allows for the reversal, by the time they reach the sixth kind of life (the poet), of soul and person, such that the person is allotted to the soul rather than soul allotted to person.[22]

Displacing the human mother and father, we have seeds sown according not to physical process but to a play between choice, action, nature, and the divine. In place of a human family, we have the gods and a fecund, generating but ungenerated, soul. Instead of sexual intercourse productive of children, we have the self-creation of the lover as a lover of wisdom and the shared creation of his beloved in the same mold. Instead of a household (the maintenance of familial ties and the upkeep and acquisition of property) we have a friendship designed to produce both lover and beloved as self-ruling and self-composed (256b). Instead of an account of the forms of human life, we have a taxonomy of men's βίοι, of what is ἀνδρός, not ἄνθρωπος. We thus have an element that courts the fantasy of a world without women – a fantasy operative at least since Hesiod and toyed with (although ambivalently) elsewhere in the dialogues (e.g., the *Timaeus*, *Statesman*, and, by some accounts, the *Republic*).

To be sure, it would be misleading to treat this as an anthropogeny. Unlike the *Timaeus*, the concern here seems to be not with the first occurrence of human beings (beyond making a stipulation about this first occurrence) nor, as with the *Statesman*, with an account of the advent of sexual reproduction; the biodiversity at stake in this passage is not that of

---

[21] My emendation of Scully's translation, to correct for the use of ἀνήρ that the translator does not observe. See also Ryan (2012, 197) on 248c8–d1: "What agency would do the planting is left moot" (197) and his comment on γονή at 284d2: "Not offspring or stock, but seed or birth, the soul being a separable thing that is inserted at birth and departs at death."

[22] See 248e and the shift from genitive case for the kinds of people previously mentioned, to indicate "planted in the seed of *x*" to nominative to indicate "*x* apportioned to or residing in *y* kind of soul."

all living things but of human life, with the conditions at play in determining the particular kind of life particular individuals have, and with examining all human life from the perspective of its expression of greater or lesser proximity to truth. But the language is appropriative of the language of sexual reproduction – as though Socrates' praise of truth cannot be sung without this invocation of germination, inception, growth, maturation, life. In this, the law of Adresteia, a name one commentator glosses as "she from whom one cannot run away," yields a fantastical birth, one that appropriates the roles of human ancestry, family history, social status, and sexual reproduction and that treats human generation as a direct function of soul's access to truth.[23]

And yet one does still, somehow, choose this life: "In all these men, the one who lives justly has a better portion; the one who lives unjustly, a worse one" (ἐν δὴ τούτοις ἅπασιν ὃς μὲν ἂν δικαίως διαγάγῃ ἀμείνονος μοίρας μεταλαμβάνει, ὃς δ' ἂν ἀδίκως, χείρονος, 248e).[24] There is, then, a productive tension, resonant with the myth of Er, between an assertion of choice with respect to one's manner of life and a meditation on the deep, constitutional, and ontological limitations on choice. That is, like the *Republic*, the *Phaedrus* includes a sustained consideration of a particularly human vulnerability. Because of the kind of beings human are, we both sense differences with respect to value and are likely to have that sense skewed, warped, obscured; or, in terms borrowed from the *Republic*, all souls sense that the good is something but very few know what it is (VI.505e). This ignorance cannot but have implications for humans' knowledge of themselves, insofar as they are living the particular lives they are in accord with their orientation toward and distance from truth. That is, to the extent that the good is mysterious to humans, so are humans mysterious to themselves. As an object of choice, βίος is bound to the *ēthos* of the chooser, and yet this *ēthos* is itself neither simply a law, like that of Adresteia, nor simply a choice, but rather the accretion of choices over multiple lifetimes and the penalties enacted for them.

We see this reflection on the nature of human choice more clearly in the second taxonomy Socrates produces in his palinode, in which the tension of embodiment, expressed in forgetfulness and the striving for recollection, is elaborated by an account of the effects of exposure to beauty, figured as

---

[23] Ryan (2012). Compare this with the laws' claim in the *Crito* that they are Socrates' father, mother, nurse, and teacher.

[24] I take this to mean that justice is distributed among most of these lives, even if some are more predisposed toward justice and at least one is so maimed as to be nearly entirely unjust.

the sprouting and regrowth of wings, and whose central tension is driven by the presence or absence of the beloved. The immediate purpose of this account is to support the characterization of love as the fourth kind of madness (252b). Once it has been so identified, Socrates then turns to continue his elaboration of the experience of love by presenting a typology of kinds of lovers and their "objects" determined on the basis of the god whom human beings choose to follow (252d–e). The goal of this typology is to explain differences with respect to loving, that is, differences with respect to what one chooses as one's object (what one sees as beautiful; i.e., what is relevant here are not only differences with respect to judgment but also differences with respect to perception) and how one behaves toward one's object (as well as toward everything/everyone else, thus indicating the totalizing effect desire can have on one's life such that orders of life emerge out of orders of desire). Followers of Zeus, for instance, seek a noble beloved, followers of Hera one who is regal, etc. "Each walks in the footsteps of the god he chooses, joining in that choral dance, living out his life in honor of that god, and imitating him to the best of his abilities" (252d), and in selecting his beloved, "each person chooses his love from among the beautiful after his own tastes, and sculpts and fits that person out like a statue as if he were a god for him to honor and to worship with secret rites" (252d–e).

There is a profound tension here between the ideas of *choosing* both a god to follow and a beloved, *being inclined* to see certain things as beautiful, *being overwhelmed* by this perception, *being possessed* by the divine, *being seized* by the beauty of one's beloved, and *being impelled* toward the truth, the latter two of which resonate with the nympholepsy Socrates invokes at the start of the palinode (238d).[25] Here we again encounter the horizon of taking, only in this case it is the lover who is taken and, in being taken, is inspired to make of himself and his beloved something that is like what has taken him. I would also add that this highlights precisely the way in which seduction itself swings between the poles of making and taking. And yet one's attraction to the beloved seems, at the same time, to come from one's deepest sense of what is one's own. And perhaps the best one can say here is simply that this is one reason why an account of eros is so philosophically valuable, precisely because it forces one to confront what theoreticians of human morality from Spinoza to Nietzsche have also found to be the

---

[25] Various forms of verbs for taking and being taken (e.g., λαμβάνω (to take), αἱρέω (to capture), and ἐνθουσιάζω (to be possessed)) abound in this passage (252c–253c).

greatest spur to the moral imagination – the thinking of choice within the horizon of constraint.

Socrates then offers an account of how to "capture" the beloved. Here is where we might anticipate the most explicit talk of power and overpowering, and in a sense we do encounter this, but mainly in the intrapsychic realm: the lover does battle with himself and attempts to overpower certain inclinations for the sake of others. Here there is violence and insult, blood and constraint.[26] But when it comes to the relationship between lover and beloved, the effort is to procure a shared perception of and transformation by the beautiful. This is, relative to cultural norms and interpsychic conflict, nonhierarchical. To be sure, the lover leads the beloved, so some asymmetry remains; nevertheless, the goal is to overcome this asymmetry, not enshrine it. The lover shapes the beloved into that in which the lover is also trying to shape himself, into becoming god-like, and this is done within the trope of service to and adoration of the beloved, and with the goal not of conquest or victory but of self-mastery and self-composure on both their parts.[27]

Truth, then, and philosophy are presented as having an equalizing effect on the erotic relationship, as mitigating the asymmetry that drives the account of the erotic relationship in Lysias' speech and in Socrates' first speech. The seduction of the beloved takes place by sharing the beloved's beauty with the beloved, offering him a mirror by means of which he can be as stricken by his beauty as the lover is. In such circumstances, a delightful play of images is born, and love unfolds with the circulation of these images – the image of Beauty that is the beloved and the image of the beloved's beauty the lover gives to him. But in order to avoid the obvious danger of narcissism here, that the beloved will simply fall in love with himself (that his love will be a tyrant) and not experience his own beauty as transporting and transforming, he must already have been inclined to such transports, and this depends on the kind of soul both lover and beloved possess.

This infecting, transporting power of beauty on the beautiful anticipates the account of the power of *logos* in the ensuing discussion of rhetoric. It will also be at work in the extension of rhetoric to cover not only the speech of the law courts and the assembly (public speech) but conversation between individuals (private speech).

---

[26] Forms of βία: 254a and e; ἀνάγκη, 254a, b, and c.
[27] Indeed, the only place κράτος appears in this discussion is in the composed self-mastery of both parties (ἐγκρατεῖς αὑτῶν καὶ κόσμιοι ὄντες, 256a–b).

7·3

For all of their talk of beautiful boys, the most consistently observed object of beauty in the *Phaedrus* is not another human being but *logos* itself, and the second half of the discussion shifts to a discussion of the beauty of *logos* (258d). It is this that is Phaedrus' true beloved, and so the question is: What kind of lover will Phaedrus be? If Socrates is to succeed in turning Phaedrus in one direction rather than another, that is, if he is to succeed in attracting Phaedrus' deepest capacities for attachment, Phaedrus must be able to recognize himself (or his ideal self) in the portrait of the lover of wisdom Socrates creates, or in words that Socrates offers to Phaedrus, he must offer Phaedrus an account of a man, "such as you and I might pray to become" (278b). And so, the task set for Socrates is to show why a lover of *logos*, who also has some attraction to its power and capacity to rule, should become a lover of wisdom (261a).[28]

We can see a repetition of several of the essential features of the palinode in this discussion of rhetoric: here too there is a captivating object of beauty, here too there is a typology of souls (271b), here too there is a vision of immortality (277a), here too there is a transmission and transformation of both another and oneself. And here too we find a sustained reflection on the generativity of beauty. Moreover, the generativity of beautiful *logos*, like that of the beautiful beloved, is an excessive generativity. This excess is figured with the language of seeds and sowing – the *logos* is a seed that sprouts more seeds. The person who uses dialectic "selects an appropriate soul, sowing and planting his speeches with knowledge, speeches that can defend themselves and the one who plants them; these speeches are not fruitless but bear seed from which other speeches, planted in other places, have the means to pass this seed on, always immortal, and to make the person possessing them as happy as humanly possible" (λαβὼν ψυχὴν προσήκουσαν, φυτεύῃ τε καὶ σπείρῃ μετ' ἐπιστήμης λόγους, οἳ ἑαυτοῖς τῷ τε φυτεύσαντι βοηθεῖν ἱκανοὶ καὶ οὐχὶ ἄκαρποι ἀλλὰ ἔχοντες σπέρμα, ὅθεν ἄλλοι ἐν ἄλλοις ἤθεσι φυόμενοι τοῦτ' ἀεὶ ἀθάνατον παρέχειν ἱκανοί, καὶ τὸν ἔχοντα εὐδαιμονεῖν ποιοῦντες εἰς ὅσον ἀνθρώπῳ δυνατὸν μάλιστα, 277a).

And yet we can also detect the anxiety of paternity – or, better, a coupled set of anxieties. On the one hand is the anxiety of producing a

---

[28] Hence the alignment of philosophy not only with Zeus but also with the oldest of Muses, Kalliope and Ourania, those who "send out the most beautiful voices and are especially fond of heaven and speeches, both divine and human" (259d).

barren seed or a seed that is no seed, that is, the anxiety of creating a product that is empty, powerless, lifeless – the anxiety of writing – relieved by the legitimate son of living *logos*. And on the other is the anxiety of losing one's paternity, the anxiety that motivates the claim that one is the father not only of living *logos* but of the seeds that this living *logos* also produces, even if those seeds come to fruition in another.

The person whom Socrates and Phaedrus pray they might be like believes written speeches are playful reminders, whereas speeches written in the soul "should be regarded as his legitimate sons, first as the sons within himself (if any are discovered therein), and then any of that speech's sons and brothers springing up simultaneously in a worthy manner in the souls of others" (δεῖν δὲ τοὺς τοιούτους λόγους αὐτοῦ λέγεσθαι οἶον υεῖς γνησίους εἶναι, πρῶτον μὲν τὸν ἐν αὐτῷ, ἐὰν εὑρεθεὶς ἐνῇ, ἔπειτα εἴ τινες τούτου ἔκγονοί τε καὶ ἀδελφοὶ ἅμα ἐν ἄλλαισιν ἄλλων ψυχαῖς κατ᾽ ἀξίαν ἐνέφυσαν, 278a–b). Here is how Hackforth articulates this anxiety and tries to "solve" it:

> A man's legitimate spiritual children are primarily those truths which he himself has discovered by a process of dialectic, and secondarily those which, while logically consequent upon the former, are actually reached, again dialectically, by others. The distinction no doubt reflects the relation between the head of a school (such as Plato himself) and its members or disciples building upon his teaching.[29]

At its best, the resolution of this anxiety yields a sense of philosophy as an intergenerational enterprise, held together by the very generative force of thought itself. However, it also includes the risk of failing to acknowledge one's indebtedness to a community of thinkers. This image of paternity threatens to become an even more monstrous Kronos: not content with consuming his own children, he devours the children of others as well, denying all other claims to paternity. In order to maintain this illusion of ultimate paternity, he must forget that he, too, is a son, that his thoughts too were the seeds of others.

7.4

In producing an image of a man whom Socrates and Phaedrus would pray to resemble, Socrates seems to want the best of both worlds: a polymorphic, excessive generativity and a clear and indisputable paternity.

---

[29] Hackforth cited in Scully (2003, 69 n. 157).

Or, perhaps better, he strives to bring together a few desires/fantasies that would tend to pull apart, presumably for the sake of attracting Phaedrus' attachment.

The *Phaedrus*, then, with its dual reflections on eros and rhetoric, is about the fantasies by which we live and to which we will cling even at the threat of loss or diminishment of our lives, the fantasies about ourselves that we require others to underwrite, the fantasies that need a community of some sort in order to come into being, be preserved, and do their work. Plato knew what Freud would go on to make explicit, namely, that the ties that bind a group of people into a crowd are erotic (libidinal).[30]

This is why love of *logos* is not enough, why it must give way to, or be transformed into, love of wisdom. For it is through their erotic connection, their attachment to the traditional rhetorician's words and the image of themselves these words create, that people become crowds, or, in the language of the *Republic*, become the beast that forms the true object of the sophists' expertise.[31] Phaedrus' love of *logos* may predispose him to a love of wisdom, but on its own it is not sufficient to save him from potentially disfiguring entanglements. Reflecting on this power in the hands of fascist leaders and in terms he borrows from Freud – they tend to be "oral character types" – Theodor Adorno observes that "the famous spell they exercise over their followers seems largely to depend on their orality: language itself, devoid of its rational significance, functions in a magical way and furthers those archaic regressions which reduce individuals to members of crowds."[32] And while speaking of language as devoid of rationality is *almost* an oxymoron for Plato, for whom the phrase "rational language" would be *nearly* redundant, Plato's *Phaedrus* shows us the gap that exists between them. It is a gap we also encounter in Homer, for whom the greatest sign of strength that linguistic homogeneity grants the Achaean forces (against the heterogeneity of the Trojans) is the *silence* with which they move to deploy their strategy.[33] Whatever misology means, it does not mean silence. Plato's misologist does not stop speaking, but he does stop trusting in *logos*. Plato does not explicitly catalogue the effects of this distrust, beyond a certain sickening,[34] but it is telling that he describes misology as worse than misanthropy, and we can see how the love of *logos* turns to hatred if one feels oneself to have been betrayed. Would that the misologist remained silent, rather than turning to feed and generate fantasies of a decidedly sickening nature.

---

[30] See Freud (1990).   [31] *R.* VI.493a–b.   [32] Adorno (1982, 132).
[33] *Il.* 3.1–9.   [34] *Phd.* 89d–e.

But the *Phaedrus* is also about how to handle these fantasies, how to analyze them, determine their worth, criticize them, excise them, and create new fantasies. The tools Plato offers for analyzing and critiquing collective fantasies and for illuminating the communal nature of fantasy-creation are hardly the least of his contributions to political theory. And Plato is certainly not above deploying the spell of language; he is a composer of incantations as well.[35] He does not simply destroy fantasies but suggests that if we must live with fantasies, let them be the right ones. The philosopher too must be an image-maker. And, for Plato, the right fantasies are fantasies that feed a human attachment to truth and being and that are, thereby, in the service of a self-knowledge aimed at self-overcoming.

---

[35] *R.* X.608a.

CHAPTER 8

A Toil-Loving Soul*

Jeremy Bell

Tell me not, in mournful numbers,
Life is but an empty dream!
For the soul is dead that slumbers,
And things are not what they seem.
– Henry Wadsworth Longfellow, "A Psalm of Life"

In the *Alcibiades* I, Socrates famously identifies the self with the soul (127e–132a).[1] While this declaration is remarkable for its forcefulness and clarity, that to which it gives voice is commonplace throughout the Platonic corpus – the self is either implicitly or explicitly identified with the soul in dialogues ranging from the *Apology* (29d–30b), *Crito* (47e–48a), and *Phaedo* (114d–115b) to the *Charmides* (156d–157c), *Protagoras* (313a–c), *Republic* (V.469d–e), and *Laws* (X.896a–e). For this reason, Plato holds both that self-knowledge requires – indeed that it is nothing other than – knowledge of one's soul and that the soul, as the existential principle of the self, is sovereign over the self (*Alcibiades* 130d–e).[2] Unsurprisingly, he does not conceive of such sovereignty as tyrannical; indeed, far from placing the soul in a position of supreme power over the self or rendering it indifferent to the self, this sovereignty has the effect of entrusting the soul's well-being to the self – our words and our deeds affect both its health in this life and its fate in the afterlife. The greatest danger arises from the fact that, though the self is soul, it is nevertheless capable of

---

* Author's note: This chapter is the result of research done while I was a postdoctoral fellow at Emory University's Fox Center for Humanistic Inquiry. I am deeply indebted to the Center for providing me with both the time and the vibrant intellectual community that made this work possible.
[1] Especially 130c and 131c. All translations of Plato are those listed in the Bibliography as published by Harvard University Press, unless otherwise indicated; I have amended these translations where necessary.
[2] Socrates declares that "nothing has greater sovereignty (κυριώτερόν) over ourselves than the soul."

failing to recognize itself as such. As a result of this self-forgetting, the soul loses itself in the self – it neglects itself in favor of those things that appear good to each of us in our daily lives (wealth, pleasure, honor, political power, etc.), and it accepts as known things that are merely opined. Occupied with such mundane goods and satisfied with its pretension to knowledge, the soul neglects that which lies beyond the obviousness of our everyday experience, believing the Good to be nothing more than the various goods that we daily enjoy and the Being of things to be unproblematically given in our experiences of them. Disburdened of any need to strive or inquire beyond its mundane commitments, the soul becomes lethargic and corrupt, and we assure our own unhappiness. Thus, the failure to know ourselves and to know in what way or ways we may best care for ourselves results in the depravation both of our soul and of the self over which it is sovereign.

In what follows, therefore, I will examine this dynamic between the soul's sovereignty over and vulnerability to the self and argue that Plato identifies the good life with the activity of the soul and the bad life with its opposite. The former state will prove to entail a knowledge of oneself – that is, of one's *soul* – which recognizes that the relation to Being, and in particular the Being of the virtues, is constitutive of the soul itself, while the latter will be defined by a failure to achieve such a recognition. This position is consistently articulated by reference to the complementary tropes of wakefulness and sleep, which Plato aligns with activity and indolence, respectively. For this reason, I will employ these terms as the north and south of the compass orienting my reading. Remarkably, this alignment remains consistent even as it is situated in relation to the changing ontological and epistemological topography of dialogues as disparate as the *Apology*, *Republic*, and *Laws*. Therefore, following the trajectory that they establish, I will demonstrate that wakefulness, i.e., the activity of the soul, is indicative of self-knowledge and the good life and the active attempt on the part of those who have achieved these states to sustain themselves therein. In contrast, its opposite, sleep, serves as a metonym for self-forgetting and for a life of such careless prodigality that Plato regularly likens it to death. The most poignant expression of this is found in the figure of the tyrant, whose unparalleled turpitude Plato ascribes to the fact that he has become in waking life what he had rarely been in dreams. With this gesture, Plato discharges the power and appeal of tyranny by revealing the tyrant to be essentially powerless; characterized by somnolence and self-neglect, the life of the tyrant turns out to be no better than death.

8.1

In light of my hermeneutic approach, I will begin by providing a cursory account of the two dominant pre-Platonic conceptions of wakefulness and sleep. Through this we will see that Plato strategically transforms the tradition he inherits in order to align both the truth and the health of the self with the noetic activity of the soul. By inverting the traditional account, he recasts sleep as a metonym for the occurrence of untruth and self-neglect – those who are asleep (either literally or metaphorically) are said to be both ignorant and unconcerned with themselves and are, to this extent, likened to the dead. Wakefulness, by contrast, is posited as the true form of the life of the self. While this holds first and foremost for wakefulness understood as the noetic activity of the soul, we shall see that Plato is not discriminating in his praise, which he likewise pays to wakefulness on the level both of the body and of the soul's pre-noetic activity.

Perhaps the most pervasive understanding of sleep in the pre-Platonic tradition is as respite from toil and suffering. Here, sleep signifies a therapeutic relief from one's cares. Thus when, in the *Iliad*, the grieving Achilles finally rests, Homer proclaims, "sleep seized him, loosening the cares of his heart" (23.54). And when, in the *Odyssey*, Odysseus is reunited with Penelope, he begins to tell his wife that "hereafter there is to be measureless toil," yet cuts himself short, declaring: "But come, wife, let us to bed, that lulled now by sweet slumber we may take our joy of rest" (23.250–255). Or, again, in Sophocles' *Philoctetes*, the play's namesake, speaking of his agonizing snakebite, says that "sleep will take me when this agony has passed, and only then will free me" (770). Expanding the therapeutic understanding of sleep into the sphere of diagnostics, Hippocrates claims, "In whatever disease sleep is laborious, it is a deadly symptom; but if sleep does good, it is not deadly" (II.1). Presented in the form of a medical axiom, one here finds a remarkably clear expression of the Greek belief that Hypnos (sleep) and Thanatos (death) were twin brothers who worked toward opposite ends and were marked by opposing values: Hypnos is gentle and sweet and may even assist us in staving off his brother for a time, while Thanatos is merciless and hated by all, even the gods.

In addition to this, there is the understanding of sleep as the site of prophetic dreams and visitations from the gods. In the fourth book of the *Odyssey*, for instance, Pallas Athena sends a phantom to the sleeping Penelope in order to assure her that, though Odysseus' travails will be both many and dangerous, he has no lesser a guide through them than

Athena herself (4.835). And in Aeschylus' *Libation Bearers*, Clytemnestra has a dream-vision that she bore a snake that tore at her nipple as she attempted to feed it – a vision portending her death at the hands of her son Orestes (510–550). Or, again, in the *Histories*, Herodotus recounts one of Cyrus' many prophetic dreams in which the king, having foreseen an attempt on his life, says, "The gods care for me and show me beforehand all that is coming" (1.209). Throughout these passages, and others like them, one sees that sleep and the dreams arising therein bear a crucial relation to truth understood in the manner that the Muses expressed to Hesiod, that is, as "the telling of things that are and that shall be and that were aforetime" (38).[3] While the gods would occasionally send false dreams, like the dream that Zeus sent to Agamemnon in the second book of the *Iliad* (2.8), such incidents were rare; far more common was the sentiment expressed by Clytemnestra's ghost who, in Aeschylus' *Eumenides*, proclaims, "The sleeping mind has clear vision, but the day-time fate of mortals is unforeseeable" (105). Here, it is sleep, not the waking life, which is said to be the site of truth. Echoing this belief, Euripides writes, in *Iphigenia in Taurus*, that "Earth gave birth to dream visions of the night; and they told to the cities of men the present, and what will happen in the future, through dark beds of sleep on the ground" (1261–1266).

8.2

With a single stroke, the *Apology* upends much of the traditional under-standing of sleep. For, when Socrates likens himself to a gadfly who cares for the city by relentlessly goading its citizens out of a life of somnolence and self-neglect, he effects a realignment of the traditional categories of value and signification associated with ὕπνος.[4] Evacuated of its therapeutic effects and severed from the truth, sleep is transformed into a metonym for the failure to know and, consequently, to care for oneself. Wakefulness is now the precondition for both health – that of the city and of the soul – and *alētheia*. Thus, in one of the most striking and well-known scenes in Plato's corpus, Socrates declares that his philosophical practice is essentially

---

[3] For more on this understanding of *alētheia*, see Detienne (1999, 45).
[4] Plato's appropriation of the tropes of wakefulness and sleep appears to be deeply indebted to Heraclitus, who, to the best of my knowledge, offers the earliest revaluation of these terms in the Greek-speaking world. Like Plato after him, Heraclitus aligns wakefulness with truth and castigates those who speak as if they were asleep. See, in particular, fragments 73 and 89.

and primarily a countermovement to the oblivion of sleep – he awakens
the Athenians from their dogmatic slumber:

> I was attached to this city by the god . . . as upon a great and noble horse
> which was somewhat sluggish because of its size and needed to be awakened
> [ἐγείρεσθαι] by a kind of gadfly . . . I never cease to awaken [ἐγείρων] each
> and every one of you, to persuade and reproach you all day long and
> everywhere I find myself in your company. (30e–31a)

That to which Socrates awakens his fellow citizens, and that for which he
reproaches them, is the belief that they know things of which they are in
fact ignorant. Through this, he discovers a life that stands in opposition to
and seeks to overturn the somnolence of his fellow citizens. This is the life
of wakefulness wherein one works ceaselessly to distinguish *epistēmē* from
doxa and to guard against the belief that one knows things of which one is
either partially or entirely ignorant. In other words, it is the life dedicated
to human wisdom (20d–e). And so, just as Odysseus rescued his companions from an existence pleasantly wasted on the narcotic effects of the lotus
flower, Socrates attempts to rouse his fellow citizens from a life squandered
in complacent slumber.

   This arousal occurs in two distinct yet related registers. On the one hand,
Socrates refutes those interlocutors who suppose that they know or possess
the virtues when they do not. Thus Charmides and Critias are shown to be
incapable of adequately defining *sōphrosunē*; Lysis and Menexenus fail to
explain the meaning of the friendship they believe they share; Euthyphro
proves tragically inept in his attempt to educate Socrates in piety; the list, of
course, goes on. On the other hand, Socrates recognizes that the preceding
entails not only ignorance of the object of inquiry but ignorance of this
ignorance; for one would presumably not suppose oneself to know that
which one was aware one did not know. Yet, unlike ignorance of the virtues
or the arts, this does not involve a relation to something that is either
conceptually or actually distinct from oneself; rather, it entails a relation
between oneself and oneself. It is this relation that Socrates points to at
21c–d, where he recounts his elenchus of the politician: "I thought that he
appeared wise to many people and especially to himself, but he was not.
I then tried to show him that he thought himself wise, but that he was not."
The politician did not merely take the object of inquiry to be otherwise
than it was, he took *himself* to be otherwise than he was – he took himself to
be knowledgeable and wise, though he was neither of these things. But this
means that he supposed he knew himself, i.e., as someone wise, when he
did not, since he was in fact ignorant.

Here, then, the sleep from which Socrates seeks to arouse the Athenians is revealed to entail a forgetting or oblivion (λήθη) of oneself. He utilizes the elenchus to awaken his interlocutors to the fact that they are ignorant not merely of the issue under consideration but of themselves as well. In this way, Socrates advocates for a peculiar form of self-knowledge wherein one comes to know oneself qua unknowing. That is to say, he goads the self out of the forgetting of itself by provoking a new self-relation wherein one is stripped of the false pretense of knowledge and wisdom and made to stand before oneself in unadorned ignorance.

Yet a single act of introspective self-awareness is not sufficient for a life of wakefulness. For it is not clear that or how my ignorance of piety would also entail ignorance of, for instance, friendship. Consequently, refutation of my understanding of the former would not involve a refutation of my understanding of the latter. Therefore another elenchus would be required for my understanding of friendship, another for my understanding of justice, and so forth for the rest. Moreover, since there is nothing to prevent me from developing other opinions regarding these same matters at other times, and nothing to prevent me from later formulating objections to an earlier refutation, there is no reason to suppose that any given refutation will guarantee an amaranthine recognition of my ignorance. Furthermore, were I to suppose the impossibility of knowing a given virtue based on one or even a series of refutations of my understanding thereof, I would by that fact take myself to know something that I do not. That is, I would take myself to know that that virtue is unknowable even though the evidence provided by my own failure offers scant proof at best. Wrongly supposing myself to know that this virtue is unknowable, I would find myself once more eating lotus flowers. This means that the pursuit of self-knowledge is not a finite activity but a way of life dedicated to daily self-examination.

The processual nature of self-knowledge reflects the dynamic nature of the self. This reveals what is perhaps the greatest danger that Socrates finds in the belief that one knows things of which one is ignorant. This belief does not simply and fallaciously negate the need for further inquiry; it anesthetizes the vital noetic functions of the soul, thereby disempowering those psychical activities that are most valuable to human existence – thinking and inquiring. Moreover, because these *are* activities, one cannot relate to them as one might an object such as a chair or a statue, for this would be to treat as complete that which is a process. Yet the effect of the Athenian claim to knowledge is to arrest thought and inquiry, encasing them in the amber of certainty. Consequently, Socrates' fellow citizens fail to know themselves not only because they claim a knowledge that they do not possess but because they fail to perceive the active principle of their souls *as* active. True self-knowledge requires that one perceive oneself in the process of thinking and inquiring, and this, Socrates maintains, may be achieved only through the philosophical examination of the virtues and oneself. Moreover, because it promotes and preserves the vital activities of the soul, Socrates claims that this processual understanding of self-knowledge constitutes the good life itself: "to talk every day about virtue and the other things about which you hear me talking and examining myself and others is the greatest good for humans" (38a). *The good life is the active life* – the life spent laboring daily over the virtues and over oneself.

Importantly, these do not constitute two distinct spheres of concern; rather, inquiry into the virtues turns out to be inquiry into the soul. This is the case not simply because Socrates asks after his interlocutor's understanding of justice, piety, etc., thereby situating the interlocutor at the center of their inquiry. On a still more fundamental level, this is the case because the very nature and character of the soul is implicated in our relation to the virtues. The claim that the greatest good for humans consists of inquiry into matters such as justice and piety – into what they *are*, and not merely how they appear – implies that the soul is, in some way, always already related to the Being of the virtues, for it is through this relation that the soul is made excellent or fails to be made so. This is the case even when, as in the *Apology*, our noetic faculties remain incommensurable with this Being. This relation, then, is not a secondary or accidental feature of the soul; insofar as it determines the qualitative state of the soul, that is, insofar as it determines the goodness or badness of the soul *in respect to its being a soul*, this relation is constitutive of the soul itself. Self-knowledge therefore entails the perception of oneself in – indeed, *as* – a relation to the Being of the virtues. It is this that is at stake in the activation of the soul's noetic faculty, for the philosophical inquiry into the virtues fosters the recognition that the soul, and the health of the soul, are always already determined by that to which the soul may assimilate itself but which it can never simply assimilate to itself. This contrasts with the tendency to equate opinion with knowledge, a process whereby one disregards the Being of the virtues in favor of their appearance, thereby rendering them fully assimilable to oneself. Thus, when Socrates accuses his fellow Athenians of being asleep because they have supposed themselves to be knowledgeable and wise when they are in fact ignorant, he is indicting them not only of a failure to perceive their own ignorance but of a failure to perceive their souls' essential relation to the Being, rather than the mere appearance, of the virtues. Their inability to care for themselves and one another follows from this somnolence, for being ignorant of that which is most proper to the soul, they are unaware of that on which its goodness or badness rests.

Transformed from the restorative cessation of laboring over the field and the home to the deleterious cessation of laboring over one's soul, sleep now serves as a metonym for the failure to tend to oneself and is thereby aligned with a lapse in the vigilance necessary to fend off untruth, complacency, and viciousness. Henceforth it is the waking life that is identified with self-care and the pursuit of the truth, i.e., the truth of one's *self*. Not only is rest no longer seen as a palliative; it is now transformed into a danger and a temptation. Thus, in recognition of the ease with which we may succumb to the belief that we know things merely opined, the wakeful life is seen as a life of ever-renewed vigilance and toil. When, therefore, Socrates declares that the unexamined life is not worth living (38a), he simultaneously elides the difference between the twin brothers Hypnos and Thanatos – sleep and death – and advances the philosopher as the one who overcomes a living death through the exercise of an almost insomniac vigilance against sleep.

8.3

Though typically placed at opposite ends of Plato's career, the *Apology* and the *Laws* share a strikingly similar commitment to the view that life in its truest sense is identified with wakefulness, while sleep and inactivity are identified with death. In the *Laws*, however, the concern over sleep has become radicalized to such an extent that daily toil over oneself is no longer sufficient – one must now minimize the time spent asleep in order to fend off the danger that it poses and to extract from each day the greatest possible benefit. Thus the Athenian Stranger proclaims that the "most demanding task" that he and his companions will face in founding the city of Magnesia is to convince its citizens to dedicate every waking moment to the care of both their bodies and their souls:

> For as compared with the life that aims at a Pythian or Olympian victory and is wholly lacking in leisure for other tasks, that life we speak of – *which most truly deserves the name "life"* – is doubly (nay, far more than doubly) lacking in leisure, seeing that it is occupied with the care of bodily and psychical virtue in general. For there ought to be no other secondary task to hinder the work of supplying the body with its proper exercise and nourishment or the soul with ethical training; nay, every night and day is not sufficient for the person who is occupied therein to win from them their fruit in full and ample measure. (VII.807c–d, emphasis added)

Reminiscent of the *Apology*, this passage again affirms that life in its truest sense is the active life and that it is therefore opposed to leisure and rest. Yet the tone has become noticeably more severe, for the demands placed on us by the need to care for ourselves now press up against the very limits of our lifespan – we would fail to exercise sufficient care even if we labored over ourselves night and day. As it is, then, we must extract from each as much as we are able.

Toward this end, the Stranger offers two innovations. First, it will be necessary to establish a program governing how the citizens "shall pass their time continuously from dawn one day until sunrise at dawn the next day" (VII.807d–e). Second, the heads of the household must awaken before their servants and believe it shameful to be woken thereby (VII.807e–808a), and, in general, all citizens must sleep as little as possible: "For when asleep no one is worth anything, any more than if they were dead: on the contrary, every one of us who cares most greatly for life and thought [τοῦ ζῆν . . . καὶ τοῦ φρονεῖν] keeps awake as long as possible, only reserving so much time for sleep as health requires" (VII.808b). No longer appealing to the metaphor of wakefulness invoked in the *Apology*, the Stranger here declares that life in its truest sense is identified with wakefulness in its literal sense. Moreover, by reaffirming with still greater severity the understanding of life as activity and toil, Plato advances the identification of sleep with death to a point of near perfection: when asleep one is worth no more than if one were dead.[5]

The equation between wakefulness and life, on the one hand, and sleep and death, on the other, has ethico-political implications that are both broad and subtle. Indeed, the Stranger's concern over this matter is so great that he prescribes practices that would be deemed unnecessarily dangerous or difficult if their true purpose were not seen. For instance, at VI.778e–779b, he denounces the custom of building walls around the city because they are "by no means an advantage to a city in regard to health . . . and usually cause a soft habit of the soul [μαλθακὴν ἕξιν ταῖς ψυχαῖς]." By providing physical security for the city, walls invite ease and laziness into the souls of its citizens, who, no longer having to keep watch both night and day, "go to sleep, like people born to shirk toil" (ibid.). Offering a singularly cunning concession, the Stranger proclaims that the city's wall should consist of the citizens' houses, which will be joined together to form a single barricade surrounding the *polis*. With this nod to the importance

---

[5] This is anticipated at *Phd.* 71c–d, where Socrates claims that being awake is opposed to being asleep as being alive is opposed to being dead.

of securing the physical safety of the citizenry, the Stranger in fact places the inhabitants of Magnesia at the point of greatest danger, thereby inculcating their private lives in the martial defense of the *polis* and assuring that they will internalize a sense of urgency and vigilance wrought by the ever-present threat of violence from without. Contrary to its stated purpose, then, the aim of this rather extraordinary measure is not first and foremost to protect the citizens' bodies but to assure the health and wakefulness of their souls. Thus the very architecture of the city will be designed to prevent the softening of the soul produced by a slackening of toil and the ease of sleep.

Similarly, at VII.823d–824b the Stranger denounces methods of fishing and hunting that, though proven effective, nevertheless promote laziness. Declaring that he will offer "praise of the kind [of hunting] that renders the souls of the young better, and blame of the kind that does the opposite," the Stranger denies the city's fisherman the use of creels, since they "do your lazy hunting for you, whether you are asleep or awake." He likewise rejects the use of traps, nets, and snares for catching land animals. However, he reserves a special disdain for the practice of night hunting, which, "being the job of lazy people who sleep in turn, is one that deserves no praise." He further disavows any form of hunting that allows for "intervals of rest from toil," all of which he denounces as shameless counterparts to the active and athletic forms, which display "the victorious might of a toil-loving soul." Just as the protection of the city is subordinated to the inculcation of the habit of wakefulness in its citizens, so too is the nourishment of the city. No activity is too slight that it cannot serve to reinforce a commitment to the values of activity, vigilance, and toil, because the very life of the city depends on the wakefulness of its citizenry. Such passages highlight the remarkable lengths that the Stranger goes to in order to assure that the inhabitants of Magnesia do not succumb to the allure of leisure and forsake the toil required to care for themselves. This is to say that they emphasize a preoccupation with the role that the governing body of the *polis* plays in affecting the relation that each citizen has with him- or herself.

The *Laws* does not limit its concern with wakefulness to matters of architecture and venatics; it shares in common with many of Plato's dialogues a commitment to the view that the function of education is to awaken the soul. For instance, at V.747a–b the Stranger praises the study of numbers for its unparalleled influence over economics, politics, and all the arts; yet he asserts that the true importance of this study does not rest in the breadth of its pertinence; rather, "its chief advantage is that it wakes up [ἐγείρει] the person who is by nature drowsy and slow of wit, and makes them quick to learn, mindful, and sharp-willed." And when discussing the proper education of children, he suggests that lessons in numbers should begin in infancy and continue throughout childhood, since the study of mathematics is "of service to the pupils for their future tasks of drilling, leading and marching in armies, or of household management, and in every way renders them both more helpful to themselves and more awake [ἐγρηγορότας]" (VII.819a–d). Though necessary for many of the arts crucial to the survival and prosperity of the *polis*, the greatest advantage gained from mathematics is that it awakens the soul. It is studied less for the knowledge that it bestows than for the state of the soul that it promotes; by awakening the soul, mathematics sharpens the intellectual faculties and makes those who study it both more adept in future educative endeavors and more useful to themselves. This is to say that it is placed in the service of the care of oneself that the Stranger claimed was necessary for Magnesia to come into being.

8.4

A similar thesis is advanced in Book VII of the *Republic*, where Socrates argues that the study of numbers and calculation is crucial to the educative program and success of the city (VII.522c).[6] The centerpiece of this argument occurs in the famous discussion of "the summoners." Here Socrates notes that everyday sense perception "will not provoke or awaken [ἐγερτικὸν] reflection and thought" because the senses grasp things as simple, unproblematic wholes (VII.523c–e); sight, for instance, perceives a finger as numerically one and identical to itself, so it fails to promote a sense of *aporia* or wonder capable of stimulating a noetic response. However, it is also possible to perceive this same object as the embodiment of a multiplicity and as a unity of opposites. For instance, a finger may appear simultaneously hard and soft, or, in the case of the ring finger, both large (in respect of the pinky) and small (in respect of the middle finger); moreover, any whole grasped by the senses will prove infinitely divisible to the mind. Attempting to reconcile these disparate modalities of perception, the soul seeks to determine if the object perceived is one (a finger numerically identical to itself) or two (both small and large); therefore,

---

[6] References to the *Republic* are from the Bloom translation (1991); I have amended the translation when necessary.

it "first summons calculation and understanding [λογισμόν τε καὶ νόησιν] and tries to determine whether each of the things reported to it is one or two" (VII.524b). Consequently, the soul posits each universal (smallness, largeness, etc.) as one and distinct, and finds that the senses confound these, perceiving a multiplicity as if it were a unity. Thus, by distinguishing between the numerical multiplicity underlying sense perception and the numerical unity given in such perception, we discover "the origin of the designation *intelligible* for the one, and *visible* for the other" (VII.524c–d). Referring back to VII.523c–e, Socrates tells Glaucon that those things are provocative of thought "that impinge upon the senses together with their opposites, while those that do not ... do not tend to awaken [ἐγερτικὰ] thought" (VII.524d); a few lines later he affirms that the study of number serves this function preeminently (VII.524d–525b).

As in the *Laws*, then, the study of mathematics is desirable because it awakens the soul; here, however, this awakening is provided with a distinctly ontological content that was not present in either the *Apology* or the *Laws*. In the former, such awakening occurred first as the realization that a given thing is not what one had taken it to be (justice, for instance, is not the same as retribution) and second as the realization that one is not as one had supposed oneself to be (one is neither knowledgeable nor wise). In the latter, it was defined more vaguely, if with greater vehemence, as a means of fostering mental acuity. Here, the study of mathematics is undertaken as a means of awakening the soul to the ontological difference between the visible and the intelligible – it serves as a propaedeutic to the study of being (VII.525a), though it itself merely "dreams about being" (VII.533b–c). Once again, then, mathematical education is desirable first and foremost for the analeptic effect that it has on the soul.[7]

Throughout the *Republic*, Socrates regularly distinguishes the guardians from the other members of the *polis* by reference to the city's educational program, arguing that all other citizens are insufficiently trained in *mousikē*, overly attached to the visible, and, as a consequence, live their lives asleep. As early as Book III, he asserts that one will become a misologist if she trains her body but has no contact with the Muses, since the soul of such a person "is not awakened [ἐγειρόμενον] or fed, nor are its perceptions purified" (III.411d–e). And when distinguishing between the guardian and soldier classes in Book VI, he argues that the steadfastness

---

[7] On the relationship between mathematics and self-knowledge, see Andy German's Chapter 9 in this book.

that the latter exhibit in the face of danger frequently translates into recalcitrance in the face of the education required by the former. He therefore excludes the soldier class from the education enjoyed by the guardians since "[t]hey are not easily aroused, learn with difficulty, as if benumbed [ἀπονεναρκωμένα], and are filled with sleep and yawning [καὶ ὕπνου τε καὶ χάσμης ἐμπίμπλανται] when given an intellectual task" (VI.503d).[8]

Yet the most crucial distinction that Socrates draws is not between the philosopher and the athlete or soldier but between the philosopher and the lover of sights, whom he distinguishes from the philosopher along the lines of their mutual attraction to beauty. While the philosopher delights in the sight of the Beautiful itself, the lover of sights "neither believes in beauty itself nor is able to follow when someone tries to guide him to the knowledge of it." Consequently, Socrates asks of such a person: "don't you think that he is living in a dream [ὄναρ] rather than in a waking state? Isn't a dream, whether one is asleep or awake, just this: mistaking the likeness of a thing for the thing itself of which it is a likeness?" (V.476c). The lover of sights is like someone asleep because she assumes an unproblematic identity between the Being or *eidos* of beauty and the various appearances thereof. Therefore, her thought languishes on the visible and is not summoned beyond the images of beauty to that of which these images are images. This is in opposition to the philosopher who denies that a thing can be known through its images and who therefore strives to distinguish the one from the other. Socrates thus asks: "the person whose thought recognizes the beautiful itself and is able to distinguish this from the things that participate in it, and neither supposes the participants to be it nor it to be the participants – is their life, in your opinion, a waking or a dream state?" Glaucon's response: "He is very much awake [Καὶ μάλα . . . ὕπαρ]" (V.476c–d).

The lover of sights is described as being asleep because she fails to perceive that beautiful things are made beautiful by participating in the Beautiful itself (V.476c–d). Thus she fails to see that the Beautiful itself constitutes the true object of her love. From this it follows that she is ignorant not only of the Beautiful but of herself as well, for she does not know what it is that she truly desires. Moreover, because this self-ignorance has the effect of collapsing the intelligible into the visible, she fails to attend to the ontological difference required to summon thought and awaken the soul's noetic powers. She is therefore oblivious

---

[8] Cf. *Men.* 80a–b.

to that which is most vital and valuable within herself. This is in contrast to the philosopher, who is aware of this ontological difference and of the fact that her love is directed beyond the visible to the intelligible. While this awareness does not necessarily entail knowledge of the Beautiful (it only entails an awareness that the Beautiful differs from its images and that the latter exist through the former), it does make possible a form of self-knowledge unfamiliar to the aesthete, for the philosopher knows what it is that she loves. Furthermore, because this love directs her beyond images of beauty to that of which these are images, i.e., the Being of Beauty, it has the effect of summoning thought and awakening the soul's noetic powers. Here, in the coadunation of self-knowledge and νόησις, the philosopher discovers not only that which is best and most sovereign in her soul; she discovers that which is most proper to this part of her soul: Being.

Despite their differing ontological commitments, we see that both the *Republic* and *Apology* advance an understanding of self-knowledge as the soul's awareness of that in relation to which it exists, i.e., Being. It is this awareness that distinguishes the philosopher from the aesthete and Socrates from his fellow Athenians. Self-knowledge, then, is not simply a matter of introspective self-examination wherein one catalogues the totality of one's opinions on a given matter or dissects the soul into its various parts and faculties. While such activities are necessary to achieve a knowledge of oneself, they nevertheless prove too inward-looking to be sufficient. The wakefulness and self-knowledge to which Socrates refers in these dialogues is, in an important regard, outward-looking. They constitute an awareness of one's inextricable belonging to that which is not only irreducible to the soul itself but which, even in the most optimistic reading of the dialogues, the soul may be said to approach only with great difficulty. It is for this reason that Plato champions the life of wakefulness, activity, and toil and condemns the life of somnolence – the former directs the soul toward that which is best and most proper to it, while the latter settles for mere images thereof. The philosopher is therefore uniquely capable of self-knowledge, since she knows not only the various faculties of the soul but what, by nature, is proper to each. This discovery is crucial to the project undertaken in the *Republic*, for in light of the tripartite division of the soul, Socrates maintains that it is only when one knows what is proper to each part of the soul "that each part may, so far as other things are concerned, mind its own business and be just" (IX.586e). This is to say that the wakefulness and self-knowledge of the philosopher serve as the condition of possibility for a justly ordered soul.

8.5

By differentiating the visible from the intelligible and casting the former as a semblance of the latter, Plato introduces an ontological problematic for which the trope of sleep proves insufficient. Thus, while this trope still serves as a metonym for the psychical state wherein one supposes oneself to know that which one merely opines (the lover of sights, for instance, believes she knows beauty), dreams have become a metonym for the ontological structure subtending this misguided pretense to knowledge: whether one identifies beauty with the face of one's beloved or with his or her portrait, one mistakes an image of beauty for Beauty itself, and this is no different from what happens when dreaming. The lover of sights, therefore, lives in a world bounded by the heavens above as if by the ceiling of the cave in which the god Hypnos was believed to reside. Still, there is an ontological difference between one's beloved and his or her portrait such that the latter stands in relation to the former as the former stands in relation to the intelligible. Thus, if a house, for instance, is a dream image of the Form "house," a painting thereof is a dream image of an image: "the art of painting makes another house, a sort of human-made dream [ὄναρ] produced for those who are awake [ἀπειργασμένην]" (*Sph.* 266c). Plato therefore concludes that the products of the imitative arts are three removes from *phusis* and *alētheia* (*R.* X.597e, 599d). Bearing only the slightest relation to truth, the mimetic arts are capable of producing not only all the other arts (as when, for instance, a painter paints an image of a cobbler or a carpenter) but "the greatest and finest things" as well, i.e., the virtues (X.598b–599d). Yet the conditions for the possibility of such production deny the product any authoritative claim to the truth – for a painter need not know carpentry in order to depict the carpenter's art, and a poet need not know courage, justice, or statesmanship in order to depict these.

If the products of the mimetic arts are dreams created for the waking, this is because dreams exist at a remove from, and therefore lack any authoritative claim to, the truth. This does not mean that they are a priori false: in the *Meno*, for instance, the true opinion that the slave boy eventually arrives at "has been stirred up in him, like a dream" (85c); in the *Phaedo*, Socrates is found writing poetry in order to test a recurring dream in which he was told to "make music and work at it," and which he had previously understood as an exhortation to practice philosophy (60d–61a);[9] and in

---

[9] Cf. *Ap.* 33c, where Socrates claims that the god commanded him to philosophize by oracles and dreams.

the *Timaeus*, divination in dreams is said to be granted to us so that we "might in some degree lay hold on truth" (71d–e). While such passages do not insist on the falsehood of dreams, they do present the relation between truth and dreams as either tenuous or indeterminate and underscore nothing so much as the necessity of actively and wakefully inquiring into one's dreams in order to determine their alethic value.[10] Timaeus is insistent on this point, claiming that one must be awake and *emphronos* to interpret one's dreams, "for it was well said of old that to do and to know one's own and oneself belongs only to one who is sound of mind [σώφρονι]" (71e–72a). Here, again, self-knowledge is granted only to the waking, i.e., to those who do not merely accept as true that which is given as such but who subject such revelations to active and critical inquiry.

Frequently, however, dreams prove to be false images that arise through self-neglect and prevent self-knowledge. In the *Theaetetus*, for instance, the dialogue's namesake confesses that dreamers "have false opinions when some of them think they are gods and others fancy in their sleep that they have wings and are flying" (158a–b). Or, again, he admits that in his dreams he has said to himself that the odd is the even (190b). And in the *Statesman*, the Stranger insists that he and the young Socrates exclude false opinions from their account of statesmanship, "so that it [statesmanship] may be present to us in our waking state instead of in a dream" (278d–e). What is remarkable about such passages is not simply the frequency with which they portray dreams as false but the fact that they identify dreams as a species of *doxa*. The soul's perception of dream images is not merely analogous to its perception of the shadowy objects produced by the imitative arts; the *dunamis* through which it relates to each is the same. And no one suffers so greatly from the ill-effects of the false opinions that occur in dreams – that occur *as* dreams – as the tyrant, whose soul is twisted into monstrous proportions by the desires and visions emerging in sleep.

In the *Republic*, explaining how the tyrannical individual is produced through a concatenation of external influence, ever-expanding desire, and the commission of various lawless acts, Socrates claims that their opinions regarding the noble and the shameful are "mastered by opinions newly released from slavery, now acting as eros' bodyguards and conquering along with it. These are the opinions that were formerly released as dreams in sleep [αἳ πρότερον μὲν ὄναρ ἐλύοντο ἐν ὕπνῳ]" (IX.574d). These newly liberated opinions serve to ratify the unnecessary desires "that are

---

[10] In the *Charmides*, for instance, Socrates directs the dialogue's namesake to "Listen, then ... to my dream to see whether it comes through the gate of horn [truth] or ivory [falsity]" (173a).

awakened in sleep when the rest of the soul, the rational, gentle, and dominant part, slumbers, but the beastly and savage part, repelling sleep, endeavors to sally forth and satisfy its own instincts" (IX.571c). Included among these are the desire for murder, riches, and feasts, as well as incest, bestiality, and intercourse with the gods. While such desires exist within us all (IX.571b), the tyrant differs from others insofar as he yields to the enduring opinion that the pleasures associated with such desires are good – indeed, that they are *the* good. Enslaved to this perverse eros, the tyrant "is continuously and in waking hours what he rarely became in his dreams [ὄναρ], and he will refrain from no atrocity of murder nor from any food or deed" (IX.574e–575a). Here we discover an astonishing similarity between the tyrant and the products of the mimetic arts – both are dream images produced in waking life. It is not merely in his dreams that the tyrant entertains false opinions regarding justice, moderation, piety, and the other virtues; he allows these opinions to become attached to his soul, like the barnacles and seaweed attached to the statue of Glaucus, so that they are transported out of his sleeping life and into the waking world.

The tyrant's dreamlike existence has far-reaching implications. First, there is Plato's suggestion that the tyrant exists at the same ontological remove from the truth as the mimetic arts and that he is therefore no more human than a painting of a house is actually a house. This claim appears to reflect the fact that the unnecessary desires ruling the tyrant's soul are not only vicious but are alien to the soul's nature (VIII.558d–559a). This is not say that their existence within the soul is contrary to nature. However, it is to say that they are by nature both separable from and incapable of producing any good in the soul (ibid.). We here find perhaps the most conspicuous and consequential difference between the soul of the philosopher and that of the tyrant. The former orders her soul by apportioning to each part that which is by nature best and most proper to it, and this, as we saw above, is possible only because she knows herself and what belongs to her. The latter effects the disorder of his soul by allowing it to be ruled by that which is entirely foreign to it. As a result, his soul is denatured and rendered no more substantial than an image in a dream.

Second, there are political and ethical implications. The tyrant's brutal rule and lawless enslavement of the city reflect his own enslavement to the lawless desires that rule within him. Yet this lawlessness is not merely desiderative in origin; it is also epistemological. For the tyrant's waking life is transformed into a nightmare of lust, gluttony, and blood only once he has adopted the false opinions regarding the good and the virtues that first preyed on him in the madness of his dreams. Subsequently, he rules over both himself and others with the conviction not only that his good is *the* good but that the good just is the pleasure gained from feasts, wealth, sex, political power, etc. In other words, he identifies the good with the pleasures of the visible realm.

Here, then, we find a final implication of the tyrant's dreamlike existence: he is rendered ignorant of himself, and this, on two separate levels. First, from the fact that (1) the good transcends the visible realm (VI.505a–509b) and (2) the tyrant desires the pleasures associated with the visible realm because he believes them to be the good, it follows that the tyrant is ignorant of what he truly desires (IX.587a–b) – he has confused an image of the good with the good itself.[11] In this regard he is like the lover of sights who is unaware that what she is truly drawn to is not the beautiful object but that through which this object is made beautiful, and whose thought is therefore never awakened to the intelligible and the true. This, as we have seen, reveals a second and still more fundamental level of self-ignorance, for it entails a failure to recognize that the soul is constituted through its relation to Being, or here through its relation to the Good beyond Being. Thus, in contrast to the philosopher, who attempts to assimilate herself to that which is incommensurable with her soul, who, that is, attempts to become virtuous by assimilating herself to the Being of the virtues, the tyrant, recognizing nothing with which his soul is incommensurate, attempts to assimilate all things to himself. In other words, his nightmarish desires for blood, wealth, incest, etc. are authorized by his self-ignorance. He does not know that element within himself which is best fit to determine what ought to be desired, i.e., the part of his soul wherein its love of wisdom, its φιλοσοφία, resides and where its relation to Being comes to light with greatest clarity (IX.586e). Yet this is the part of the soul to which Socrates says one must look in order to truly see the soul itself, for it alone is awake and looks not to visible images but to the *eidei* of which these images are images, and is, as such, akin to the divine and the immortal (X.611d–e). When the tyrant looks to himself, he sees only the barnacles, seaweed, and accumulated detritus which he has, in his ignorance and shamelessness, acquired. He never sees the godlike figure slumbering beneath.

As a result of his self-ignorance, the tyrant not only lives the most wretched form of life (IX.587b); he suffers the most wretched fate in the afterlife. Speaking of one who fails to distinguish between the visible and

---

[11] As Brickhouse and Smith note (1994, 88), "what the tyrant really desires is typically not what the tyrant thinks he desires."

the intelligible, and who therefore perceives neither the good itself nor the other *eidei*, Socrates says that such a person "does not know the good itself or any other good thing. And if he gets ahold of some image of it . . . it's through opinion, not knowledge, for he is dreaming and asleep throughout his present life, and before he wakes up here, he will arrive in Hades and go to sleep forever" (VII.534b–c). Though this comment is made in Book VII, it anticipates the fate of the tyrant recounted in the concluding myth of Book X. Here, in the final pages of the *Republic*, we learn that, while all other souls (both human and animal) are reborn into new bodies and new lives, the souls of the wicked – tyrants being foremost among them – are stripped of their skin and condemned to Tartarus (X.615c–616a); banished from the cycle of birth and rebirth, these souls alone truly die.[12] Within the nightmare of the tyrant's lack of self-knowledge, then, the unity of Hypnos and Thanatos is perfected: asleep throughout his life, the tyrant is condemned to death in Hades.

---

[12] A similar image is offered at *Grg.* 525c–e.

CHAPTER 9

Mathematical Self-Ignorance and Sophistry
Theodorus and Protagoras

Andy German

A striking feature of the *Theaetetus* is the repeatedly highlighted friendship between Protagoras and Theodorus. Protagoras is called Theodorus' comrade (ἑταῖρος) and, on one occasion, even promoted to "teacher."[1] Indeed, several times, Socrates simply identifies the two men, calling Theodorus "Protagoras" and making the former stand in for the latter whether he likes it or not.[2]

Now, why this should be the case is something of a mystery given the radically divergent inclinations of these two men. Protagoras, the great sophist and "father" of the *homo mensura*, is portrayed in the eponymous dialogue as someone with a pronounced disdain for mathematics (which might reflect the historical personality if the fragment preserved by Philodemus is to be believed).[3] Theodorus, in turn, fancies himself a strictly neutral bystander at a verbal duel. He is, he tells Socrates, "unused to this sort of conversation" (146b3), by which he apparently means that sort of conversation which raises general questions (like "Whatever is knowledge?") that are above the pay grade of any recognized expertise. As he indicates later, he has long since turned away from "mere" or "abstract" speeches (ψιλῶν λόγων) to the safe harbor of geometry (165a2). In turning his back on *logoi* he feels that he has left behind, with barely concealed relief, the empty speechifying of *both* philosophy and sophistry.[4]

Each man, then, looks down his nose at the pursuits of the other and yet they are something of a pair. In forcing us to ask 'Why Theodorus and Protagoras?' Plato also forces us to ask what their respective areas of expertise – mathematics and sophistry – could have to do with one another.

---

[1] *Tht.* 161b9–10, 162a4, 164e2–165a5, 168c3, e8, 171c8. On Protagoras as Theodorus' teacher, see 179a10. All translations from Greek are my own, though I have consulted Benardete (1984) and Burnyeat (1990). The Greek text of the *Theaetetus* comes from the newly edited version of *Tomus I* by Duke et al. (1995).
[2] *Tht.* 170a6, c1, 178c1, e4. [3] Cf. *Prt.* 318d5–319a2 with Fragment 7a in Sprague (1972, 22).
[4] See Benitez and Guimaraes (1993, 305) on Theodorus' "conflation of philosophy and sophistry."

By means of their juxtaposition, I will argue, Plato sheds light on a kind of self-ignorance that can lodge itself at the heart of his own conception of παιδεία as a περιαγωγή – the mathematically inflected, psychic revolution culminating in dialectic.[5] In Theodorus (and Theaetetus himself, for that matter), Plato affords us an occasion for sober reflection on the astounding intellectual vistas he opened up in *Republic* VI and VII.[6]

At least one link between Theodorus and Protagoras is immediately obvious. Both men are teachers, professors of wisdom about elevated matters. Like the sophists, Theodorus is an itinerant teacher who has come from Cyrene to Athens, the "School of Greece."[7] And he too is one of those with whom the youth eagerly associate. Socrates mentions that Theodorus has amassed a significant following (143d7–e2).[8]

The dialogue has thus been well described as a custody battle of sorts over Theaetetus' education.[9] But one cannot decide who is the true teacher without inquiring into what real teaching is, an inquiry that links the *Theaetetus* most closely to the *Republic*.[10] Why? Note that at 145a6–9 and 145c7–d2, Theodorus is said to have a professional competence in all of the mathematical studies that *Republic* VII calls dialectic's "assistant" arts (συνερίθοις τέχναις): geometry, astronomy, harmony and calculation, and "everything concerned with education."[11]

---

[5] *R.* VII.533c8.

[6] The *Theaetetus* has been a locus for interpretative struggles over its dating and, since antiquity, its philosophical import (is it a purely skeptical dialogue which initiates the abandonment of the "metaphysics of Form" or a calculated "aporetic" dialogue meant to point to the indispensability of Forms or one yielding some positive results of its own?). Though I read the *Theaetetus* alongside the *Republic*, the question of compositional chronology is irrelevant here. Whenever Plato wrote these two dialogues, and in whatever order, they represent two mutually enriching viewpoints on a common theme – the activity of knowing in its various manifestations. Regarding the second question, there is truth in both lines of interpretation. The *Theaetetus* indeed shows the limits of a strictly mathematical conception of knowledge, and this "skeptical" result points to the necessity of Form. But, I will argue, it is also a critical reflection on the ascent toward the Forms in *Republic* VII, and thus has something *positive* to say about what is needed to make *nous* most fully present in dianoetic thought, namely, a kind of self-knowledge. For a useful survey of the debate on the *Theaetetus*, see Sedley (2004).

[7] The Ἑλλάδος παίδευσιν, Thucydides, *Historiae*, II, 41, or the "Greece of Greece" (Ἑλλάδος Ἑλλας Ἀθῆναι) in the epigram on Euripides in *Anthologia Graeca*, VII, 45.

[8] See Theodorus' own boast at 144a2 that he has "consorted" (πεπλησίακα) with very many.

[9] Benitez and Guimaraes (1993, 308).

[10] Ibid. That these two dialogues are to be thought together is also hinted by Theodorus' description of Theaetetus, which ascribes to him many attributes of the philosopher-king in the *Republic*. See Friedländer (1969, 148–149).

[11] *Tht.* 145a9. Cf. *R.* VII.533d3–4. In the *Theaetetus* no mention is made of the distinction between plane geometry and stereometrics, and the studies are not listed in the same order as their presentation in the *Republic*, an order that Socrates emphasizes is crucial (VII.528a6–7, d5–10). In other words, Theodorus has the elements of the total synoptic education, but no understanding of what makes them into a whole.

He is, then, a possible representative of that genuine spiritual cultivation that Socrates, in the *Republic*, consistently opposes to merely vulgar, mechanical learning.[12] But is Theodorus at all aware that the mathematical arts are assistants, are subordinate to anything at all? This is tantamount to asking whether Theodorus displays any awareness of dialectic and its relation to mathematics, and if not, why not. Only by answering this question does Theodorus' openness to Protagoras' teaching become explicable.

9.1

The five mathematical sciences of *Republic* VII have been the subject of profound investigations that have illuminated the choice of subjects in the Platonic *Quadrivium*, their precise order of study, their interrelation, etc.[13] While many interpretive points remain contested, two elements of Socrates' description should, I think, be uncontroversial (though not, for that reason, simple). To begin, (1) calling mathematical studies "preludes" or "assistants" to dialectic does not imply a merely instrumental relationship between them. On the contrary, mathematics and dialectic are akin, essentially related through their respective content.[14] And yet, (2) despite this kinship, they are potentially separable, in the following sense: the mathematical preparatory teaching, the προπαιδεία, can be used incorrectly (VII.523a2), in which case it is useless (VII.531c6–7) or without profit (VII.531d3) since it fails to lead the soul upward to dialectic. This is why Socrates can assert that it is surely not the case that every man who is "clever" at mathematical sciences is *eo ipso* also a dialectician (VII.531d8). Let us begin, then, with the kinship of mathematics and dialectic before turning to their estrangement in Theodorus, a clever mathematician whom no one could mistake for a dialectician.

In his study, "Plato on Why Mathematics Is Good for the Soul," Myles Burnyeat notes that, in developing his pedagogical program, Plato was interested only in certain kinds of mathematics:

---

[12] *R.* VII.522b3, 525c1–d3, 526c11–e2, 527d5–6.
[13] Cornford (1932), Von Fritz (1969), Gadamer (1986), Miller (1999), Burnyeat (2000).
[14] Burnyeat (2000, 46): "The famous image of dialectic as the coping stone of the curriculum … implies the completion of a single, unified building, not a transfer to different subjects in a different building." Cf. Hackforth (1942, 2).

[T]here was quite a lot of mathematics in existence which he [Plato] did *not* want on the curriculum ... Pythagorean harmonics, contemporary mathematical astronomy, mathematical mechanics and, I believe, mathematical optics ... These studies would all keep the mind focused on sensible things. They do not abstract from the sensible features as much as Plato requires.[15]

However, as any deeper reading (including Burnyeat's) shows, Plato's criterion for choosing among the mathematical sciences is not only a preference for "abstraction" over sensible concreteness. Nor is it simply a preference for purely contemplative number theory over utilitarian, calculative mathematics (λογισμός).[16] There is a further distinction made, *within* pure theoretical mathematics, among kinds of numerical ratios. Only those that express concord (συμφωνία) and attunement (ἁρμονία) are of ultimate interest to Socrates, thus forging a tight thematic link to the concord and attunement we aim at in ordering our soul, or the city, or any unity within multiplicity.[17] But to speak of certain mathematical relations as better or more beautiful is to admit that mathematics is part of a larger noetic realm having *normative*, not only epistemic, significance.[18] Only because of this can it make sense to say that dialectic is at one and the same time the ability to give a logos of the "being of each thing" (the ὅ ἐστιν ἕκαστον) and simultaneously of the Good itself (αὐτὸ ὅ ἐστιν ἀγαθόν, VII.532a6–b1).

It should not be surprising, then, to find *agathon* and *kalon* present at every stage of the ascent in Book VII, even where not explicitly mentioned.[19] Even in passing references to the correct (ὀρθῶς) use of mathematics, one sufficient (ἱκανῶς) for initiating dianoetic thought

[15] Burnyeat (2000, 17).
[16] Of the kind used by generals, farmers and men of business. See *R.* VII.525d3, 526d1–5, 527d2–5. Note: In all these rejected cases, some abstract numerical thinking nevertheless *does* take place. A businessman, for example, must eventually turn from counting sensible objects to the manipulation of pure monads if he is to do anything beyond basic inventory. The problem is that the narrowness of his concerns forecloses on any possibility of reflection about the wider noetic realm of which these numbering units are a part. In other words, an actuary may well engage in *perfectly abstract* mathematical thinking of stupefying complexity and still this will not lead "upward" toward being and the Good, because it cannot lead outward beyond the narrowness of its point of origin.
[17] For numerous examples from the *Republic*, see Burnyeat (2000, 52–56).
[18] On the Greek proclivity for attributing aesthetic and moral qualities to numbers, see Marrou (1965, 270–272).
[19] At VII.530a4–7, the true astronomer will believe that the heavens were crafted to be as beautiful as possible. And at 531c1–4, Socrates hints that the true "*harmonikos*" would rise to an investigation of the διὰ τί, "that through which" numbers are concordant. This can only be the Good as the ultimate principle of measure, which is why proper harmonics is useful πρὸς τὴν τοῦ καλοῦ τε καὶ ἀγαθοῦ ζήτησιν (VII.531c6–7) but useless for anything else. See *Phlb.* 64c1–e7 on the relation between ἀγαθόν, καλόν, and μετριότης.

(VII.523a2, VII.524d9), Socrates is already speaking of goodness and beauty since judgments about fitness (or rightness) and sufficiency are incomprehensible except as implicit judgments about goodness. For example, something is fit – or, as we would also say, *well*-suited – to attaining some chosen end.

It is this normative kinship between mathematics and dialectic that has disappeared entirely in Theodorus.[20] This cannot be because he has a merely instrumental view of mathematics. On the contrary, the dialogue emphasizes that Theodorus is a pure theoretician to an almost comical degree. He identifies wholeheartedly with the philosopher of Socrates' "Digression," whose body alone resides in the city while his soul flies out beyond the petty concerns of practical life and "geometricizes the plane" (173e4–6), unsure of whether his own neighbor is a human being or not.[21] What ultimately disqualifies Theodorus from being a dialectician is something else altogether: his marked aversion to engaging in reasoned conversation, in logos. As Socrates gets Glaucon to agree in the *Republic*, those incapable of giving and receiving logos can never be knowers in the strict sense.[22]

In Theodorus, then, mathematical competence has apparently combined with dialectical impotence. How does such a combination come about, and why?[23] Theodorus' breathtaking self-ignorance or self-forgetfulness seems the obvious answer.[24] But this does not take us very far since self-ignorance, too, is said in many ways, each with its distinctive history and inflection. In order to relate mathematics to sophistry, on the one hand, and to dialectic, on the other, we need a phenomenologically faithful account of the unique character of a *mathematician's* self-ignorance.[25]

---

[20] Rendering Theodorus' refusal of Socrates' invitation to investigate knowledge (146b3–4) as "I am not used to this kind of discussion" (Levett) or "to conversation of this sort" (Benardete) is a blamelessly accurate translation. Nevertheless, it hides the fact that, in Greek, Theodorus is literally saying that he is unused to τῆς τοιαύτης διαλέκτου.

[21] See Theodorus' reactions at 173b7–c6, and especially 175a7. Elsewhere, I interpret the systematic importance of Theodorus' reactions to the Digression for assessing the presentation of philosophy in the *Theaetetus* more generally. See German (2017, especially 624–629).

[22] *R.* VII.531e3–4.

[23] *That* it happens – that Theodorus represents a recognizable human type – is something we are all passably familiar with, as Adam remarks in commenting on *R.* VII.531d8. See Adam (1902, 1963, 136).

[24] Friedländer (1969, 161), Stern (2008, 192), Tschemplik (2008, 151).

[25] See Gadamer's observation (1986, 45) that "one will only be able to understand the *Theaetetus* fully once one has properly evaluated the complete paradox in Theaetetus' giving a sensualistic answer to the question: 'What is knowledge?' For Theaetetus is a brilliant mathematician."

9.2

There is a general pattern in Theodorus' behavior up to, and including, his grudging acquiescence in becoming Socrates' main interlocutor at 169c3–7. Just as his student, Theaetetus, seems blind to the incompatibility between the mathematical objects he studies and his definition of knowing as sense perception, Theodorus refuses to note the broader practical implications of Protagoras' doctrine when assessing it, even as Socrates all but clubs him over the head with those implications.

At 161c2ff., Socrates begins his "examination" of Theaetetus' definition by a direct attack on Protagoras, the gist of which is quite straightforward: if each person "alone by himself" opines his own things truly, how can it ever be that Protagoras is wise (σοφός) and worthy of teaching? (161d1–e1). Theodorus responds:

> Socrates, the man is a friend, as you just now said. So I would not consent that Protagoras be refuted through an admission of mine (δι' ἐμοῦ ὁμολο-γοῦντος); nor would I choose to resist you against my opinion (παρὰ δόξαν). (162a4–7)

Now, in a Platonic dialogue, any answer this convoluted is virtually crying out for a minute analysis. Note that there are two different things Theodorus wishes to avoid: refuting Protagoras and getting involved in an argument with Socrates. In both cases, though, the wishes result from the *same* fact: viz., he sees perfectly well where Socrates' argument is headed. If each is the last court of appeal on his own opinions, then no one can be an expert or a teacher of someone else. That Theodorus sees this explains why does not want to "admit" (ὁμολογεῖν) something that he knows will hoist Protagoras by his own petard,[26] and also why he does not want to resist (ἀντιτείνειν) Socrates against his sober judgment that Protagoras is already well and truly hoisted in any case. Interestingly, however, the fact that Protagoras' speeches directly undercut his deeds as a teacher is not enough to fatally undermine the *homo mensura* in Theodorus' eyes (or Theaetetus' either). Nor does he seem to make the connection that if the *homo mensura* makes the teaching of rhetoric impossible, it would have a like effect on geometry since it overthrows all claims to superior expertise. Indeed, even when Socrates directly confronts Theodorus with just this possibility at 169a1–5, inviting him to investigate whether everyone is now

---

[26] It is unfortunate that in an otherwise remarkably insightful study of the 'ironic and comic elements' in *Theaetetus* 161–171, Edward Lee has nothing to say about this passage. See Lee (1973, 225–261).

to be admitted to be as competent in geometry as he is – that is, even when Socrates forcibly places the status of mathematics into question – Theodorus submits to him only with the greatest reluctance.[27]

This obliviousness to the relation between *logos* and *erga*, together with a sense of being entitled to neutrality, manifests itself throughout the dialogue. Most telling for our purposes, though, is the point at which Protagoras' doctrine encounters questions regarding the good, beautiful, just, and so on. Here, just as Theaetetus earlier seemed willing to let the good and beautiful be subject to the flux of genesis (γίγνεσθαι ἀεὶ ἀγαθὸν καὶ καλόν, 157d7–12), so too is Theodorus unconcerned about allowing the chips to fall where they may, at least where the fate of the good or the beautiful is concerned.

At 170a3–171e8, Socrates gets Theodorus to agree that Protagoras' speech leads either into absurdities, when it forces him to deny the possibility of opining falsely (171c9), or straight self-contradiction (the table-turning, or "*peritropē*," argument at 171a–c).[28] Socrates then suggests a revision that might mitigate some of these difficulties. We are less interested in whether this "revised Protagoreanism" actually holds any water than in the distinction that constitutes its nerve: Socrates suggests that perhaps the *homo mensura* ought to apply to (1) perceptual contents (hot, dry, and sweet and "all such things," 171e2–3) and (2) judgments about political things (beauty and ugliness, justice and injustice, holy and unholy, 172a1–2). However, it will not apply (that is, each man or polis will *not* be the measure) for (1) "objective" expertise, such as medicine (171e4), and (2) calculations of benefit or advantage (172a5–6, 177d2–7). In other words, considerations of beauty and justice will be consigned to the same level as sense perceptions – irrefutable, but only because they are inescapably private and doxastic – while the good earns a privileged epistemic status, but only in the guise of advantage.

It should be easy to see that Socrates' revision rests on a supremely dubious move. It assumes that advantage can be cleanly peeled off from justice, beauty, etc., thus allowing utilitarian calculation to proceed unencumbered by criteria of value. Once we assume that, just as every man knows that health is better than sickness, every city knows how to identify

---

[27] See Theodorus' invocation (169c5) of the tragic fate (εἱμαρμένην) that Socrates, like Clōthō the daughter of Necessity, is spinning out for him.

[28] On the senses in which Socrates does indeed "defuse" Protagoras' position, regardless of whether the argument at 171a–c goes through or not, I agree with the chess player analogy in Lee (1973, 247–248).

its own advantage, it becomes mere common sense that some people are better than others in future-oriented calculations of advantage.

But let us do what Theodorus did not do at this point: reflect. Is this separation really so neat? Even when, for example, a man or a city chooses to act exclusively according to utilitarian criteria, they must precisely *choose* so to act. And each can only do so in light of some larger opinion about what is good for that man or that city. But this good derives from a conception, however implicit, of what the good is for human life taken as a whole ("Life and limb before all else," say). To abandon one's allies and look out exclusively for one's own skin, for example, implies a considered judgment that it is good for me to look out only for my own skin and, more than this, that when life and death are on the line, considerations of honor, for example, have no standing. Stated otherwise, pure utilitarian calculus gains the appearance of immunity to flux (and hence the status of a "real" expertise) only so long as we ignore the fact we must *decide* to engage in pure, utilitarian calculus, that we must decide to separate it from all normative criteria. But this separation itself expresses a normative criterion.

At any rate, Theodorus has nothing to say about the possibility that just and holy things have no essential being of their own (172b4–5), and, from a certain, mercenary perspective, he appears to have good grounds for doing so. After all, like the doctor, he is an expert, and expertise has now been lifted clear of the Protagorean-Heraclitean flux. The relation between the square built on the hypotenuse and the sum of the squares built on the other sides of a right triangle will hold just as well no matter what we think about the beautiful or the just. What is remarkable here is the fact that while *Republic* VII insists that geometry is crucial for helping the soul make out the idea of the good more easily (VII.526e2) and that there is a general and complete difference between someone who has been devoted to geometry and someone who has not (VII.527c5–8), these high hopes are utterly unfulfilled in Theodorus. Despite his mastery of these sciences that turn the soul toward the Good, the geometer remains exactly where most people are, with an unexamined opinion that the just and holy are purely conventional. He simply cannot see how any of this relates to him and his intellectual vocation.

We turn now to another, later, passage where Theodorus does not seem at all indifferent but, instead, abandons his Olympian detachment and joins battle with a vengeance: Socrates' final refutation of the Heraclitean doctrine of φερομένη ὀυσία, being in flux (179d3). We shall inspect this passage in detail in a moment, but first we should note Theodorus' open detestation of the "comrades of Heraclitus" who, he says, behave like those driven mad by the sting of a gadfly (179e7), shooting off impenetrable enigmas (180a4) and appearing spontaneously from some unknown source of inspiration, rather than in the proper manner – as pupils of an acknowledged master like his pliable (and certainly not manic) Theaetetus. It is not initially clear why the Heracliteans suddenly come in for such vituperation. Is this simply a case of a professorial *Streit der Fakultäten*? Or does Theodorus see more clearly, in this case, that if *all* things are in motion (τὰ πάντα κινεῖσθαι, 181d9), as the Heracliteans insist, stable unity of any kind becomes incomprehensible and, with it, mathematical sciences, whose intelligibility presupposes the unity and stability of the arithmetic monad?

Whatever the answer to that question, Theodorus does *not* see something else, namely, the significance of the contradiction between the Heracliteans' speeches and their deeds. The Heracliteans, he complains, are simply swept along just like their own writings and are literally incapable of standing still (179e7–180a1). In a wonderfully rich moment, the same Theodorus who disdains mere logoi and shrinks from giving an account of himself now complains of the Heracliteans' refusal to give and receive logoi (180a5, c4–5) since they permit nothing to be stable, whether in their speech or in the soul (180a8–b1). To this Socrates responds:

> Perhaps, Theodorus, you have seen those men fighting, but have not been together with them when they are at peace (εἰρηνεύουσιν), for they are not your comrades. But I suppose they do say such things [i.e., stable things] at their leisure to their students, those whom they want to make like themselves. (180b4–8)

Socrates is pointing directly to a fatal flaw in Heraclitean doctrine: it is impossible to live it coherently. The Heraclitean tries to teach, but by this very act indicates that he does possess "some stable self-conception" to which he wants to liken his student.[29] Similarly, he must assume that his student, too, is a stable *someone*, since only such a being can be addressed, can understand, agree, and decide. Simply put, even the orthodox Heraclitean must speak. But since to speak is to weave together semantic elements that must themselves exhibit some stability in order to convey meaning, the Heraclitean cannot articulate his own doctrine (183b3–4).

Once again, however, an overt contradiction between speech and deed does not, by itself, decide the issue for Theodorus. Instead, he insists that

---

[29] Stern (2008, 193).

he and Socrates must take over the flux doctrine and examine it as if it were a πρόβλημα, a geometrical construction (180c6).[30] For Theodorus, whatever refutation we provide must be *ordine geometrico demonstrata*. A pragmatic refutation, of the kind Socrates has just put on the table, simply does not occur to him. Seth Benardete puts the point well: "He [Theodorus] presents the soul-destroying and logos-destroying character of the [Heraclitean] doctrine and yet does not conclude that this would refute the doctrine. It could still be true of being even if one could not live it on the level of either speech or soul."[31]

Of course, the combination of Heraclitean φερομένη οὐσία and Protagorean *homo mensura* is so radical that it would act like acid on all human activity, practical or theoretical, reducing it to nonsense. Socrates' resurrected Protagoras, for example, indicates in no uncertain terms just how far he is willing to go in defending his position. Unlike Socrates (or Theaetetus) he would not scruple to surrender the temporal unity of consciousness in order to preserve the strictly private, momentary, and irrefutable character of appearance. Protagoras would be willing to countenance an argument that states that the subject to whom something appears at t_1 is simply not the same subject to whom something else appears at t_2. This is the direction in which Protagoras points when asking, at 166b6–c1, whether Socrates really thinks he (Protagoras) would have a problem granting that there is no "he" – that is, no unified, temporally enduring conscious subject – but rather only a series of radically disparate "*hes*" having a radically disparate series of appearances extending to infinity.[32]

Protagoras made no mention of mathematics, but the implications of his doctrine are unmistakable. How could it be possible to understand and make use of number unless the soul itself were in some sense one? As Socrates gets Theaetetus to agree later, it is only the soul itself through itself (αὐτὴ δι' αὑτῆς ἡ ψυχή, 185e1) that could possibly stand in relation to being, nonbeing, similar and dissimilar, same and other, one and the rest of number (ἕν τε καὶ τὸν ἄλλον ἀριθμόν, 185c9–d1). But the soul must be a unity, "some one single look" (μίαν τινὰ ἰδέαν, 184d3), in order for descriptors like "examining by itself" or "through itself" to gain any traction. Theodorus has nothing to say about any of this, either during or after Protagoras' speech. When Socrates concludes his defense of

---

[30] On this "ridiculous suggestion," see Benitez and Guimaraes (1993, 314).
[31] See Benardete (1984, 136).
[32] The Greek reads as follows: ἢ ἐάνπερ τοῦτο δείσῃ, δώσειν ποτὲ τὸν αὐτὸν εἶναι τὸν ἀνομοιούμενον τῷ πρὶν ἀνομοιοῦσθαι ὄντι; **μᾶλλον δὲ τὸν εἶναί τινα ἀλλ' οὐχὶ τούς, καὶ τούτους γιγνομένους** ἀπείρους. Cf. 160b5–8.

Protagoras, with its annihilation of psychic identity, Theodorus merely remarks that it was νεανικῶς, spirited (168c6–7).

9.3

How best, then, to understand the philosophical significance of Theodorus' presence in this dialogue? We have seen in some detail that he has no difficulty following the logic of an argument. What he consistently fails to see, or remark on, is the existential import of these arguments and especially the stake that he might have in any of them. It is this failure that distinguishes his self-ignorance as specifically mathematical. The primary cause of that ignorance, I submit, is not the absence of knowledge but the *presence* of a particular assumption: Theodorus assumes that whatever the results of the argument, and however outrageous they might be, they are still "mere logoi" *when compared with mathematics*, the independence of which continues inviolate. This assumption best explains the neutrality he claims for himself, since it renders him incapable of seeing geometry, and himself qua geometer, as something requiring any explanation or justification.[33]

That Theodorus is the literary incarnation of a more general problem very much on Plato's mind is clear enough if we remember the discussion of mathematicians and geometers in the Divided Line:

> Those who occupy themselves with geometry, calculation and the like set down the odd and the even, the figures, the three forms of angle and other things related to these in each inquiry *as known* (ὑποθέμενοι ... ὡς εἰδότες), making their hypotheses about them, *and do not think it worthwhile to give any further account* of them to themselves or to others *as though they were clear to all* (ὡς παντὶ φανερῶν).[34]

It is clarity and precision that lend the mathematical sciences their overpowering self-evidence and their pedagogic status.[35] But this same quality blinds the mathematically inclined to the question of the source of that clarity and precision. That is, mathematical thought taken by itself does not go "to the beginning" (οὐκ ἐπ' ἀρχὴν ἰοῦσαν, VI.511a5–6), does not

---

[33] As Tschemplik (2008, 145) intimates, Theodorus combines the metaphysics of the Digression's "flying philosopher" with a Protagorean politics but does not see this combination as in any way questionable.

[34] *R.* VI.510c2–d1.

[35] Socrates emphasizes this overpowering quality by his repeated use of the language of compulsion to explain the effect of mathematics on the soul. *R.* VII.526b1–2 (προσαναγκάζον), 525d6, 526e3 (ἀναγκάζει).

feel the need to elucidate the link between mathematical νοητά and the ἀρχή of the noetic realm.[36]

Theodorus displays a variant of precisely this blindness.[37] The universally acknowledged clarity of mathematics nourishes his assumption that mathematics is a kingdom apart from the more encompassing context of reasoning treated by sophists and philosophers, the reasoning expressed in evaluating, judging, choosing, etc. For him these two realms are independent forms of rationality – "mere" logoi versus geometry (165a1–2) – without any common root. As soon as we realize that Plato identifies this common root as the real target of Protagorean sophistry, we are in a position to understand how it could be that sophistry finds an unwitting ally in mathematicians, of all people.

On Socrates' account, the most decisive consequence of Protagoras' collapse of being into appearance is its necessary implication that speech does not register and elucidate the various modes of being (sensible particulars, mathematical entities, justice, beauty, etc.) whose interrelationship constitutes an ordered multiplicity accessible to different observers. That is, the *homo mensura* renders inoperative any sense of a *shared* world, and with it any sense of rationality as a project carried on in a discursive medium. Socrates admits that if Protagoras is right, then σύμπασα ἡ τοῦ διαλέγεσθαι πραγμαετία, the "whole business of conversation" in which appearances and opinions are examined, refined, or refuted by mutual appeal to the *difference* between appearing and being, is "one long and immense piece of nonsense" (161e4–162a1). The *homo mensura*, no doubt, also leads to incredible logical and ontological consequences,[38] but Socrates' focus on the impossibility of διαλέγεθαι points to another difficulty, closer to home. Later in the *Theaetetus*, thinking (τὸ διανοεῖσθαι) is described as:

> A speech (λογόν) which the soul by itself goes through before itself about whatever it is examining ... Soul thinking looks to me as nothing other than conversing (διαλέγεθαι), asking and answering itself, affirming and denying. But whenever it has come to a determination ... and asserts the same thing and does not stand apart in doubt, this we set down as opinion (δόξα). (189e6–190a4)

---

[36] In this, I agree with Boyle (1974, 10). λογόν διδόναι here does not mean giving a definition of the even or the odd, but providing a "causal" explanation of them, explaining their relationship to the "supreme αἰτία."

[37] Cf. *R.* VI.484c6, on the difference between the blind and those who have a pattern in the soul of the being of each thing. My thanks to James Ambury for pointing me to this passage.

[38] As noted by Aristotle, *Metaph.*, Γ, 5, 1010b26–28: "such views [like those of Protagoras] leave nothing to be of necessity, as they leave no *ousia* of anything."

Now, if διαλέγεθαι gains no purchase on the being of things, what becomes of the soul's faculty of judgment, which it can exercise only by means of dialogue (internal or external)? And if judging is reduced to the serial exchange of δόξαι, what then becomes of *choosing*? The full compass of the *homo mensura* problem reveals itself to us only if we do not lose sight of human *pragmata* at this, ostensibly "quotidian," level. A passage in the *Cratylus* confirms this.

After Hermogenes asserts his linguistic conventionalism, which has it that correct use of names is exclusively a product of agreement and lacks all natural basis,[39] Socrates wonders whether the same applies to beings (τὰ ὄντα), namely, whether "the *being* of each of them is a private matter for each person, just as Protagoras used to say."[40] He investigates this possibility, however, by means of an abrupt shift from the ontological question to the difference between decent and worthless (πονηρόν) human beings. Socrates asks if Hermogenes has encountered people of both types and receives an affirmative answer. He then continues:

> And how do you figure that? Or is it in this way: those who are entirely decent (πάνυ χρηστοὺς) are entirely sensible (or reasonable, φρονίμους) while those who are entirely worthless are entirely senseless (πάνυ ἄφρονας)? ... And this too, I imagine, seems completely the case to you, that *if there is "being sensible" and "senseless"* (φρονήσεως οὔσης καὶ ἀφροσύνης), it's completely impossible for Protagoras to speak truly, since presumably one person could be no more sensible than another if whatever seems to each one to be the case is going to be true for each.[41]

Here too, just as in the *Theaetetus*, a specific mode of being – φρονήσεως οὔσης, being sensible (or reasonable) – is invoked as a touchstone for deciding whether Protagoras can do justice to how things stand with *ta onta* more generally. It is a comportment that cannot be reduced to either theory or practice because there is a sense in which it underlies both.[42] The link between φρόνησις and praxis is perhaps more immediately familiar, but we ought to remember that even purely "theoretical" activity emerges from a phronetic context. Our decision to engage in theoretical work emerges from, and is a refinement of, our capacity for being reasonable in the most basic sense: that is, motivated by the distinction between true

---

[39] *Cra.*384c11–d2: οὐ δύναμαι πεισθῆναι ὡς ἄλλη τις ὀρθότης ὀνόματος ἢ συνθήκη καὶ ὁμολογία.
[40] Ibid. 385e5–6: ἰδία αὐτῶν ἡ οὐσία.   [41] Ibid. 186b9–d1.
[42] In Plato, the uses of φρόνησις range rather more loosely than in Aristotle, sometimes referring to practical judgment and sometimes to something of a more theoretical cast. For example, it seems to be close to theoretical knowledge at *R.* X.603b1 or in the passage at *Men.* 97b5–7 that speaks of knowing the road to Larissa φρονοῦντος.

and false and better and worse. This capacity is that "common root" of which I spoke and, for Socrates, the *homo mensura*, when thought down to its foundations cannot but take deadly aim at it. Theodorus, of course, shows little evidence of having thought through Protagoras' teaching at all. But taken at a more superficial level, we can immediately discern its appeal for him and, with it, the "friendship" between mathematician and sophist.

If the encompassing horizon of sensible behavior is ineluctably doxastic and if the opinion of each is based strictly on what appears to each, then Protagoras effectively grants Theodorus what Socrates was unwilling to grant him: a pass on the need to explain and justify himself. And this is a situation congenial to someone who assumes that a justification of mathematics is otiose in any case.[43]

Burnyeat, in treating the "critique" of mathematics in the third stage of the Divided Line, argues that in attributing to mathematics a degree of cognitive clarity that is only intermediate (above opinion about sensibles but below dialectical knowledge of Forms) Socrates is not criticizing mathematics, but rather "*placing* it," in a "larger epistemological and ontological scheme."[44] This is true, except that Theodorus shows that a fully competent mathematician can be completely unaware *that he needs to be placed*, because he is unaware, or has forgotten, that even the purest theoretical discipline shares, with praxis, a common rational whole bound together by the internally complex nature of the Good.[45]

In *Republic* VI, the Good functions as an *archē* in at least two ways. It is the *archē* of the intelligibility, the "being known" (τὸ γιγνώσκεσθαι) of things known (τοῖς γιγνωσκομένοις) (VI.509b5–6) and of the power of knowing. It is also, however, the source, or ultimate referent, of all choice and action; it is "what every soul pursues and that for the sake of which it does everything" (VI.505e1–2). The Good is thus the source both of the special clarity of mathematics (its being knowable) and of the choice-worthiness of knowing it. In this way, it establishes the normative kinship between mathematics and dialectic mentioned earlier. Theodorus is unaware of this double relation since he cannot see how anything outside mathematics could bear on its own nature and subject matter.

---

[43] See Benardete (1984, 116): "Theodorus can live his own life if he is safe from the opinion of others. Protagorean skepticism guarantees his neutrality in philosophy." See also ibid., 125, "the attraction Protagoras had for him consisted in his doctrine that apparently guaranteed his [Theodorus'] right to be left alone."

[44] See Burnyeat (2000, 42).

[45] Perhaps this, or something very like it, is what Leo Strauss refers to (1959, 40) as "the charm of competence, which is engendered by mathematics and everything akin to mathematics."

Now, being unaware of this does not interfere at all with the ability to grasp and manipulate mathematical or geometrical forms. It will not interfere with Theodorus' ability to "do" mathematics. But it will make it impossible for him to understand fully what he does when doing mathematics; that is, how mathematics is an expression of rationality more broadly (and correctly) understood. This latter understanding requires that mathematical intelligence "know itself" by coming to realize that the mode of being peculiar to μαθήματα is not self-explanatory. It is constituted by the activity of a principle that transcends those μαθήματα.[46] It is a form of self-knowledge, then, that transmutes mathematical sciences into dialectic.[47]

Let me try to state that last point more fully. Mathematical science that knows itself would subordinate *itself* to dialectic in a manner analogous to the relation, in Aristotle, between physics as the study of sensible beings in motion and πρωτή φιλοσοφία as the study of separate, motionless being. As the study of τὰ πρῶτα καὶ τὰς ἀρχὰς τὰς πρώτας among natural beings, physics is the highest theoretical knowledge of nature (περὶ φύσεως ἐπιστήμης).[48] As Aristotle tells us explicitly, "*If* there were no other kind of *ousia* besides composite natural ones, then physics would be πρώτη ἐπιστήμη"; that is, it would be πρωτή φιλοσοφία. "But if there is some motionless *ousia*, the knowledge of *it* would be first and would be first philosophy."[49] And this is exactly what transpires. The investigation into physical phenomena, by its own internal dynamism, leads to the necessity of positing separable *ousia* (because of the problem of the eternity of motion) and so physics of its own accord, as it were, cedes pride of place to metaphysics.[50]

Stated in the terms of our case, if Theodorus had truly known what he is *qua mathematician*, he would not need Socrates to drag him by the ear onto the wrestling mat of logos. He would already share Socrates' "terrible love" (ἔρως δεινός) for the activity of logos because he would recognize in that activity the completion of his own activity – certainly as a mathematician, but also as a human being (169a6–c3).

---

[46] This, I take it, is Burnyeat's meaning (2000, 77) in saying that only "in light of the Good" does one understand what mathematics really is.

[47] On dialectic as a form of self-knowledge, see Baracchi (2004, 33), Gadamer (1986, 42–43), and Gonzalez (1995, 160–161).

[48] Arist. *Ph.* 1, I, 184a10–15.   [49] Arist. *Metaph.* E, 1, 1026a27–30.

[50] See *Euthyd.* 290b7–c6 on how geometers, at least those who are not totally devoid of *nous*, must hand over their μαθήματα to the dialecticians who know how to "use" them. On the "use" of knowledge, see Brian Marrin's Chapter 6 in this book.

9.4

But how does this recognition occur? How can mathematical intelligence know itself in such a way as to carry it beyond mathematics? In the *Republic* and *Theaetetus*, Plato gives us two different accounts, with the latter perhaps serving as a corrective to the former.

Republic VII describes a smooth ascent powered by the relation of mathematics to its proper objects. By purging the accumulated dead weight of our sensuous and passional entanglement in the flux of genesis (VII.519a7–b3), the "mathematical arts . . . have this power to release and lead what is best in the soul up to contemplation of what is best in the things that are" (VII.532c4–7).[51] The ability to grasp synoptically the relation between all parts of the noetic realm and the "best" among them is the "species difference" of the ἀνήρ διαλεκτικός: "For the man who is capable of an overview is dialectical, while the one who isn't is not" (VII.537c6–7).[52] Mathematical training in the appreciation of concord and attunement is described as a preparation for a synoptic view of kinship, ultimately visible only in light of the Good, because it itself is an intimation of that kinship.[53]

While Socrates does not hide the magnitude of the task or the fact that many might fail at it, these caveats remain largely in the background of *Republic* VII. The general tenor is "optimistic," perhaps in keeping with the overarching aim of convincing Glaucon and Adeimantus that a city governed by "wholly beautiful" (παγκάλους, VII.540c3), mathematically refined dialecticians is difficult but not impossible.[54]

The *Theaetetus* presents a different, more sobering, aspect. As regards Theodorus, it really seems that precious little ground is won and held. He takes his leave as eager to be rid of λογόν διδόναι as he was reluctant to engage in it at the outset (183c4–5). Socrates is more sanguine about the younger Theaetetus, but he, too, never acquires a definition of knowledge. At most, he learns the moderation that comes with knowing that one does not know (210c3–4).

The two dialogues, I suggest, are two different reflections on one problem: how to understand together what sophists like Protagoras put asunder – the interrelation of truth and goodness or, in contemporary

---

[51] *R.* VII.532c4–7: τοῦ βελτίστου ἐν ψυχῇ πρὸς τὴν τοῦ ἀρίστου ἐν τοῖς οὖσι θέαν.
[52] See Burnyeat (2000, 67).   [53] *R.* VII.531c9–d3.
[54] *R.* VII.540d1–3. On the 'optimism' of this account, see Burnyeat (2000, 64–65).

terms, rationality and value.[55] The *Republic* presents a program for full self-knowledge achieved through knowledge of the intelligible grounds of being.[56] The *Theaetetus* reveals the potential wrench in the works; viz., the self-same "assistants" to dialectic may obstruct the path to dialectic. The luminous clarity and precision of mathematical knowledge can "lead the soul upward" but can, by virtue of this same characteristic, also lead the soul *away* from the inextricability of true and good, which is the root of our desire to know in the first place.

This would explain why, although the *Theaetetus* is a dialogue with a geometer and his young student who naturally identifies mathematics as knowledge (146c7–d3), we get no analysis of the intelligible structure common to all mathematical sciences. Instead, it focuses on a different kind of apprenticeship. Theaetetus is being trained to do what Socrates, unlike Theodorus, is keen to do: use praxis as one measure of theoretical logoi, so that even an implacably coherent doctrine must answer to our ability to actually live it. Praxis certainly lacks the clarity and distinctness of mathematics. But what it lacks in these it makes up for in salutary proximity to those experiences of distinguishing better and worse that are the medium in which deliberate choice occurs. Theodorus' turn from mere logoi to geometry, like every other choice, implies reasons, namely, reasons why that choice seemed decisively better.[57] And we human beings choose hoping that what seemed to us to be so really *is* so.[58]

Sensible behavior, then, perpetually rotates around the same axis – the inextricability of true and good. And in seeking a logos of the being of each thing *and* of the Good, dialectical science aims to reveal the intelligible horizon in which this sensible behavior "makes sense."[59]

---

[55] See Stern (2008, 125).   [56] See Lloyd Gerson's Chapter 1 in this book.

[57] Therefore, Glaucon said more than he knew at VII.522e1–4 in asserting that one must study λογίζεσθαί τε καὶ ἀριθμεῖν if one is going to be a human being (εἰ καὶ ἄνθρωπος ἔσεσθαι).

[58] Now, what if someone were to object that Theodorus did not become a geometer for *any* discernible reasons? After all, he doesn't mention any. The best he can manage is to say that he turned to geometry "somehow" (πως), and for all we can ferret out of the text, it might simply have been an unreflective "inclination." But this is neither here nor there. Inclinations are expressions of preference – here, a preference for clarity and precision – and hence implicit rank orderings. The implicit becomes explicit the moment we are forced to reflect on an inclination by the fact that it conflicts with another inclination and we must choose between them. On this point, then, I agree with Benardete (1984, 123): Theodorus refuses to come to grips with the πως in his autobiographical statement.

[59] Vegetti (2013, 213): dialectic is able to "understand both the conditions of truth of sciences and the reason why they are valuable in themselves and desirable for mankind."

The two activities are isomorphic, but in the *Theaetetus*, mathematical intelligence needs to be *made* aware of its links with both of them, which means that the coexistence of *l'esprit géométrique* and *l'esprit de finesse* is a live problem for Plato's pedagogic vision. But it is one of which he was quite well aware. The *Parmenides* is hardly Plato's only exercise in self-critical probity.

CHAPTER 10

Why Is Knowledge of Ignorance Good?*

Marina McCoy

In Plato's *Apology*, Socrates claims for himself a uniquely human wisdom, the wisdom of knowing that he does not know (*Ap.* 21d). As interpreters, we often take for granted that knowing that one does not know is good. However, the reasons why such knowledge of ignorance might be good are numerous. Is it good to know of one's ignorance because it allows for the possibility of future knowledge? Is it good because knowing one's ignorance is an epistemically accurate state and therefore inherently better? Does it help one to avoid hubris? Does it help the individual to live more virtuously? This chapter examines the evidence for and against various alternatives, with focus on textual evidence from Plato's *Apology* and *Meno*. Each of the above positions has merit, but I argue that Socrates' main reasons for advocating knowledge of one's own ignorance are two-fold. (1) Knowledge of one's own ignorance is an epistemic virtue that allows one to progress in inquiry. The experience of *aporia* allows interlocutors such as Meno to recognize what they do not know, and so to be open to what else they can learn. However, without the existential and proper affective sense of oneself as limited as a result of this *aporia*, there may not be any progress in virtue. (2) In the *Apology*, Socrates shows that the possession of "human wisdom" is a practical wisdom that allows one to act more virtuously in concrete circumstances. "Human wisdom" is more than knowing that one lacks some specific propositional content. It also includes an existential and affectively appropriate understanding of oneself and others as limited. Socrates reacts to ignorance with a response of care. Such self-knowledge enables one to respond more virtuously to one's own emotions and to others. Socrates demonstrates this kind of human wisdom in the *Apology*.

* Thanks to Anne Marie Schultz and Nicholas Smith for helpful comments on earlier drafts.

169

10.1

In the *Meno*, knowing one's own ignorance is presented as an epistemic good. Meno is able to progress to offering a universal and philosophical definition of virtue only when he recognizes that the kind of answer he initially offers is lacking. Only in recognizing the shortcoming of one's views can they be replaced by better, truer views. However, for Meno, these particular experiences of his epistemic shortcomings are still insufficient to produce moral virtue. Meno experiences *aporia* but does not come to a deeper sense of his own or others' limits in a way that allows him to live virtuously. As I will argue, Meno's failure to recognize a particular limit intellectually does not move him to a further existential insight into himself as lacking or imperfect. Meno recognizes some of his epistemic limits but does not grow in self-knowledge in this more personal and lived sense. Thus we can see that simply recognizing that one does not know what one thinks one knows about a particular intellectual matter is insufficient for the full possession of self-knowledge.

The *Meno* opens with Socrates praising Meno for having learned from Gorgias how to answer nearly any question as if he were an expert (70b–c). Socrates contrasts this Thessalian wisdom with the relative lack of wisdom in Athens (70c–71a). Socrates says that he, like all other Athenians, if asked whether excellence (ἀρετή) can be taught or not, will only laugh and say that he does not know, and does not even know what virtue is (71a).[1] While Plato's reader may suspect that Socrates' description of Athenian humility may not be realistic, it allows Socrates to deny that he knows what excellence is, and invites Meno to explore his own possession of wisdom or its lack. Meno's response is to wonder whether Socrates really does not know what excellence is, and whether he would want such a reputation for not knowing to be circulated abroad (71b). Here, Meno displays concern with honor and being believed to be a person who knows. He also seems genuinely to think that his teacher, Gorgias, does know what excellence is, and is surprised that Socrates does not also think so (71c).[2]

Plato's reader is presented with two contrasting views of excellence and the ease or difficulty with which it can be known, and with two characters

---

[1] Here I translate ἀρετή as "excellence" rather than "virtue" in part because the dialogue begins without even a shared agreement as to whether it is moral concept or not.

[2] For a thorough analysis of Meno's character, see Gordon (1999, 199). For Meno's concern with honor, see ibid. (97–98).

who embody different states of self-knowledge: one who denies knowing and another who expresses surprise even at the possibility of not knowing. Plato's reader is implicitly invited to consider her own view of whether excellence is easily and widely known and to consider her own self-knowledge with respect to whether she is the sort of person who claims to know it or not. The reader is invited to consider whether she lives in a world more like the purportedly wise Thessalia or the relatively unwise Athens.

Meno's first reply to Socrates is a mere "swarm" of ideas (72a–b), lacking unity and universality of a singular form (εἶδος). Meno's description of excellence simply lists a variety of actions appropriate to different stations in the current social-political context of ancient Greek cities. It is essentially conservative in that Meno takes for granted the goodness and appropriateness of the various roles conventionally assigned to men, women, slaves, elderly people, and so on. Men are to rule in the realm of public affairs, women are to run the household well and to obey their husbands, for example (71e).

With some difficulty, Socrates leads Meno to offer a different kind of answer, a singular account of excellence: "What else than to be able to rule over human beings?" (73c). In some ways this definition still fails to be completely universal, for it picks out only one part of the many roles listed in the initial swarm of ideas: the conventional excellence of young, free men. However, at least Socrates has been given a singular concept of excellence that is the same for all in its meaning, and it reveals Meno's view that the sort of excellence that he desires is to rule rather than to be ruled. This move from the "swarm" to a unified account of excellence requires that Meno experience doubt about whether he understands what Socrates was after in asking for a singular *eidos*.

When pressed to give an answer that has one and the same *eidos*, Meno says, "It seems to me that I understand (δοκῶ γέ μοι μανθάνειν), but I indeed do not yet have hold (κατέχω) of the question as I want to" (72d1–2). Meno's word choice here of κατέχω (to grasp) already points to the significance of self-knowledge in his process of coming to give a better kind of an answer to Socrates' question: he says that it *seems* to him that he knows, but he also does not have a firm "hold" on the problem. That is, Meno recognizes that he understands only partially the meaning of Socrates' question, and he admits this lack of full understanding while expressing a desire to have a better hold on it. He uses a metaphor of having partial physical grasp on something not yet fully under one's control in order to express this sense of partial intellectual understanding. Socrates then goes on to explain to Meno more about what he is after, by comparing virtue with a concept such as health and strength, which might not be common to all but has the same "form" for all instances. Meno's answer that virtue is the capacity to rule over others still emerges from a conventional view of male achievement, but Socrates is able to move him away from the initial manner in which he answered the question. Meno learns how to give a more unified explanation of the form that excellence takes, rather than simply listing a series of virtuous actions.

In this passage, we see a person who recognizes what he does not know, asks for assistance, and progresses a bit toward knowledge. Of course, this does not mean that Meno knows what excellence is. In fact, given the movement of the remainder of the dialogue toward an exploration of the centrality of justice, moderation, and other moral qualities as central to excellence, Meno's definition is quite insufficient. At this juncture, he improves only with respect to the *kind* of answer that he is willing to offer. But this forward movement is real and demonstrates the value of self-knowledge for philosophical progress. Meno recognizes his own epistemic limit and so progresses in his answers. Here, knowing one's ignorance does not mean simply the total absence of knowledge. Meno has a partial grasp of what Socrates is saying. Ironically, Meno shows that one *can* "know what one does not yet know," thus contradicting the paradox that he will later offer (80d5–9), provided we understand such knowing not to mean already being in a state of secure knowledge about the totality of one's subject matter – ἐπιστήμη in its strictest sense – but rather a partial understanding of a complex totality. Meno's statement that he does "not yet have hold of" the answer provides a phenomenologically compelling way of describing his recognition of ignorance. He has a sense of *something* making sense about Socrates' request for a common form – the question is not complete gibberish to him – and yet he cannot quite see exactly what the right kind of answer would look like. Plato does not treat all knowledge as binary, that is, as either total and present or completely absent, but rather as progressive. One can grasp part of what one seeks, without comprehending all of it.

Later definitions of excellence exhibit this same partiality of grasp. For example, Meno's understanding of excellence as "desiring beautiful things (τῶν καλῶν) and having the capacity to acquire them" (77b2–5) is shown to be problematic because some people seek bad things, or only apparent goods like wealth, honor, and social position, sometimes through unjust means (78c–79a). Meno also misses the connection of excellence to justice and other moral qualities. However, his broader intuition that excellence is a desire for what is καλόν gets something right.[3] Socrates later claims that excellence is wisdom (89a3–4), but this definition is compatible with "desiring beautiful things," if one understands philosophical wisdom as precisely such a kind of a desire. After all, Plato's *Symposium* presents love as desiring the beautiful and the good (*Smp.* 201a, 201c, 204b). There, Socrates emphasizes the human as "in between" knowledge and ignorance. While we cannot assume that Socrates in the *Meno* holds exactly the position that he holds in the *Symposium*, the point is that the view of excellence as "desiring beautiful things" is not necessarily mistaken. The problem is with which goods Meno takes to be the best and most beautiful, and whether human beings have only partial or complete access to these highest goods. Meno has a grasp of human excellence while not grasping it fully.

Meno makes progress in his conversation with Socrates, more than once.[4] However, Socrates is not successful with Meno, if by success we mean that Meno learned enough about excellence to go on to live his life virtuously. The dialogue's drama alludes to events from near the end of Meno's life, when he commits injustice for the sake of personal gain. According to Xenophon, Meno was motivated by an excessive desire for wealth and honor, and desired friends with power so that he could commit injustices without penalty in the course of pursuing these ends (*Anabasis* 2.6.21). Xenophon portrays Meno as deceptive, incapable of genuine friendship, and prone to deception and the mockery of friends (*Anabasis* 2.6. 25–26). Meno took Thessalian troops to assist Cyrus in the overthrow of his older brother, King Artaxerxes of Persia, but deceived his troops as to the true purpose of their mission until they reached the bank of the Euphrates, and they were considerably angry with him. When Cyrus died in battle, the Greek troops allied themselves with the Persian Ariaeus, Meno's host, under the leadership of Clearchus. Meno, along with Tissapherenes – a friend of Ariaeus – plotted to overthrow Clearchus and betray the Greek troops. While most of the men were beheaded, Xenophon says that Meno was tortured for a year before being put to death (*Anabasis* 2.6.29). Xenophon presents Meno as a man willing to betray his own troops and to pursue his own self-interest without concern either for justice or for friendship to the Greek troops whom he initially

---

[3] Τὸ καλόν is not easily translatable into English, and means both beautiful and fine. Meno does not separate the conventionally noble and the objectively beautiful, but the definition expresses the idea that excellence means wanting what is best.

[4] Gordon (1999, 98–99) takes Meno to dodge Socrates' attempts to draw him into dialectic, while I see the root of his problem as his avoidance of a deeper sense of self-doubt.

commanded, and so as suffering the consequences. Even if Xenophon's account in the *Anabasis* is biased, he insists that the facts are well known to all (*Anabasis* 2.6.28). Moreover, as Klein has argued, the Platonic text itself makes allusion to these historical events, although they are dramatically later than the conversation of the dialogue. At one point in their discussion, Socrates says, "Well then, to acquire gold and silver is excellence, says Meno, the ancestral guest friend of the great king" (78d). Here Plato alludes to both Meno's greed and his relationship to the foreign king, suggesting that Plato shares at least some of Xenophon's view of Meno.[5]

The question, then, is why Meno's capacity to know of his own ignorance in the course of conversation with Socrates does not result in any kind of moral conversion. Instead of looking more deeply into himself, he describes Socrates as being akin to a torpedo fish who numbs him in both soul and tongue (80a5–6). Meno says, "Socrates, I used to hear before I met you that you are always in doubt (ἀπορεῖς) yourself and make others doubt (ἀπορεῖν), but now it seems to me that you are bewitching and drugging me with potions and really subduing me with incantations, so that I have become wholly aporetic (μεστὸν ἀπορίας)" (79e–80a). Rather than attributing the cause of this deficiency to himself, Meno attributes the problem to Socrates. Socrates replies that he is only like a torpedo fish if he himself is numb as he numbs others, and he reasserts his claim not to know what excellence is (80c3ff.). Meno, however, does not believe this disavowal. Turning away from that possibility, he poses the well-known paradox.

10.2

If knowing of one's own ignorance as an epistemic state is not sufficient for self-knowledge, then what else might be necessary? I suggest that Plato's *Apology* provides a rich understanding of self-knowledge through the portrayal of Socrates' "human wisdom." In the *Apology*, Socrates seeks to defend not only himself against the charges that his practice is impious and corrupts the youth, but also the very practice of philosophy. Far more of his speech is spent defending his own practice of questioning others and the meaning of this practice than, for example, discussing whether he attended Greek religious festivals or not. Socrates argues that his questioning of others is good and does not corrupt them. Part of his defense consists in asserting both a similarity and dissimilarity between himself

---

[5] For Plutarch and Cornelius Nepos as sources, see Klein (1989, 44).

and his interlocutors. Socrates questions others because they are ignorant regarding many matters, and in this regard, they and he are alike. He, like the politicians, poets, and craftsmen, lacks knowledge of many moral and political matters (21d3–4). However, Socrates alone possesses a self-awareness of his own ignorance, while others falsely claim to know beyond the true scope of their own knowledge. This dissimilarity makes Socrates better than those he questions and is part of his justification for why he continues to question others. Yet this higher status with respect to self-knowledge does not necessarily indicate a higher status with respect to "being human." As I will argue, Socrates is also careful to emphasize a kind of democratic, universal aspect of ignorance as part of the human condition. His discourse thus moves between claims of radical equality of human persons, who all do "not know," and special status for those who possess self-knowledge about such ignorance. The question is why Socrates thinks this form of self-knowledge is worthy and beneficial.

Socrates denies his own knowledge throughout *Apology*. The opening lines begin with the claim that he does not know (οὐκ οἶδα) how his accusers have affected the jury, before reporting with irony his own state of being carried away by the opposition's rhetoric (17a1–4). He denies Aristophanes' portrayal of him (*Clouds* 19b–c) as possessing knowledge (ἐπιστήμη) of "things under the earth and in the heavens."[6] He denies being an expert in human excellence, like the sophists who take a fee and purport to teach young men to excel (20c1–3). In quick sequence, Socrates states that he lacks knowledge of rhetoric, natural science, and the capacity to teach moral and political excellence, precisely the sorts of knowledge that the sophists might claim to possess.[7] He then contrasts his own wisdom to the knowledge of others who claim a more than human wisdom:

> I, men of Athens, have acquired this name through nothing other than a certain kind of wisdom. What kind of wisdom? That which is perhaps a human wisdom (ἀνθρωπίνη σοφία). I venture that I am wise with this wisdom. (20d6–8)

While others may claim a more-than-human wisdom, Socrates locates himself within the conceptual space of being "only human." This claim is contextualized within the contrast between his own practice and that of

---

[6] All translations of the Greek are my own, based on the Greek text in Duke et al. (1995).

[7] For further argument on the relationship between philosophy and sophistry, see McCoy (2008, 23–55). See also McPherran (1996, 86–90) for evidence of the popular perception of a link between impiety and sophistry.

the sophists: rather than carefully parsing different ways one can know, or offering epistemological classifications, Socrates focuses on praxis. Others might practice rhetoric, claim to teach political and moral excellence, or investigate natural phenomena, but if he knows anything, he has wisdom that helps him deal with human matters. His statement is also existential – he takes himself out of the more specific identities of being a talented courtroom speaker, expert teacher, or gifted scientist and asserts instead that he is only human. He thus begins a movement in his speech away from professional practices and identities into an exploration of what it means to be a human being, and how the philosophical activities in which he engages are intended to enhance his own and others' humanity.

Socrates presents the nature of human wisdom as a kind of a puzzle by introducing Chaerephon's reported visit to the oracle at Delphi to ask whether anyone was wiser than Socrates. The oracle's reply is that "no one is wiser" (21a). Before analyzing how Socrates interprets this reply, it is worth noting what the oracle says and does not say. First, the Pythia did not say that Socrates is uniquely wise or possesses more wisdom than others. She merely replied that no one is wiser. In theory, this could mean everyone else is equally unwise. Second, the oracle's reply does not even mention Socrates. Read apart from Chaerephon's initial question, her statement is only: "no one is wiser (μηδένα σοφώτερον εἶναι)" (21a). The oracle's statement thus also potentially invites an even more universal interpretation: with respect to human beings, no one is wiser (i.e., than anyone else).

In keeping with Greek practices that understood the oracle as in need of interpretation, Socrates compares his self-understanding with the content of the oracle's proclamation.[8] His hermeneutic is to assess the meaning of the oracle's statement according to how it may be harmonized with his own assessment about his actual state of knowing. While he never doubts the veracity of the oracle, his initial state is one of puzzlement, as he attempts to reconcile Chaerephon's interpretation – that Socrates is especially wise – with his own self-understanding. This moment of *aporia* is significant, for it not only precedes Socrates' eventual solution to the puzzle but also already exhibits precisely the sort of human wisdom that he will claim for himself. Socrates is comfortable questioning the veracity of what he thinks he already knows about himself: he is willing to doubt whether his self-knowledge is

---

[8] Not all authors see Socrates' aim in refuting the oracle as interpretive. For example, Taylor (1932, 160–161) takes Socrates' mention of the oracle to be purely humorous. Others see the oracle as a directive to pursue the mission of philosophy, for example, Friedländer (1964, 162) and Grote (1888, 284–287). Carvalho (2014, 41–47) understands Socrates to be cross-examining the oracle and reinterpreting its meaning in order to salvage his own view that he is not wise.

really accurate. At the same time, he also does take seriously what he so far believes about himself – that he is not really wise at all – in order to interpret the oracle's meaning, in the absence of any other measure. He thus takes a middle position between relying on his own current self-knowledge as the basis for unraveling the riddle and exploring the possibility that *how* he understands himself and his own state is not yet adequate. In other words, Socrates takes a middle way between assuming the adequacy of his self-understanding and total skepticism about it.

Socrates says that his long-term practice of questioning others is a means to discover whether the oracle could be refuted (21b–c).[9] He begins by going to others with a public reputation for wisdom. While Socrates claims at the outset that his initial reason for questioning others was only to discover whether the oracle was correct, he quickly extends his own mission to include improving others' knowledge of themselves. He remarks that he tries to *show* others that although they think themselves to be wise, they are not (21c). He concludes from these experiences: "I am wiser than this human being, for while neither of us knows what is beautiful and good (καλόν κάγαθόν), he believes that he knows something while not knowing it, while I, just as I don't know, don't believe that I know. I seem then in this little matter to be wiser, in that what I do not know, I do not think that I know" (21d3–8).

Of course, Socrates' additional practice of demonstrating to others their own ignorance is hardly necessary in order to understand the truth of the oracle's words with respect to himself. Socrates might well have discovered the ignorance of others and humbly and quietly walked away with a better sense of his own wisdom, without showing others their own limits and angering them. Socrates' sense of others is more than a sense that they are epistemically or morally limited. He also wants to care for their souls through his questioning. This suggests that Socrates' wisdom is not restricted to knowing himself and includes care for others grounded in understanding the human person.

Moreover, talking about how his interlocutors have reacted to questioning demonstrates to Socrates' current audience, the jurors, some of the moral implications of self-knowledge. Most people whom Socrates questions become defensive when they recognize their ignorance. Socrates says that they react by hating him rather than attending to their own state

---

[9] Perhaps Socrates questioned others in some way before Chaerephon went to the oracle, but minimally Socrates tells us that the long-term *meaning* he gives to his philosophical questioning arose from his exploration of the oracle's meaning.

(21e1). The bystanders who witness this process similarly come to dislike Socrates, perhaps because they have some stake in maintaining the honor of others or fear being questioned themselves. For the purposes of his defense, telling this story explains the anger leveled at Socrates that, he thinks, led to his trial. For the deeper purposes of his defense of philosophy, Socrates provides a further lesson here for the jurors: believing that one knows when one does not know has consequences for our affective and moral lives. An inability to admit one's own shortcomings often leads to falsely directed anger and hatred (Socrates uses the verb ἀπέχθομαι, to incur hatred, at 21d1). That is, not knowing ourselves well can also lead to not caring for others well.

Socrates, in contrast, is not especially reactive in the face of either praise or blame. Both when Chaerephon praises him as the wisest of all human beings and when his fellow citizens express anger, Socrates stays focused on actively seeking the truth about himself rather than relying on others' honor or dishonor as the primary source of his own self-knowledge. Socrates reports to the jury that when he first realized how unpopular he was becoming, he felt "grieved and afraid (λυπούμενος καὶ δεδιὼς)" (21e2).[10] Nevertheless, his commitment to discovering the truth of the oracle remains unwavering. Later, he will compare his steadfastness to that of Achilles in his decision to remain at his post rather than flee the danger of death (28b–e). His steadfastness stems not from a lack of a strong affective response to being disliked but rather from his chosen reaction to grief and fear. While his own lack of good reputation among those whom he questioned was "difficult and heavy" (23a1–2), Socrates bears the burden without lashing out. He maintains that his goal throughout the process of questioning others was both to understand himself better and to help others to grow in their own self-understanding. He seems to recognize his practical limits as a teacher. He is not in full command of a precise method by which he can unfailingly improve all those whom he questions. Rather, he openly acknowledges the difficulty and sorrow that he has felt because of being disliked and misunderstood. However, these initial emotions are only a first response, and he willingly takes the longer path of exploring more fully whether he is worthy of Chaerephon's praise or the politicians' blame.

Both Socrates and those whom he questions lack honor in the eyes of others. Both lack knowledge of the good and beautiful. However, if we

---

[10] As Schultz (2015, 132–134) argues, Socrates' narration shows that he is keenly aware of his own and others' emotional responses throughout the trial.

trace out their long-term responses, we see some distinct differences. The politicians, poets, and craftsmen react with anger and contempt for Socrates. Their anger is directed outward toward the perceived source of pain, as a means of release from pain (23c8–d2). Socrates compares himself to a gadfly who is swatted for the irritation that he causes, despite his potential value in awakening others to virtue (30e–31a).[11] His interlocutors, however, generally do not stand back and assess whether the honor they have previously received is now no longer proper to their own actual reality. They refuse to attend to the gap between received honor and whether it is deserved. Perhaps even more importantly, they do not understand that the source of this pain stems from a lack of fit between what they claim to know and what they actually know about themselves.

Part of the process of arriving at greater self-knowledge includes recognizing that things that one thought one knew about oneself may not be true. It is not simply the case that any given politician, once questioned, does not know as much as he claims to know about a particular *topic* such as courage. It is also the case that the politician once considered himself the *sort of person* who was wise about courage but now must doubt that self-assessment. In other words, Socrates' questions do not simply lead others to doubt the veracity of their truth claims about particular matters, such as the relationship between courage and knowledge. His questions lead others to recognize a fundamental problem in second-order judgments made about *themselves* – that they are wise, courageous, or just people. Socrates' interlocutors ought to be willing to reconsider their own judgments about themselves and to replace their false views of themselves with a more accurate self-assessment. However, they refuse to do so because of the emotional responses that tend to accompany such self-doubt. Instead, they turn their discomfort with themselves against Socrates: "those being examined are angry at me, not themselves" (23c8–d1).

If we recall Socrates' own prior description of puzzlement at the oracle's declaration that "no one is wiser," we see an alternative response. Socrates also experiences a gap between his sense of himself and what others say: here, what the oracle says (that he is wise) and his sense that he is not wise. He feels puzzled and confused, but his response is not to reject the external assessment immediately nor to accept it at face value. Rather, he spends time in *aporia*, allowing himself to stay with his sense of puzzlement, and he then explores through interactions with others whether the judgment is

---

[11] Naas (2015, 43–59) notes the peculiarity of this self-reference insofar as a gadfly not only awakens but also mindlessly disturbs, annoys, and goads.

correct. And, in fact, Socrates' self-assessment shifts significantly after exploration. Rather than simply believing that he lacks wisdom, he discovers that the knowledge of his own ignorance is a worthwhile and noble aspect of being human. Socrates learns from the tension between Chaerephon's praise and his own sense of lack. He discovers a duality in himself as, on the one hand, merely human in his lack of knowledge about the good and the beautiful, and, on the other hand, possessing a human wisdom in knowing of such ignorance, in recognizing that this human state has its own kind of value and beauty. His wisdom includes not only knowing that he does not know about some particular factual matter, but also his sense of care for himself and for what is human – the proper affective response to his own human state.

Socrates also provides Plato's reader with a different model for a possible emotional response to the experience of losing honor with those about whom one cares.[12] When Socrates experiences difficulty and pain at being rejected by the politicians, he does not immediately react to their displaced anger but is patient and compassionate in understanding it as a common human response. Perhaps for this reason, Socrates is often shown in the dialogues continuing to question and so to care for the souls of others, such as Alcibiades, Meno, Callicles, or Thrasymachus, who are complicated in their emotional reactions to his questioning.

In contrast to many of his interlocutors, Socrates reacts to his emotional experiences of grief, difficulty, and burden that result from others' judgments by reminding himself of his own limits. He does not attempt to bolster his own honor or direct anger back at those who are angry with him. Rather, he places himself on level ground with all other human beings. Immediately after he describes his emotional response to slander and unpopularity, he explains: "Men, it is likely that the god really is wise and through his oracle says this, that human wisdom is of little value or none at all. And he seems to say 'this man Socrates,' using my name, making me a paradigm, as if he were to say, 'This one of you, oh human beings, is wisest who like Socrates recognizes that he is in truth of no worth regarding wisdom'" (*Ap.* 23a5–b4). Socrates rejects Chaerephon's interpretation that the oracle was offering special praise of Socrates and instead interprets the oracle to be making a general proclamation about the

---

[12] I am indebted to Anne Marie Schultz's extensive work on emotional regulation in the character of Socrates and on how his narration functions to allow us as readers to gain insight into Socrates' state of mind and motivations. Her work on the connections between philosophy as practice and emotional self-regulation offers new insights into Socrates. See Schultz (2013 and 2015).

relative lack of value of human wisdom. Socrates seems to experience a kind of compassion for those who criticize him, in that he understands their lack of self-knowledge, and hateful and angry reactions, as an instance of a more universal lack of wisdom and as a common human reaction to *aporia*.

Thus, we see that Socrates describes the genesis of knowing his own ignorance as good both because it is a realistic existential understanding of what it means to be human and because it is a practical virtue that allows a person to respond differently to others and their limits than he would without such self-knowledge. Although knowing his own ignorance is first described as an epistemic state, Socrates' emphasis in the *Apology* is largely on its moral and political value. Socrates' claim to wisdom is not only a claim about knowledge of propositions. It also includes the larger set of affective responses to such ignorance that form part of his moral virtue.

10.3

What sort of wisdom, exactly, does Socrates claim in the *Apology*? One possibility would be to say that Socrates has the correct cognitive content about his own epistemic state of ignorance and that this knowledge alone has a practical value. However, as the case of Meno shows, this is not necessarily the case. One can understand correctly one's epistemic state as ignorant and one still may not have a sense of its practical or moral value, or live differently. A second possibility would be to say that Socrates knows that he does not know and also (separately) has some good emotional skills that allow him to make good use of that epistemic state. However, I think a third possibility better fits the textual evidence: Socrates' wisdom is a *practical wisdom* in which knowing how to act well includes both epistemic and affective aspects. Meno is perfectly willing to accept that he lacks some propositional knowledge. He has an emotional response to it, in describing his own *aporia* as feeling "numbed." However, he never reaches a state of *care* for himself or others as ignorant. Both the correct cognitive recognition of his and others' ignorance and the appropriate affective response toward that ignorance (care) *constitute* Socrates' state of human wisdom. Such wisdom is part of self-knowledge and allows him to live in a better way with other human beings.[13]

---

[13] Of course, the Platonic view of wisdom as a virtue is developed much further in other dialogues. Socrates must not only know that he and others are ignorant and that they need a care of the soul but must also develop a kind of "knowing how" that extends beyond these aspects of human wisdom as presented in the *Apology*. Thanks to Nick Smith for pointing out this aspect of the problem to me.

These differences in self-knowledge and response to one's emotions also result in different moral judgments and political actions undertaken by Socrates and the politicians. The politicians who are angry with Socrates bring him to trial. Meletus and Anytus display their anger and defensiveness by turning to the legal system to prosecute and even to kill Socrates. In his cross-examination of Meletus, Socrates shows that such actions display a lack of genuine "care" for others (24c).[14] In contrast, Socrates' knowledge of his own ignorance had practical effects in his moral judgments that it would be wrong to try the ten generals as a single body or to kill Leon of Salamis (32a–e). The connection between knowledge of ignorance and such actions may not immediately be clear. After all, Socrates gives these two instances as proof that he acts for the sake of justice and not out of a fear of death (32a). This explanation seems to indicate that Socrates acts from positive knowledge of justice and therefore that he is not as ignorant as he claims to be.[15] I agree with commentators who have argued that Socratic ignorance does not entail a total incapacity to speak wisely about moral or political matters.[16] Moreover, some of what Socrates believes relies on divine sources.[17] However, Socrates' awareness of the limits of his own knowledge, and his sense of sharing in a universal human *weakness*, are both arguably at play as well.

First, it is important to distinguish between Socrates' claim that human wisdom is worth little or nothing and a claim that Socrates never makes, namely, that he never knows how to act in any particular instance. When Socrates describes human wisdom as worth little in the eyes of the oracle, the main contrast he draws is between divine and human wisdom (20d–e). Human beings are not gods in what they can know. From the point of view of the oracle, human knowledge is "only" human and worth nothing. However, this does not mean that everything that is said about matters of justice is worthless. Socrates is not a skeptic who refuses to engage in all political activity, although he eschews many of its traditional forms. He is

---

[14] Socrates teases Meletus for lacking "care" for others, even playing on the link between Meletus' name and the Greek verb for care, μέλω.

[15] See McPherran (1996, 178–185). See also Brickhouse and Smith (1994, 189–201). As Brickhouse and Smith argue, the *daimonion* opposes Socrates' actions, suggesting that the internal prompting against action arises only when Socrates' rational discernment process has failed to yield the right answer for action. Such actions remind us that Socrates is fallible in moral judgments. In contrast, Vlastos (1989, 1393) argues that rational argument always supersedes religious sources, which can never trump it.

[16] See Gerson (1992, 124), who argues that one must distinguish between the capacity to offer a *logos* about a topic and the claim to knowledge.

[17] See Brickhouse and Smith (1984, 125–131).

not unconcerned with matters of human justice simply because human beings are not gods. Human knowledge is not oracular. This does not mean that we cannot make reliable judgments about how to act, even if those judgments are in principle revisable in light of future inquiry.[18] Socrates has a kind of "know how" about how to act. This "know how" partly comes from recognizing his own ignorance but also must include a sense of how to apply that knowledge of ignorance to particular situations.

Socrates refuses to arrest Leon of Salamis and protests the decision of the council to put to death the generals after the battle of Arginusae. But he does not claim expertise in either of these matters. He never articulates a theory or set of reasons for why the governments in question were acting unjustly. Rather than possessing secure knowledge of the innocence of the generals or the positive virtues of Leon, Socrates refuses to act precisely because of his own and others' ignorance. In the case of the generals, Socrates opposes the decision to kill them without a trial because it is illegal and unjust (32c). But the injustice of the action can be understood as an instance of recognizing one's own ignorance. Socrates and the Assembly did not know whether the generals ought to be held responsible for the rescue of survivors of the battle. A trial is designed precisely in order to allow the reasons for or against such a judgment to be laid out, deliberated, and acted on.[19] In the absence of a lawful trial, the Assembly ought to have deferred judgment and followed the law's requirement for a trial. Similarly, when the Thirty Tyrants asked Socrates to bring Leon from Salamis to be executed, he went home rather than follow such an order. His stated motives were to act neither impiously nor unjustly (32d). Again, such an action need not be understood as simply an instance of secure knowledge of the justice of whether Leon deserved death or not. Socrates' motivation could have been as simple as refusing to harm a person in the absence of any knowledge as to whether he deserves it, especially in the absence of lawful reason to do so.[20] Knowing that one does not know about the particular justice of either case is already in itself sufficient reason not to act against the law. Socrates' reasons to act justly in these instances

[18] Ibid., 127.

[19] Here it may be helpful to recall the connection between the Greek δίκη (trial, indictment, justice) and δικαιοσύνη, the term Plato uses most in philosophical descriptions of justice.

[20] Unfortunately, the exact identity of Leon of Salamis is unclear. One author has argued that Leon of Salamis may well be the general Leon mentioned by both Thucydides and Xenophon, highly respected as a virtuous democratic leader. He speculates that the Meletus who arrested Leon of Salamis might well be identified with the Meletus of Plato's *Apology*. See McCoy (1975). If McCoy is right, then Socrates' case is strengthened even further: Meletus was willing to arrest a leading democratic general and unjustly put him to death, but Socrates refused to participate in the action.

may well have been limited to a strong belief *that* killing when in a state of ignorance about the justice of a particular matter is itself unjust.[21]

Socrates thus gives us ample evidence that his knowledge of his own ignorance is already a kind of practical wisdom that assists in his interactions with others. Self-knowledge of one's own ignorance and the recognition that others are likewise ignorant both contribute to Socrates' capacity to live a moral and just life. Socrates' ignorance about himself helps him to avoid inappropriate reactions to praise and blame that are not well founded in reflection and deeper self-exploration. His understanding of his own epistemic limits prevents Socrates from harming others unlawfully and contributes to a sense of self-restraint in such circumstances, even when his own life might be endangered as a result.[22] Socrates finds strength in pursuing his mission of acting as the city's gadfly through recollecting the shared and universal nature of human ignorance, which allows him to continue his questioning of others despite anger, rejection, and other emotional reactions that are the consequence of such questioning.

To the claim that Socrates has a sense of shared humanity with others that leads him to a general sense of equality with others, one might object that Socrates also makes some rather self-aggrandizing remarks about himself in the course of his defense. For example, Socrates calls himself a "gift from the god" to Athens (31a8–9) and suggests an initial counterpenalty of free meals at the Prytaneum, like the Olympic victors (36d–37a). Clearly, Socrates sets himself apart from others in noting his special role and particular gift as a benefactor to the city sent from the god. Such remarks, coupled with his refusal to entreat the jurors to take pity on him, might easily have been seen as arrogant by the jurors, but Socrates himself takes pains to deny such an interpretation:

> Perhaps you think in saying this, in what I said about pity and supplication, that I speak boldly (ἀπαυθαδιζόμενος), but that is not the case, Athenian men. Rather, I am persuaded that I have never willingly done wrong (ἀδικεῖν) to any human being, but I am not persuading you of this. (37a3–7)

---

[21] Here I am not arguing that Socrates knows nothing at all. As Brickhouse and Smith (1989, 128–137) make clear, Socrates definitely asserts that he knows that it is evil and unjust to disobey one's superior, whether divine or human (29b). Obedience to the law would be a case in point. My point here is only to say that knowledge of ignorance can itself be a powerful motivating force for choosing action or nonaction.

[22] Gerson (1992) also argues that self-knowledge is central to moderation, especially insofar as care for the good of one's soul rather than the good of one's possessions limits unjust actions undertaken in order to gain material goods.

Socrates insists that his own goal is neither self-aggrandizement nor false self-diminishment. Instead, he tells the truth about himself as he best understands that truth. In the larger context of his account of his human wisdom, he sees himself both as like others in being ignorant of many things and as being unlike them in taking on a distinctive political role due to having a clearer sense of what it means to be human and the centrality of self-knowledge.

In this political role, Socrates is somewhat successful, insofar as others, much younger than he, will follow who will continue to test and to examine (39c–d). Here Socrates implies, though he never explicitly states, that among his followers are those who have also encountered their own ignorance and who will take on similar philosophical and political roles in the city. Plato as one of these followers is another clear instance of Socratic success. Socrates is no longer unique in possessing this human wisdom and acting on it for moral and political purposes. Self-knowledge begins but does not end with the self.

CHAPTER 11

Self-Knowledge in Plato's Symposium

Eric Sanday

In this chapter, I will use Plato's *Symposium* to examine a tension that I believe to be key to self-knowledge. On the one hand, knowledge proper refers to noetic insight into the ultimate explanatory principles and causes, which "objects" are often referred to in the dialogues as forms. On the other hand, self-knowledge refers to basic modes of self-awareness and self-understanding that are at once embodied and interpersonal, and which are not explicitly related to the study of form. I believe these two basic commitments, to knowledge and self-awareness, tend to obscure one another in the dialogues and in contemporary interpretations. My basic thesis is that the demands of theoretical knowledge and self-awareness are in tension with one another but that Platonic philosophy demands that we understand the nature of these opposed demands and endure the strife between them. Self-knowledge, understood in its most encompassing sense, is the life of reflectively enduring that strife, of reconciling the existential burdens of philosophy with the demands of theoretical knowledge proper.

Plato's focus on erotic matters in the *Symposium* is well suited to this inquiry, for it is in erotic experience that one is both drawn outside oneself *and* reminded of one's own fundamentally situated position in the world. It is a fitting arena in which to draw the contrast between the nature of theoretical understanding and the sometimes excruciating personal demands of the path of philosophical education. I will first focus on the speech of Diotima, especially the notion of nonpossessive "reproduction in [the presence of] the beautiful (τόκος ἐν καλῷ)" (206b7–8) and the recognition of form *as form* in the "highest mysteries" (210a1).[1] I then

---

[1] I will subsequently be referring to these as the "higher mysteries," wanting only to distinguish them from the lower mysteries. A word of clarification: there is also a distinction to be drawn between lower and higher within the lower mysteries. For the sense of "highest," cf. Diotima's reference to "attaining the highest point" (*Smp.* 211b7). For discussion of the sense in which one has "nearly (σχεδόν ... τι)" (211b6–7) reached the highest point when one has grasped the form of the beautiful

focus on the speech of Alcibiades in order to illustrate the tension between theoretical insight and our embodied self-awareness. Finally, I consider Plato's use of the character of Diotima in light of the use Hesiod makes of female characters in the *Theogony* as a way to understand the distinction between image and principle in the project of knowing oneself. I conclude that Plato's *Symposium* serves as a philosophical recapitulation in both body and mind of the Delphic command to "Know thyself."

II.1

My aim at first is to introduce Diotima's speech and then explain the distinction between higher and lower mysteries. My main focus is on Diotima's notion of "reproduction in the presence of the beautiful," which I will interpret as appreciative activity that seeks to know the Beautiful itself (and the Good) indirectly, by working to rethink and renew the animating norms of personal ethical life, of law, and of the sciences. This section will explain who we are when we engage in theoretical inquiry and how, in our theoretical engagements, our relationship to ourselves and others is transformed.

The main body of the dialogue consists of six deliberately ordered speeches given at a dinner party hosted by Agathon just a day after he won highest prizes in the poetry competition of 416.[2] Although the dinner guests agree to forgo the customary drinking and instead to spend their evening speaking in praise of love, what follows is as much praise of love as it is a series of competitive speeches by men who are concerned for the most part with outdoing, and being outdone by, each other. In each case, the praise reflects on the person doing the praising: Phaedrus praises love within the framework of traditional Homeric values; Pausanias situates that wisdom within the context of Athenian legal custom; Eryximachus responds to Pausanias by situating his praise of love within an account of the opposites studied and managed by medicine and the other arts. Aristophanes introduces a critical note in his comedic account of human hubris, and Agathon responds to Aristophanes with a demonstration of the

---

as form, see later. All translations are my own. I am using the Greek of Burnet 1901, and I am referring to Dover (1980), Groden's translation (Plato 1970), and Fowler's translation (Plato 1925).
[2] Of course, the order is introduced as following the seating arrangements, which are mostly contingent, and one narrator recounting the conversation, Apollodorus, was not present at the event himself but heard of it from Aristodemus, who acknowledges not remembering all details. On the subject of the date of the retelling, see Nussbaum (1979) and Miller (2015). On the subject of the characters present, see Nails (2002).

poetic talents that won him the prizes at the competition the day before. Socrates refutes Agathon's basic approach and concludes the praise of love by situating it within the philosophical framework of the higher and lower mysteries. Thus, although the speakers are tasked with eulogizing love as a god, many of them are satisfied to show that his own concerns are worthy of respect and honor. Having agreed to praise a god, the speakers compete with and focus on themselves and each other, and they risk falling prey to the desire to outdo one another, a danger that is only increased by the fact that four participants are speaking in the presence of their lovers. The desire for approval and appreciation of the competitors is so strong that Agathon finishes his speech to boisterous applause, Aristodemus reports, "befitting both himself, the young man who had delivered it, as well as the god" (198a2–3), as if to confirm that the speech was vying for prominence not only with the other speakers but also with the god.[3] The challenge of self-awareness is evident: if one claims to be praising a god but is in truth concerned primarily with oneself, one has failed to notice and take responsibility for what one is doing with one's words.

Socrates answers Agathon by drawing attention to the competitive context of the speeches and turns the group's attention to truth, to speaking truly, and to accountability. Socrates recalls to Eryximachus the earlier prediction that Agathon would speak "wonderfully" and leave Socrates in *aporia* (198a6–7), calling Agathon's speech "beautiful and many-faceted" (198b3). But, Socrates says, it wasn't the speech as a whole so much as the end, the "beauty of the words and phrases" (198b4–5), that shamed him and highlighted by contrast his incapacity to "speak so well" (198b7). Socrates invokes the Gorgon's head and says that he expected to be turned to stone by Agathon and rendered speechless, as if there was nothing left to be said simply because all the words had been exhausted. Socrates thought that, he says, it was necessary to "speak the truth" (198d3–4), come what may, but now he finds himself having sworn an oath to which his heart (199a6) did not consent. Socrates sets the terms explicitly: he is willing to tell the truth honestly and in whatever order the words come to him, but he is not willing to speak for the sake of victory.

---

[3] Miller comments on the distinction between the καὶ ... καὶ ... and ... τε καὶ ... constructions, referring to Smyth (1963): "[καὶ ... καὶ ...] emphasizes each member separately" (#2878). Miller (2015, 5 n. 8) proposes: "Translating it as "both ... and ...," while perfectly possible, would fail to convey the implicit sense that the speech, in being "fitting" (to invoke another suggestion from Smyth) as well to Agathon as also to the god, gives Agathon prominence at the expense of the god."

Socrates may be speaking ironically, but he is speaking with serious purpose. By making reference to what it means to "speak the truth" and by invoking the nature of an oath, Socrates has made speech and our accountability to speech a subject of discussion. Discourse can bring a speaker into community with others, but it can by the same token close off community. There is a truth of matters, and that truth, not the speakers, will determine whether their speech is well spoken. Whether Socrates is simply an exception to this rule of competition among the speakers is worth asking, but it is evident that he would like us to speak and to listen in light of evaluative criteria that test the speaker's commitment to the truth of what they say.

When Socrates begins his refutation of Agathon, his first point is to show that love also aims beyond itself. In brief, Socrates argues that love is definitionally "of something" (199d1), just as "brother" is by definition the brother of someone. Love is of the beautiful because it lacks the beautiful and therefore is not beautiful. Moreover, beauty is a good, and love therefore lacks the good and is not good. But lacking beauty does not entail that love is ugly, as if everything not beautiful is ugly. Love is a daimon, an intermediate between beauty and ugliness, not having the beautiful but relating itself to the beautiful as a lack. Love seeks beauty and cares for the expression of the beautiful.[4]

In two steps, Socrates has shifted attention from the prize won in competition to the earnest striving to live up to certain objective demands. He shifts attention from the goal of possessing the beautiful to the goal of opening oneself in appreciation of the beautiful, a stance of self-aware understanding in which one both seeks true explanatory principles *and* remains alert to what one is doing with one's knowledge, i.e., how one is using it.[5] In order to make his beginning, Socrates has challenged the

---

[4] In the exchange between Socrates and Agathon, we can detect a trace of the existential weight of the philosophical path and the feeling of self-alienation that can result from philosophical engagement, but we can also see the demand for honesty and presence with one another, the intimacy, of the philosophical path. Socrates speaks to Agathon in the voice of Diotima and allows his younger self to stand as surrogate for Agathon. This shows the necessity of distance from what is being said. On the other hand, Socrates expects and explicitly directs Agathon to be fully present to the entailments and tacit commitments of speech. Socrates says: "It is not difficult to refute Socrates, ... my dear Agathon, but impossible to refute the truth" (201c8–9). We readers may share the position of Agathon. We may contemplate the overturning of our shared commitments without being directly challenged but are expected to attend to the movement of refutation.

[5] By beginning with this turn toward desire as a lack and human beings as fundamentally dispossessed or incapable of stable possession – thereby interrupting our affective bond with possessions – Socrates starts at a point parallel to Aristophanes' characterization of human beings as fundamentally wounded.

assumption governing the other speeches, namely that the competition between individual speakers takes priority. He thereby also challenges the assumption, implicit in that competition, that the particular domain of expertise from which each speaker delivers his speech has privileged access to the truth. As long as we take truth to be victory, honor, or expertise, we fall short of the happiness that Diotima associates first with encompassing virtue and, later, the contemplation of form. By freeing eros from our desire for control and subordination to lesser ends, we are prepared to come to know ourselves by recognizing the limit to which we are subject as human, i.e., to recognize our own necessary lack of the beautiful, and to become receptive to the beauty that exceeds and guides our newly appreciative activity.

By identifying ignorance as a failure to notice one's own lack and by reorienting conversation toward the beautiful that it does not possess, Socrates has prompted us to take the first step of initiation into the philosophical mysteries. Socrates' initial focus on the truth of speech is, I claim, attempting to open up a fundamental difference between ourselves and the beautiful. Without a basic awareness of our *secondness* as mortals and the transformative power of our appreciative activity in the presence of the beautiful, we cannot satisfy the specifically theoretical side of the broader duality that is self-knowledge.

II.2

The higher and lower mysteries are described by Diotima from 207c to 212a, and they are explicitly named at 209e–210a, just before the introduction of the ladder of philosophical education leading up to the form of the beautiful itself. In each case, the mysteries refer to basic motivations that govern a human life. The lower mysteries consist of various kinds of productive activity by which human beings leave behind something of themselves and, thereby, secure undying memory and participate in immortality. The lower of the lower mysteries consists in bodily reproduction, leaving behind children through which one achieves immortality. The higher of the lower mysteries consists in giving birth to thought and other virtues by the poets, craftspeople, educators, and shapers of the state. In all the lower mysteries, the beautiful manifests itself and guides the initiate, but the focus is primarily on the product, the offspring, and the memory secured, rather than on the beautiful. The initiation into the higher mysteries reverses this forgetfulness of the beautiful by aiming at explicit recognition of the beautiful itself and, ultimately, a recognition of the causal primacy of form. The mysteries have in common an orientation toward the beautiful, but the higher mysteries explicitly resist the self's desire to possess the product of its activity.

The path opened up by Diotima is a path of appropriately self-knowing and self-limiting recognition and appreciation of the beautiful. Initiation begins with the feeling of vulnerability, the desire to act, and the commitment to making a mark through one's actions. We undergo vulnerability in the presence of the beautiful, and, in the moment of vulnerability, we are reminded of the lack from which life-defining actions are launched, and reminded that such actions depend inescapably on us. But then the experience of desire projects us beyond ourselves with inspiration to act, to exceed ourselves and to produce something. The question of self-knowledge is whether we are choosing our lives in light of ultimate reasons or causes and, thereby, living seriously, or acting for the sake of self-promotion. If we fail to act or act for the wrong reasons, we are subject to forgetfulness of the beautiful and forgetfulness of ourselves.[6]

That each of the six speakers at the dinner party is an example of living seriously, in the terms I am suggesting, can be seen insofar as each lives in service of articulate values that all accept and recognize. Each has heeded the call to take a stand and speak on behalf of the core moving principles in human life. Of all six, Socrates (and Diotima) stand out for most of all embracing the vulnerability and inspiration, and thereby the existential choice, that are occasioned by love of the beautiful. Diotima indicates as much in her evaluation of the various kinds of action, with the highest and most virtuous kinds of action being those that let the beautiful act as a guide, forgetting reputation and letting the products take care of themselves. Self-knowledge, or virtue simply, would consist of a life of sustained and appreciative letting-presence of the beautiful.[7]

II.3

In Diotima's account of the higher mysteries, we see that the activity of self-knowledge consists, essentially, in not letting one's self-concern

---

[6] There are further examples of deflection earlier presented in the figures of Apollodorus and Aristodemus.

[7] I believe there is a strong connection between what I am in this chapter calling self-knowledge and virtue. Specifically, there is a connection between, on the one hand, appreciative, nonpossessive, letting-presence of the beautiful, a manifestation of moderation belonging to the theoretical side of self-knowledge, and, on the other hand, the affective and interpersonal moderation demanded in response to the existential weight of the philosophical path. However, this is a larger claim for which I am not here prepared to argue.

obscure the coming to presence of the beautiful. Critical to Diotima's presentation of this activity is to outline a path of education in which our activity allows the beautiful to reveal itself more deeply, in turn allowing us to engage in more profound activity. Diotima introduces this virtuously circular activity first with an image of Eros as a daimon that can wound us *and* heal the wound it creates. Diotima describes eros as "intermediate between mortality and divinity" (202e1), i.e., as intermediate between the sacrifices (appreciative activity) offered by human beings and the commands and responses (guidance) given by the gods. Eros "fulfills both, so as to bind the whole itself to itself" (202e6–7). It is through the daimonic intermediary that "all mingling and dialogue" (203a3–4) between mortals and the divine take place. According to Diotima's image, Eros is the child of Poverty and Plenty, embodying qualities of both parents but participating alternately in the power of each. Like his mother, eros is scheming and striving; like his father, Eros has resources and finds a way around obstacles. Eros soars each day, dies, and is reborn again in the morning. Thus, Eros orients us toward the divine both by revealing the gap between the mortal and divine and by opening up a path to cross that gap. These images of schism and return set the stage for the explicit account of the virtuously circular structure of appreciative activity.

Socrates feels persuaded by Diotima's account, but at first he continues to conceive of eros possessively, i.e., the desire to possess beautiful things and to make them one's own. The limit of virtuous activity is, for him, the possession of beautiful things. Diotima prompts Socrates to look beyond the act of possession. What else, she asks, do we desire beyond the possession of good things? On the basis of the possession of good things, we enjoy happiness, which is complete (205a3); happiness lacks nothing and needs no further explanation. All human beings would agree. But two aspects of the good undermine the paradigm of possessiveness. First, human beings love the good whether or not it is their own; they love it even if they must dismiss what is their own. Thus, she says, if part of one's very own body were no longer good, one would cut it off. Socrates can readily agree that desire for the good takes priority even over possession. Second, even if our mortal nature could, if at all, possess the good "now," our desire would remain to possess the good *always* (206a11–12). Thus, we already wish for more than possession in the present but some kind of possession eternally.

Diotima sets aside the concept of "possession" in order to address the desire for eternity using the image of "reproduction." Each of us is pregnant in body and soul, she says, and we gain our lasting share of the good by giving birth. The beautiful is what inspires us and reminds us of our mortality, it grounds us, and it allows us to deliver what we all have within ourselves. As if to continue the movement of refutation that Socrates began with Agathon, Diotima says that "love is not love of the beautiful" (206e2). Diotima calls love, our self-actualizing response to inspiration, "reproduction in [the presence of] the beautiful" (206b7–8). "Reproduction is the eternal and immortal in the mortal" (206e7–8). The process of giving birth and participating in the immortal is easiest and most spontaneous, she says, in the presence of the beautiful, and we experience it as joy (χάριν, 208b5). Rather than fulfilling our highest aim in possession of an object, through acquisition and ownership, we fulfill that aim through actualization of a latent potential that we all have as human and that in the *Republic* is characterized as an "indwelling power" and in the *Symposium* is captured by the image of pregnancy in soul. Being pregnant in soul is the presence of νοῦς within our soul.[8]

This type of reproductive activity in which we satisfy our desire for eternity provides us with the greatest happiness of which we are capable, which is increased in relation to the divinity of our offspring. The more divine the offspring, the more our happiness, and the more intimate our bond will be with others, with the most divine offspring being, she says, the *logoi* produced by the shared journey of people concerned with virtue and knowledge. The principles of virtue and knowledge are the ones that are most basic, most constitutive of who we are, and it is in relation to these principles that we are most with others, least alone.[9]

We can see in this account of happiness an attempt not only to enter into deeper intimacy with others but to reveal the difference in kind between the human and the divine and to submit, with self-knowledge, to the limit that defines us as human. Eros distinguishes, and brings into relation, the mortal

---

[8] Thus, the *Symposium* would align with the *Republic* in the important respect that we, as human beings, have an aspect in us that is divine, one that is not subject to generation and decay and that can be turned in this direction or that for better or worse. Both dialogues refer to this divine aspect as intellect (*nous*). In the *Republic*, it is "the indwelling power of the soul and that organ by which we learn" (VII.518c4–6). Insofar as this power is indwelling, it finds its analog in the *Symposium* description of each of all human beings as "pregnant" (206c1) in body and soul.

[9] In modern philosophy, one sees a tendency to treat the gaze of the other as an originary source of our own sense of embodiment and interpersonal commitment. This is especially clear in Hegel, Sartre, Levinas, and others. Something like the gaze of the other exists in Plato, for instance in the *opsis*, or face, of the beloved in the *Phaedrus*. However, whereas these modern philosophers offer an account of the gaze of the other as continuous with their theoretical insights, Plato keeps the account of self and other separate, for better or worse, from his theoretical account of form.

and divine.[10] Rather than studying the reconciliation of opposites that are the same in kind, as music studies the reconciliation of high and low tones in the notes of the scale or medicine studies the reconciliation of cold and hot in the healthy norms of the body, eros awakens a difference across which the whole is unified. Through eros, human beings exceed the limit that defines them, and at the same time they become aware of being subject to that limit and learn to attend to it properly.

Diotima's image of eros as intermediary allows us then to access our inward awareness of eros as subject to *and exceeding* mortal limit, at once earth-bound and divine, which is really the core of self-knowledge. The human experience of erotic life is, like the life of eros in the image of Poverty and Plenty, an experience of excess and deficiency. It is earth-bound in the sense that no single fulfillment can expiate our desire, and yet it is divine in the sense that we exceed ourselves toward the immortal, participating in the deepening expression and understanding of the beautiful. The erotic attitude seeks inspiration without seeking to possess beauty, to master or supplant it, which explains Socrates' earlier objection to competitive speech-making and helps prepare us to interpret the speech of Alcibiades yet to come.

In short order, Diotima has made the decisive transition from possessive eros to eros as beauty-inspired reproduction in body and soul of our connectedness to what-is. Rather than being reduced to an object of possession, beauty is allowed to shine and inspire, so as to deepen our understanding and to share it in intimacy with others. Through accepting awareness of our own mortal limit, i.e. having achieved the self-awareness that recognizes our fundamental incapacity to possess the object of desire as if we were gods, we become better able to participate in our deepest desire for happiness. The shift into the higher mysteries begins with an embrace of appreciative activity, which is not contingent on winning a name for ourselves but, instead, is undertaken for the sake of the beautiful itself.

11.4

This section discusses the nature of the theoretical insight that becomes possible on the basis of appropriately attuned self-knowledge. The specific

---

[10] Mortals are associated with the female, the mother; the gods are associated with the male, the father. The conception is clearly Greek in character, creating a hierarchy between the better and worse, where the female is the embodiment of what is worse, mortal, and lower, and the male is the embodiment of what is good, perfect, and higher. It is a challenge, however, to that convention for Socrates not only to put himself in the position of the refuted but to identify the philosopher refuting him as a woman, Diotima. See Section 11.6 of this chapter.

claim I want to make is that form, here the form of the beautiful, is the limit of a process of ever-deepening appreciative activity in the presence of the beautiful.

We have seen that in the higher of the lower mysteries the soul reproduces itself in *logoi*, and Diotima characterized this type of reproduction as the "most divine." In the activity of articulating our accounts of virtue in concert with trusted interlocutors, we are also deepening and extending our engagement with the beautiful, which guides those accounts. However, in the highest of the lower mysteries, the depth of the relationship to and appreciation of the beautiful is not the goal; the goal is those *logoi* and their articulation of the beautiful in which insight is preserved, i.e., divine "offspring" that preserve insight. In the higher mysteries, by contrast, concern for posterity does not guide the activity. The point here is the direct and true insight that informs our accounts, which in turn serve as the occasion for further insight. At each step of education, we wish ourselves to recognize the source and conditions of our activity and to grow from that understanding, but we are now aiming at the limit of our activity, and the goal is fundamentally other than ourselves.

Diotima describes a set of educationally transformative steps through which the student-initiate passes, starting with appreciation of the beauty in the body of one with whom one has fallen in love, to beauty of character, to the beauty of virtue cultivated by the laws, beyond that to the normative principles of domains disclosed by the sciences, finally arriving at the beautiful itself (211e1), the form. The path is undertaken over the course of one's life, beginning from youth (210a), and at each step, dialogue between the guide and initiate is essential (210a7) to steer the process toward discussion and shared insight.

The steps for initiation into the higher mysteries (210a–211d) are given as follows. The immediate and powerful bond of love for an individual is at first augmented by the less powerful but also wonderful beauty of the discourse produced in the context of a loving relationship. The beauty of a body, addressed as an object of discourse, cannot fail to be open, through the very determinacy of the discourse, to comparison. This awakens the student of eros to the comparative ranges in which bodies are unfolded, and attention turns away from the individual to an awareness of the beauty of bodies generally, a beauty that announces itself as "one and the same" (210b3). At this point, "the beautiful" refers to an appreciation that there is a measure on which a body can draw and, in turn, which a body can illuminate. The presence of the beautiful is arresting, and its presence grips us. Insofar as we learn more about the beauty of bodies, we deepen that appreciation and enable the beautiful in bodies to reveal itself to us more fully. None is the final or exclusive expression, but all are in principle capable of bringing the beautiful to presence.

The shift from the beauty in bodies to other kinds of beauty happens by virtue of the discursivity in and through which beauty is articulated. Once we understand that the beauty we see in bodies is *already* something discursive, we begin to grasp the measures of more and less, i.e., the measure of various indefinite ratios, that is the illumination of the beautiful. The beauty that is expressed by bodies is slowly, but organically, fulfilled as the beauty of insight into the way beauty is articulated, the insight into that articulation, and the greater intimacy fostered in this process.

Following a focus on the priority of beauty disclosed in the kind over the individual body, the student of erotics learns to see and prioritize (210b7) the beauty of the character of the beloved's soul. Specifically, the bloom of the character of the soul inspires "love and care" (210c1) for the person and produces discourses that make in principle all young persons "better" (210c2). We notice that the very discussions in which that beauty of character is expressed become a source through which the beauty of character is developed, further deepening our knowledge and appreciation of the beautiful and, at the same time, deepening our openness and receptivity to the beautiful, which I earlier identified as an aspect of moderation.[11] At this point the focus has turned explicitly to care for the soul and the ways in which our discourses will help us to recognize, understand, and cultivate beauty. Love and care for the character of the beloved and engagement with discourses that improve the young generally entail a higher-order engagement with the cultural institutions, such as legal custom. We are returning to a value first expressed by Pausanias, although from a changed perspective. Diotima says that production of beautiful discourses that improve the character of the young will necessitate "contemplation of the beauty of customs and practices" (210c3–4) as opposed to focusing on what these customs and practices can produce for the maintenance of social order. Our orientation has become less managerial and more appreciative.

Diotima here gathers the beauty of customs and practices in order to make visible their kinship (συγγενές) (210c4–5), which leads the student to the study of the sciences. Once we can appreciate laws, customs, and practices that guide education and conversation at an institutional or societal level, the specificity of the city can be contextualized within the

---

[11] See note 7.

normative structures guiding and preserving all beings, of which human cultures are one sort. We begin to see beauty in the principles of entire domains of phenomena in the sciences. It is here that the student, keying from the beauty of the sciences, transitions from the beauty of individual bodies and individual practices (i.e., the beauty of body and the education of soul) to the "vast sea of the beautiful" (210d4), giving rise to many discourses and thoughts, and being strengthened by a boundless love of wisdom (ἐν φιλοσοφίᾳ ἀφθόνῳ) (210d6).[12]

The soul, strengthened and actualized by this process, eventually catches sight of "a certain single knowledge (τινὰ ἐπιστήμην μίαν τοιαύτην)" (210d7, Groden trans.) of a unique kind of beauty, i.e. the form of beauty itself, which is the limit of our appreciative activity. The student who has followed correctly "suddenly sights something astonishingly beautiful in nature (ἐξαίφνης κατόψεταί τι θαυμαστὸν τὴν φύσιν καλόν)" (210e4–5), that for the sake of which everything else was undergone. What follows is a description of form, and it is given mostly in negative differentiation from becoming. The beautiful itself is "eternal (ἀεὶ ὄν), neither coming to be nor passing away, neither growing nor diminishing" (211a1–2). It is not subject to perspectives; it is not beautiful in one respect but ugly in another, or so at one time and not so at another, or in one relation and not another, or to some people but not others. The priority of the beautiful itself gathers together many different kinds of things as secondary to it: hands, faces, all bodily beauty, propositions, sciences, the entire cosmos and all animals, and all things generally. It is "in accord with itself, single formed with itself, always being (αὐτὸ καθ᾽ αὑτὸ μεθ᾽ αὑτοῦ μονοειδὲς ἀεὶ ὄν)" (211b1–2). Other things participate in it, and though they are generated and destroyed, it is neither more nor less, nor is it affected at all.

Diotima's description of form raises to the level of explicit recognition a source of the various types of normativity that announce themselves as beautiful and that guide the different kinds of appreciative activity. The beautiful itself is the limit of the virtuous circle followed by the initiate into the higher mysteries: the beautiful inspires my appreciative activity by its

---

[12] I think we can see in this notion of a "boundless" love of wisdom the kind of generosity that the philosopher admires and imitates in the *Republic*, first at VI.500b–c when encountering the just, divine, and harmonious order of forms, and then at VI.508e–509b, going beyond the orderliness of the forms' not-harming each other to the Good's generosity of constituting the forms. Continuing with the parallel between the indwelling power for learning, in the *Republic*, and pregnancy, in the *Symposium*, the imitation of the Good in the *Republic* generates within us a disposition toward the good as a kind of second nature that testifies to our commitment to the sources of inspiration, both in the forms and in beloved others.

self-disclosure, and through that activity, my appreciation of the beautiful deepens, allowing its self-disclosure to become more profound. The form is the limit of this process, closing the circle, punctuating the process, and revealing the inexhaustibility of expressive activity. Through our insight, the beautiful reveals itself as "single," not complex, and "suddenly." Practically, what disclosure of the beautiful itself entails primarily is the methodological awareness that we can have true insight into the beautiful but, nonetheless, cannot possess that insight and must strain to let the beautiful show itself again and again. One such disclosure is an event of plenitude, but it is at the same time a promise to be fulfilled.

Now let us turn to the other side of the account of our appreciative activity and the self-disclosure of the beautiful, the side obscured by the upward-looking course of Diotima's comments. Upward progress along this path requires that the self work to hold itself subject to the limit that defines it as mortal and to hold itself open to the guiding self-disclosure of the beautiful. What we have not explored is the reverse side of self-knowledge, i.e., the practices of ignorance through which the self refuses and shields itself from the beautiful. Alcibiades is a case study from which we can reflect on the nature and style of practices opposed to self-knowledge.

11.5

Diotima's account has focused primarily on causes. Reproduction in the presence of the beautiful, the core of the higher mysteries, requires that we acknowledge the intelligibility of higher-order structures of law-giving, fields of knowledge, the necessity that governs what is most knowable, and the form itself, i.e., the form of the beautiful. The self-disclosure of the beautiful arrests and guides us, making use of our minds and hands and skills, *as long as we have resources for this transformation.* What of the concomitant poverty of the erotic soul? In this section, I propose to examine the psychological burden of the philosophical path by looking at the way Alcibiades refuses to endure and affirm the path set forth by Diotima.

At the outset of his comments, Alcibiades promises to offer "images" (215a4) of Socrates. In these images, Alcibiades reports, first, his failed attempts to seduce Socrates into being a proper lover and, second, his encounters with Socrates on military campaigns. The overall picture of the erotic encounter and the military campaigns reflects the ambivalence of Alcibiades' feelings toward Socrates. On the one hand, Alcibiades is speaking in a prosecutorial voice assailing the party responsible for his grievance, and to further strengthen his hand, he is directing Agathon to avoid falling for Socrates' schemes. On the other hand, Alcibiades is effectively praising Socrates' martial virtue.

Alcibiades' apparently conflicting purposes of accusing and praising Socrates work in tandem with each other, and they serve as a good example of practices that resist self-knowledge. In the presence of Socrates, Alcibiades feels that his life, as he lives it, is unworthy. He can see a better life, a fundamentally different life, one that he could be living. Unfortunately, the sense of noble shame that attunes Alcibiades to this other life disappears when he is not in the presence of Socrates, when Alcibiades' internal demand to pursue the philosophical life seems to vanish. But this is a lie, one that Alcibiades is telling himself. He says that he simply loses the desire that Socrates incites in him. However, Alcibiades does not just forget himself or simply lose the proper orientation, as if he mislaid it. Alcibiades actively refuses to pursue the path that Socrates awakens within him, and his comments demonstrate this point.

The first strategy of active refusal is to reduce the presence of the beautiful to something human, i.e. to Socrates, and to something, like Socrates, that can be manipulated. The second strategy is to exalt Socrates, the presence of the beautiful, as something divine, as something beyond the human, and as a paradigm to which Alcibiades and the rest of us mere mortals need not answer. This two-fold strategy, diminishing the beautiful to something that can be controlled and exalting Socrates to the status of something more than human, is the shape of Alcibiades' refusal.

Alcibiades arrives without warning and drunkenly sits down in the party's midst. When he discovers that he has seated himself next to Socrates, he exclaims in alarm that Socrates has a habit of showing up "suddenly" (213c1) where he is least expected. Socrates describes Alcibiades as jealous, envious, potentially violent, and seized by a lover's madness. Alcibiades rejects the possibility of reconciliation with Socrates and promises vengeance on him. The tone is jesting and flirtatious, but something seems to have jarred them both.

Alcibiades compares Socrates to the sileni, the dolls that have nested within them a series of similar dolls and which, at their inside core, contain statues of the gods. Socrates is outwardly human, but he has an otherworldly effect on others. Alcibiades first describes the encounter with Socrates' words. The things Socrates says, his *logoi*, have a profound effect, whether they are spoken by Socrates or someone else. Socrates is like the satyr Marsyas, hubristic, fearsome, and wonderful. Socrates' words amaze Alcibiades, make his heart pound, bring tears to his eyes, and make him think of himself not with pride but as a slave to meaningless pursuits, his own life not worth living (216a1–2). Alcibiades compares Socrates' speeches to the Siren song, to which he must shut his ears and from which he must run away. Socrates makes Alcibiades feel ashamed and obligated to do what Socrates commands, but Alcibiades refuses to change his life and flees, he says, "like a slave" into the honors bestowed by the Athenian demos and its adoration.

It is interesting to note that Alcibiades never speaks of Socrates but, instead, of how Socrates makes him feel. Alcibiades speaks of what the *experience of* Socrates is like. It thus makes sense that Alcibiades does not respond to Socrates' words but to Socrates himself, attempting to seduce Socrates rather than struggling to come to terms with the insights toward which Socrates is pointing. In my view, Alcibiades mistakes his own experience of vulnerability as a weakness to be remedied, and he mistakes the beauty of Socrates for the beauty of his words. The attempted seduction is a bid to claim an interpretive victory, reducing the beautiful to the person of Socrates and demonstrating its vulnerability (i.e., lack of divinity) by subjecting it to bodily desire. Through the strategy of seduction, Alcibiades seeks to humanize Socrates and rob the beautiful of its divinity, which is a practice of ignorance that aims to remove incipient self-knowledge.

Alcibiades' second main strategy is to exalt Socrates beyond the human, where we can no longer be expected to answer or respond to what Socrates occasions in us. Alcibiades relates events from the campaigns at Potidaea and Delium. In both cases Socrates exemplifies extraordinary virtue of courage, moderation, and a kind of wisdom. During the siege of Potidaea from 432 to 430, the army was cut off from its supplies and troops went for long times without food. Socrates was able to bear deprivation better than anyone else. Similarly, as Alcibiades also tells us, Socrates prefers not to drink alcohol, but when forced to drink, he drinks more than anyone else, enjoys it more than anyone else, and remains unaffected. When the army was exposed to brutally cold temperatures, Socrates was able to walk around outside in his accustomed way, even in bare feet, and handle the conditions better than others who were bundled up like koalas (not Plato's image). On one occasion, when he struggled with an intellectual problem that provided him no way through, he stayed glued to the spot all night long, drawing others out of their tents to bed down outside, until finally at dawn he blessed the sun and went about his day. During the disorderly retreat at Delium in 424, Socrates was better able to keep his head than Laches and was better able to defend his compatriots than Alcibiades on horseback. In all of Alcibiades' descriptions of Socrates in the field, we hear an echo of his resentful characterization of Socrates as "more invulnerable to need [i.e. gratification] than Ajax to iron" (219e1–2). Socrates, according to Alcibiades, is simply beyond the human. In cold places, over stretches of time, in the face of necessities of food and luxuries of drink, Socrates is depicted as inhuman. Alcibiades would have us think that Socrates has despised the body to the point of losing his humanity; he is a living abstraction, and therefore the rest of us humans are excused from responding to that model.

In his anxiety, Alcibiades construes Socrates as more-than-human, I claim, so that we are not required to respond to the provocation that Socrates occasions. At the same time, Alcibiades tried to show that Socrates is vulnerable not only to desire but to desire that can be inspired by Alcibiades' body. It is as if Alcibiades is "impious" in the sense that he believes the gods don't exist (i.e., Socrates is not what he sometimes appears to be); the gods do exist but they don't care (i.e., Socrates is more-than-human); or the gods do exist and care but can be bought off (i.e., seduced).[13]

I have argued in this section that Alcibiades would like to believe, and have us believe, that philosophy is either a presence, equal to ourselves, that is available to be seduced, or is so alien to us that we could never be blamed for failing to live up to its demands. Alcibiades is actively construing Socrates in a way that excuses him and the rest of us from facing up to something that, when it is awakened, is awakened *within* and *beyond* ourselves. Whether Alcibiades is pushing Socrates away toward the divine or lowering Socrates toward bodily desire, he is using Socrates to shield himself from being accountable to the presence of the beautiful arising within him. He is engaging in practices of ignorance that work by undermining the conditions of self-knowledge, i.e., the moderation in affective and interpersonal life that is the condition for an ever-deepening understanding of and receptivity to the beautiful. On the reverse side, Alcibiades' efforts to conceal from himself the demands that Socrates has awakened within him are evidence of the difficulty of the task demanded by philosophy, which was left out of Diotima's account of philosophical education. The image of Alcibiades serves as a negative reminder of the courage required for facing up to the demands of philosophy.

Let's now return to the speech of Diotima to see how the lessons of the speech of Alcibiades are reflected at the level of the composition of the

---

[13] This tracks the three types of impiety listed in the *Laws* (X.885b6–9): (1) the gods do not exist; (2) the gods exist but they are indifferent to human concerns; and (3) the gods do exist and are concerned with human affairs, but they can be bought off.

Symposium. I propose that we should interpret Socrates' presentation of Diotima's speech in light of Hesiod's use of female characters in the *Theogony.* If we do, we will be able to see how mythopoeic images are used by Plato to serve the aim of self-knowledge.

11.6

The basic story of Hesiod's *Theogony* is the establishment of the infallible divine rule of Zeus. By defeating the Titans and, with the help of Gaia, gaining their recognition of his authority over all gods and human beings, Zeus institutes a system of divine powers in which each god has dominion over a proper part of the whole, supplanting the need for rule by violence and oppression with the principle of justice. The system Zeus establishes relies on the internalized respect of each member for the ordered whole and the principle governing their interrelation. To the extent that the subjects of Zeus' rule respect the principle of their ordering, this is a system ruled by justice rather than Zeus personally. At the same time, however, Zeus institutes and maintains his reign by force and cunning, so his rule is not simply free of the cycle of violence and oppression that preceded his reign. By repeating violence, especially at the inception of his reign, Zeus risks repeating and deepening the hold that violence and oppression have on the ostensibly "just" order. I want to focus on the ambiguous relationship between force and justice in Hesiod's account to amplify the tension between knowledge proper and self-knowledge with which I opened.

The key moment for our present purposes is what I will call the "internalization of the female." Zeus swallows Metis, who is pregnant with child, and from her he gains cunning and unerring counsel and gives birth to Athena, with whom he shares power as his "equal in power and wisdom" (*Theogony,* 896).[14] By swallowing Metis and giving birth to Athena, is Zeus giving proper place to the female other by sharing power, or is he simply repeating the cycle of violence at a more fundamental level?

---

[14] There are many other elements, and Hesiod's story is significantly more complex. I have not done justice to the complexity of Gaia's role in the final attempt to overthrow Zeus or, after his victory, her counseling the Titans on their act of submission to Zeus or her helping Zeus internalize cunning for himself. Zeus retains power after defeating the Titans only because he spies the onrushing Typhon in the nick of time, before being overthrown. Typhon is Gaia's youngest child, presumably last child, and Zeus sends the defeated Typhon to rest permanently in Tartaros. Is this a violent fulfillment of Ouranos' unsuccessful attempt to force the children of Gaia back into her womb? However that might be, it is after the defeat and exile of Typhon that Gaia counsels the Titans to recognize Zeus' authority, and it is Gaia and Ouranos who tell Zeus he will be overthrown and who give him the words to deceive Metis into being swallowed by him, where she becomes his personal source of wisdom.

On the one hand, it seems that Zeus departs from the oppressive rule of his father and grandfather. When Gaia first gave rise, through parthenogenic birth, to her offspring, she gave rise to Ouranos as her "equal" (126) and, in that spirit, to a system of interrelation. When Ouranos lies with Gaia, seemingly by force, and later when he forces their children back into her womb, Ouranos does violence to the set of interrelations of which he is a part. Similarly, Kronos violates the system of interrelation by swallowing his offspring, the children of Rhea. Both Ouranos and Kronos, threatened by the very system in which they have their identity, rule by force and oppression. Zeus seems to depart from them when he not only shares power but shares power with a female god, restoring the system of interrelation to which Gaia first gave rise at the same time as he enacts a principle of justice as the source of that system. His act of justice seems to continue when, in sexual union with Themis, he helps give rise to a new order of Eunomia, Dike, and Eirene.

On the other hand, however, in order to establish his rule, Zeus swallows Metis, who thereby loses her autonomy, and Athena is born in full armor and in the absence of a (visible) mother. In both Zeus' incorporation of Metis and Athena's warrior armor, Zeus' reign seems to be a deepening of rule by oppression and ostensible self-sufficiency rather than setting aside violence and making room for justice. Herein lies the ambiguity: although Zeus' internalization of the female gives rise to the system of recognition and institutionality by which each god possesses a proper domain, Zeus makes room for the female in terms of a masculine paradigm, maintaining his monopoly on force.

In my view, the point of the *Theogony* just is the ambiguity of Zeus' resolution of the cycle of violence. That is to say, the point is to acknowledge the risk of repeating that cycle of violence and oppression in the attempt to overcome it. Female bodies in the *Theogony* harbor the generativity from which the established order is threatened. Established identities and relations are threatened by new gods, and new gods arise from the generative power that is most explicitly a part of the female body. Male bodies, while still being a part of the system of interrelation and reproduction, stand at a greater distance from pregnancy and birth and are able to deny their interrelational dependence on other bodies, as exemplified by the oppressive rule of Ouranos and Kronos. Hesiod's accomplishment is to include both injustice and justice within a more fundamental account of justice.

We might draw a parallel here with the *Symposium*. Plato, like Hesiod, takes special care to incorporate excluded opposites within a more expansive and justly composed whole. At the level of the images, Alcibiades performatively reintroduces the unruliness the symposiasts set aside at the outset of their speeches. Diotima had turned away from self-regarding concerns to focus on causal structures and the priority of form, but Alcibiades reintroduces to the dialogue all that has been set aside, especially the psychological pressure that accompanies transformative activity. The image of Alcibiades draws our attention to the marginalized and to the feelings of marginalization and vulnerability that accompany philosophical practice.

But, more profoundly than Alcibiades, the presence of Diotima at the core of the dialogue represents an internalization of the excluded or marginalized. In the exceedingly male-oriented society of Athens and in the unreflectively enjoyment of male privilege in the *Symposium*, Diotima stands out as speaking not only as an equal but as a philosopher and a teacher. By reminding the other speakers that they are male and by encouraging the transformation of ontological understanding through the images of pregnancy and reproduction, Diotima is strongly suggestive of a Platonic reappropriation of Hesiod's account. Just as the male gods in the *Theogony* distance themselves from the possibility of decentering by forcefully displacing the emergence of a new center, and Zeus risks repeating this violence when he establishes a just order, so too human activity in the *Symposium* distances itself from the possibility of decentering by habitually overlooking the guiding presence of the beautiful in favor of amassing tokens of one's self and one's achievement in the world. To counter this, the images of reproduction in the presence of the beautiful and being pregnant in body acknowledge the priority of the beautiful and the constitutive interrelationship of parts. This was made especially clear in the transformed attitude toward the causal priority of one's own work. Rather than treating our work as the causal source, and rather than treating the product of our masterful and appreciative activity as a surrogate for ourselves in the world, we are invited to focus our appreciative activity on the beauty that guides that activity. It is through this practice of respect for the beautiful that we are educated up to a recognition of the ultimate causal source, the beautiful itself, or form. By recognizing our own essentiality, yet still allowing ourselves to be displaced, Plato presents a provocative ambiguity that, if we attend to its many facets, helps us learn to make room for form in a way that is aware of the practical burdens of doing so. The image of the female at the center of the dialogue reenacts the ambiguity, similarly operative at the core of the *Theogony*, of both inter-personal self-awareness and theoretical knowledge in a single, maximally inclusive, presentation.

11.7

It is through appreciative activity, guided by the beautiful, that we enable the beautiful to disclose itself to us more deeply. Diotima has referred to this process as "reproduction in the presence of the beautiful." I have tried to show that this process carries with it an existential weight that is not explicitly addressed by Diotima but that can be traced out in Alcibiades' strategies of refusal of the path opened up by Diotima. This alone would be sufficient to show that the Platonic account of form is true, i.e., reproductive, only if it is seen in the context of the disruptive and transformative process of self-knowledge.[15] In order to pursue the beautiful itself not solely as an object of study but as divinely inspiring, we must allow ourselves to become open, unpossessive, and transformable. What I hope to have added by reference to the "internalization of the female" in Hesiod's *Theogony* is that the existential weight of the philosophical path increases, again and again, as our appreciative activity becomes more disciplined. Once we appreciate the tension between theoretical knowledge and self-knowledge along the philosophical path, we can begin to appreciate the difficulties and risk inherent in the demand to "Know thyself!"

---

[15] There is more truth to this second point than I think most readers are willing to accept. The excessive emphasis on the beautiful itself as a universal with an account has given rise to Vlastos' familiar claim that the Platonic conception of love does not adequately address the individuality of the individual. However, if we are only willing to read the whole dialogue with an eye toward the way each part relates to and qualifies the others, we can, I think, see that Diotima's speech is highlighted in its one-sidedness by the opposing but equally one-sided character of Alcibiades' speech. The parity between the two should prepare us to at least look for further insight not confined to either speech.

CHAPTER 12

Double Ignorance and the Perversion of Self-Knowledge

Danielle A. Layne

> SOCRATES: But if you are bewildered, is it not clear from what has gone before that you are not only ignorant of the greatest things, but while not knowing them you think you do?
> ALCIBIADES: I am afraid so.
> SOCRATES: Alack then, Alcibiades, for the plight you are in! I shrink indeed from giving it a name, but still, as we are alone, let me speak out. You are wedded to ignorance my fine friend, of the vilest kind.
>
> *Alcibiades* I 118b4–7 (Lamb trans.)

As any casual reader of Plato's dialogues knows, the activity of heeding the Delphic oracle, of coming to know oneself, begins with recognizing one's ignorance. Witnessed in Socrates' often proud boasts of not-knowing, in dialogues like the *Apology* (21d) or the *Alcibiades* I (124c), and praised as a necessary feature of the erotic soul in the *Symposium* by Diotima (204b), we are asked again and again to value the lack, the poverty, the confusion penetrating to the heart of the human condition. From seemingly ethical beginnings in Socrates' pursuit of definitions of the virtues in the so-called early dialogues to his more psychological and cosmological accounts of the human soul as a mixture of knowing and not-knowing, poverty and plenty, sameness and difference, we are called to recognize, in texts as diverse as the *Apology*, the *Republic*, the *Phaedrus*, the *Timaeus*, and others that we all begin the pursuit of knowledge and the Good from the cave of shadows and illusions, from a state of tragic fallenness, from a condition, described by Timaeus as being upside down (43e). Plato continually and consistently reminds his readers that we must recognize this condition, the reality of perplexity and the genuine dissembling it can cause, before we can set things right side up, before we can order ourselves so as to become otherwise than ignorant, otherwise than disordered and confused. Contrariwise, if we fail to acknowledge our ignorance, we cannot traverse the path of learning and inquiry constitutive of the examined life regularly valorized throughout Plato's dialogues.[1]

In direct opposition to this recognized ignorance, Plato set the condition of *double ignorance* or the ignorance of ignorance often combined with haughty conceit, vain ambition, and aggrandizing self-love, witnessed in individuals as disparate as Euthyphro, Anytus, Meletus, and Alcibiades. In all of the dialogues where someone suffers from this condition, Plato is careful to show that their self-ignorance and corresponding pretense isolates them in a world of illusions and alienates them from themselves and others. It comes as no surprise, then, that such individuals are lambasted for their inability to truly enter into conversation, to join in inquiry, to carefully weigh the argument, or to maintain lasting relationships. They rush off like Euthyphro, cut the conversation short like Anytus, hurry toward a conviction like Meletus, or, as in the case of Alcibiades, they desperately love the body but not the man. In all of these examples, the doubly ignorant fail to truly and consistently acknowledge their confusion and pretense, and as a consequence, they neither know nor care for themselves or the other standing before them. Rather, they unwittingly admire appearances of themselves reflected in their reputations, their political ambition, their capital and/or youthful beauty. In short, when Alcibiades confesses in the dialogue named after him that he has long wavered on the question of whether self-knowledge was easy or hard (129a), he speaks for all of us who are caught between the deceitful image of ourselves that we reflect before our peers and countrymen and the more ambiguous and confused image of the soul that the Socratic lover exposes.

With this dichotomy in mind, this chapter will first explore the condition of double ignorance and its counterpart – recognized ignorance – from the perspective of understanding how both forms of ignorance offer images of the self, one dissembling and dangerous, the other complex insofar as it teeters between knowing and not-knowing. In the second half of the chapter we shall explicitly turn to the erotics of both double and simple ignorance, showing how the doubly ignorant, in their flight from admitting ignorance, fail to know themselves because they fail to love themselves and the other in their complexity, as beings who are between knowing and not-knowing. Contrariwise, the simply ignorant, insofar

---

[1] Cf. *Alc.* I 106d–110a or *Men.* 84c. Cf. Proclus, *In Alc.* 177.27–178.4 where he writes, "Everyone who has inquired after any subject or consulted teachers about anything can name a time in which he once considered that he did not possess this knowledge; and the reason is that men both hasten to make inquiry when they advert to their own ignorance and frequent the doors of teachers when they are not confident of being sufficient unto themselves for the removal of ignorance" (O'Neill trans.).

as they appreciate souls who recognize their ignorance, who recognize that wisdom and self-knowledge begin by overcoming versus hiding it, come to love themselves and others as what they are—ambiguous souls who, as Socrates wonders himself, could always be either Typhonic monsters, willful dissemblers, or, conversely, something altogether simpler (*Phdr.* 230a).²

12.1

Two of the most paramount descriptions of the problem of double ignorance appear in works where they are least expected, i.e., texts that are not led by Socrates and so seem less inclined to carve out distinctions between kinds of ignorance: the *Laws* and the *Sophist*.³ In the former, the Athenian Stranger, in his painstaking attempt to construct just laws, makes note of the various causes of vice (ἁμάρτημα), including uncontrolled passion (θυμός) and deceitful pleasure (ἡδονή), before turning to the expected third origin, ignorance (ἄγνοια), a hazard that he explicitly divides into two categories:

> Nor would it be untrue to say that the third cause of vice is ignorance. This cause, however, the lawgiver would do well to subdivide into two, counting ignorance in its simple form to be the cause of minor evils, and its double form – where the folly is due to the man being gripped not by ignorance only, but also by a conceit of wisdom (δόξῃ σοφίας), as though he had full knowledge of things he knows nothing about – counting this to be the cause of great and brutal evils when it is joined with strength and might, but the cause of childish and senile evils when it is joined with weakness. (IX.863b–d) (Bury trans. with minor alterations)

---

² Here, it should be understood that I am following the work of Gordon (2012, 47), who argues that "knowledge of the self is fundamentally social insofar as it necessitates a relation to the other, and it is fundamentally erotic insofar as the relation to the other is ideally an erotic relation." Gordon further argues that "the leading or guiding toward self-knowledge carried out by the lover connects the cultivation of self-knowledge to the divine, and in doing so it connects self-knowledge to the mediating role of eros" as that which is between mortal and immortal, poverty and plenty, knowledge and ignorance. In this chapter, I hope to further expand on this thesis by showing how double ignorance obstructs loving the other and, consequently, ourselves as erotic beings.

³ The Platonic problem of double ignorance was especially important for the late antique Platonist Proclus. Extensive discussion of this condition, which relies heavily on the passages from the *Sophist* and the *Laws* that are immediately given in the body of the text, can be found in Proclus' *Commentary on the Alcibiades I*, and a more limited analysis can also be found in his *Commentary on the Parmenides*. See particularly *In Alc.* 201.5–8: "Either we do know or we don't and if we don't know, either we think we do or we don't. If we do know we possess knowledge; if we neither know nor think we do, simple ignorance; but if we don't and think we do, we are doubly ignorant." See further *In Alc.* 189.10–190.8; 200.15–201.5; 236.14–19; *In Crat.* 13.1 as well as Anon., *Proleg., Phil. Plat.* 16.17–30. For further discussions of double ignorance in Plato and Proclus, see Layne (2009a), (2009b), (2015), and (2017),

Here we see the Athenian explicitly demarcating between kinds of ignorance where the greatest form results from combining ignorance with hollow pretenses to wisdom. The Athenian claims that the "extreme form of ignorance" deserves to be called the "greatest" not simply because it sentences its sufferers to lives of self-contradiction and discord (III.689a8) but also because chaos threatens to manifest itself in the state as a consequence.[4] For the Athenian, this extreme form of ignorance is intimately bound up with a form of self-deception blinding its sufferers to the value of realities outside their solipsistic worldviews, leading such persons to perpetuate a rejection of a common good in favor of valorizing their own private interests (IX.875a). As shall be discussed more fully in the second half of this chapter, the doubly ignorant person's self-deception typically ends in becoming like the tyrannical soul of the *Republic* as he often combines all three vices demarcated by the Athenian. That is, their passion (θυμός) will be misdirected and will, as such, merely defend their appearance, while their lack of understanding reality will cause them to seek pleasures that cannot satisfy the soul, creating in many who suffer from double ignorance an insatiable psychic hunger.

The second passage in Plato's corpus that most explicitly outlines the problem of double ignorance occurs in the *Sophist* where the Eleatic Stranger clearly discriminates between the worst form of ignorance and other forms of ignorance:

> I at any rate think I do see one large and grievous kind of ignorance, separate from the rest, and as weighty as all the other parts put together . . ., thinking that one knows a thing when one does not know it. Through this, I believe, all the mistakes of the mind are caused in all of us . . . and furthermore to this kind of ignorance alone the name of stupidity is given. (229c1–10) (Fowler trans.)

In this passage the Stranger is distinguishing between the mere ignorance that seems to be a necessary part of the human condition and a more heinous form characterized by pretenses that warp or deform the soul.[5] Ultimately, the Stranger argues that individuals must be purified from this severe distortion by being forced to "cast out" their vain opinions through argumentative methods that expose their bondage to "thinking one knows a thing when one does not." Describing the task of those set on purifying the doubly ignorant, the Stranger argues:

---

[4] Cf. *Lg.* IX.863a.
[5] *Sph.* 230a. See Gooch (1971) and Lott (2012) for a thorough analysis of this section of the dialogue.

They question a man about the things about which he thinks he is talking sense when he is talking nonsense; then they easily discover that his opinions are like those who wander (πλανωμένων), and in their discussions they collect those opinions and compare them with another, and by the comparison they show they contradict one another about the same things and in respect to the same things. (230b2–8) (Fowler trans.)

In their pretense, the doubly ignorant thoughtlessly trust their intuitions, never taking the time to reflect on their internal consistency. This self-assurance causes them to be completely unaware that their opinions are far from resembling stable knowledge insofar as particular methods of discussion often expose how very easily their thoughts "wander" (πλανωμένων). Think here of Euthyphro, whose responses appear to Socrates like the animated statues of Daedalus (11c), or even Alcibiades' case of bewilderment (πλανᾷ) in the dialogue named after him. In fact, in the *Alcibiades I* Socrates explicitly defines bewilderment (πλανᾷ) as the particularly uncanny response that arises when individuals discover their conceit and the consequent realization that their opinions are inconsistent or "wandering." For Socrates, we are not bewildered by our ignorance of things when we know we do not know (*Alc I.* 117d).[6] Rather, we are "bewildered in spirit (πλανᾶσθαι τὴν ψυχήν)" only when we, as the Stranger phrases it, have an "unjustified belief in [our] own wisdom" (*Sph.* 231b).

It is conceit, then, that obstructs the doubly ignorant from recognizing their internal inconsistency. As such, many Platonic commentators and scholars have argued that Socrates' methods revolve around exposing the source of such bewilderment, the intuitive but unwarranted confidence, that weds individuals like Alcibiades to their double ignorance.[7] It is only when we are humbled that we can more clearly begin to see the possibility of being "bewildered in spirit," as in this humbling we become aware of our need to tend to the relationships between our ideas; i.e., we become aware of our need for consistency. Similarly, for the Stranger, one must be cleansed from double ignorance via a refutative method that "restores him who is refuted to an attitude of modesty," an attitude he explicitly

---

[6] See Kurihara (2012, 83).

[7] See Cain (2007), who argues for the importance of seeing the value of shame and positive humbling in Plato's dialogues in general and Socrates' methods in particular. As a consequence, she offers a psychological rather than merely an epistemological reading, e.g., Vlastos, of the Socratic *elenchos*. See also Proclus *In Alc.* 210.17–211.14, and Olympiodorus, *In Alc.* 124, 10–25, who both write extensively on the connection of double ignorance and shame, arguing that Socrates' methods of refutation and exhortation are designed to relieve this shame-worthy condition of the soul.

characterizes as finally distinguishing what one merely thought one knew from what one actually knows.[8]

Alongside the condition of being "bewildered in spirit" or failing to notice internal inconsistency, the doubly ignorant are often depicted by Plato as persons who attempt to live a life of cultivating appearances or images. This is, of course, one of the main themes of the *Republic*, *Phaedrus*, *Apology*, and others. Throughout many of these texts Socrates consistently contrasts those who merely wish to appear just or knowledge-able with those who are actually just or wise, e.g., the sophist as opposed to the philosopher. Especially in the *Sophist*, the Stranger insists that the doubly ignorant are imitators who pattern their lives after a particularly strange kind of image-making. Similar to Socrates' distinctions in *Republic* X, there are two categories of imitators for the Stranger: (1) imitators who model themselves after that which they know and (2) imitators who mirror patterns without knowledge. In other words, what is suggested here is that all human beings are, indeed, kinds of imitators, producers and lovers of images, yet the former category attempts to create images of realities, of things that can be known (think here of Plato's own penchant for advancing images of intelligible reality that readers are explicitly invited to model, e.g., the cosmos of the *Timaeus* or the just soul of the *Republic*), while the latter produce images based on ignorance. As such, they haphazardly construct a kind of "fun house of mirrors," refracting images of wisdom and beauty, never knowing which image is reality. Indeed, their obsession with appearance may cause them not even to believe in reality or, more precisely, a reality outside appearance. Consider here the sight-lovers of *Republic* V.476b–e who are defined as those who believe in many beautiful things but fail to believe in the reality of beauty itself. That is,

---

[8] See Notomi (1999, 295–296) on Plato's intentional blurring of the image of the sophist's activities and Socratic method. Others who have argued that this is a description of the Socratic *elenchos* include Hackforth (1946), Sayre (1969), and Dorter (1990). Expanding on these ideas, it seems clear that the Stranger is highlighting the therapeutic nature of the *elenchos* versus its merely eristic *telos*. As such, I am more inclined to believe that Plato was drawing attention to the different ends of the sophist and Socrates – the former hopes to dissemble for the sake of supporting one's public persona, while the latter has a pedagogical purpose insofar as he hopes to bring the interlocutor to a state of self-dismantling so as to come to authentic self-understanding. Cf. *Chrm.* 157a where Socrates explicitly compares his method to a healing charm or *Tht.* 151d where Socrates repeatedly insists that his interrogative methods are for the good of those he tends. Protagoras' statements at 167a also show the moral implications of education as a kind of purification, i.e., a moving from a worse to a better state: "So, too, in education a change has to be made from a worse to a better condition; but the physician causes the change by means of drugs, and the teacher of wisdom by means of words." While these statements are made by the "resurrected" Protagoras, they are arguably also a good description of the hopes even sophists may have had in practicing elenctic type interrogations. For more on the therapeutic intent of the Socratic ἔλεγχος in particular, see May (1997).

they believe only in likenesses of beauty, the appearance of beauty, and therein fail to love or see the reality of beauty outside appearance. Similarly, for the doubly ignorant, their beautiful image or appearance is all they know. They spend their lives caring for the appearance of themselves, their reputation, and demeanor before the masses rather than their soul because they fail to believe there is anything else beyond their appearing.

Moreover, a further division is made in the *Sophist* between (1) those who are truly unaware that they lack knowledge and (2) those who suspect that "they are ignorant of the things which they pretend before the public to know" (268a). With the first, we may easily think of a variety of Socrates' youthful interlocutors like Alcibiades who, after engaging in elenctic activities, seem genuinely alarmed by their lack of knowledge and, consequently, seek to overcome such confusion.[9] Such "honest" double ignorance seems altogether understandable in the early stages of youth, where interlocutors may not have the practical or elenctic experience to know that their opinions wander or that they pursue images over reality. However, the latter imitators, those long entrenched in their conceits, are described as fearful and suspicious and are deemed by the Stranger as dissembling imitators (εἰρωνικὸν μιμητὴν) insofar as they suspect their pretense.

The appearance of such a "dissembling imitator" in the Platonic corpus is striking insofar as it suggests that the doubly ignorant may be aware of their chicanery and are willfully hiding their ignorance. Is this possible? Would this not be akratic? How can the doubly ignorant be aware of their ignorance and still be doubly ignorant? Would they not be persons of recognized ignorance, and if so, how are they not compelled to live the examined life? The crux of the issue centers on why these "dissembling imitators," while suspecting their ignorance, feel they must hide it by putting on an air of wisdom.[10] To understand this, it behooves us to think of one of the most classic examples of double ignorance in Plato's dialogues – the double ignorance associated with the fear of death in the *Apology*. As Socrates famously argues:

---

[9] As Gordon (2012) notes, Alcibiades admits ignorance six times in the first half of the *Alcibiades* (108e4, 112d10, 113b6–7ff., 116e2–3, 118a15–b3, 127a9–13).

[10] See Lott (2012, 47) for an excellent account of the εἰρωνικὸν μιμητὴν, its relationship to shame and fear, and the problem of pretense. Cf. *Phdr.* 242e–243a: "[B]ut their foolishness was really very funny besides, for while they were saying nothing sound or true, they put on airs as though they amounted to something, as if they could cheat some mere manikins and gain honor among them."

For to fear death, gentlemen, is nothing else than to think one is wise when one is not; for it is thinking one knows what one does not know. For no one knows whether death be not even the greatest of all blessings to man, but they fear it as if they knew that it is the greatest of evils. And is not this the most reprehensible form of ignorance, that of thinking one knows what one does not know? (29a–b) (Fowler trans.)

Double ignorance, here, is characterized by unwarranted fear of the unknown, in this case death. The masses' double ignorance is a particular pretense: they believe they know that death is an evil. In other words, double ignorance is specific. It is not merely the ignorance of ignorance in general or being dissembling imitators more broadly. Rather, it results from holding pretenses about specific ideas; in this case, the Athenians hold a conceit regarding death and as a consequence fear or regard it as evil. Similarly, the fear of the dissembling imitators derives from thinking they know ignorance is something shameful, something to be avoided at all costs (much like death). They conceitedly believe that associating with ignorance harms one's *appearance* or reputation for wisdom. In other words, such individuals are unaware of their ignorance regarding the nature of ignorance itself and so they create an image of themselves as wise, beautiful, just, or pious, untouched by any association with ignorance or doubt.

Put otherwise, the doubly ignorant think they know that acknowledged ignorance in these arenas is always shameful, that admitting ignorance about their own virtue or expertise is an evil and will damage what is most valuable, their reputations and/or self-images. The dissembling imitator is unaware of his ignorance about ignorance, failing to see how recognized ignorance can be part of the life of wisdom or virtue. As such, while suspecting/knowing his ignorance, he holds the conceit that it is better to appear wise, just beautiful, etc.[11] Consequently, the doubly ignorant person creates an image of himself without knowledge, projecting a fantasy about what wisdom looks like, a fantasy that is reflected to others and is further reproduced in others. In the end, the dissembling life of the doubly ignorant centers on the pretense that all that matters is their appearance,

---

[11] Consider Proclus' discussion (*In Alc.* 210.17–211.1) of why Alcibiades hides his ignorance despite being aware that he may be ignorant: "For Alcibiades looks on ill-repute with apprehension, and would endure anything rather than shame and condemnation; and what need is there of words, seeing that he admits real evil that he may not endure apparent shame?" In other words, Alcibiades would rather admit of double ignorance, the real evil, than be associated with ignorance, only a seeming shame. For the Neoplatonist, discovering ignorance or becoming simply ignorant is the first step toward the path of learning and inquiry. See *In Alc.* 236.15.

their image as powerful, wise, beautiful, etc. For them, this image is all that is real. As such, the philosophical life, insofar as it troubles such appearances, is regarded as something to be avoided; i.e., the examined life is the dangerous life that pressures the doubly ignorant to dismantle all they know to be good, their appearance.

To be sure, the life of double ignorance is threatening not only to one who possesses it but, more poignantly, to those who are duped by the pretense of the doubly ignorant. In the *Philebus*, Socrates explicitly describes his fears about the political power of the doubly ignorant when he describes the condition of the "ridiculous," a state defined as involving "the opposite of the condition mentioned in the inscription at Delphi" (48c). Contrasting self-knowledge with self-deception, Socrates maintains that the "ridiculous" are those who deceive themselves by believing that they are wealthier than they are or that they are more endowed with physical beauty than they really are. The most abhorrent, as already suggested, think they excel in virtue when they do not (49a). Said differently, all categories of the ridiculous arise from the ignorance of ignorance combined with self-deception in the arenas of money, beauty, and human virtue. For Socrates, this absurd self-deception contagiously fills the masses with "strife and false conceit of wisdom" (49a), creating cultures that pretend away their ignorance to the point that Socrates boldly declares such pretense an evil (49e). Such cultures create people who consider it an insult, a threat to their livelihood, when their projected self-image is threatened and, as such, it creates people who believe they must strike back at those who attempt to expose their pretense.

In this vein the Socrates of the *Philebus* warns, in tune with the Athenian's argument in the *Laws*, that the doubly ignorant person who possesses false conceit, who deceives himself and others, falls into two distinct categories: the weak and the strong. Socrates argues:

> [T]hose of them who have this false conceit and are weak and unable to revenge themselves when they are laughed at you may truly call ridiculous, but those who are strong and able to revenge themselves you will define most correctly to yourself by calling them powerful, terrible, and hateful, for ignorance in the powerful is hateful and infamous – since whether real or feigned it injures their neighbor – but ignorance in the weak appears to us as naturally ridiculous. (49b–c) (Fowler trans.)

In other words, those without power who attempt to dissemble are simply absurd and tragic, reducing others, who know better, to laughter (49e), while persons who combine ignorance and false conceit with power are something truly terrible and hateful (49c). Their self-deception does not merely end in making horrific decisions about how to run the state, about those with whom to go to war (*Alc.* I 106c–113d) but, perhaps more importantly, saturates the worldviews of all those who come into contact with them. As such, the doubly ignorant threaten to mold the state into their own image – creating a state mired in a life of appearances either tragic and ridiculous in its impotence or terrifying and unpredictable in its potency.

Harkening to the *Republic* and the ship of state analogy, the Eleatic Stranger in the *Statesman* warns of the very real dangers of rulers suffering from this condition. They are as hazardous, he says, as captains who feign the requisite knowledge of how to steer ships, leading not only themselves into a life of pretense but creating crews that steer the country toward disaster:

> Many, to be sure, like ships that founder at sea, are destroyed, have been destroyed, and will be destroyed hereafter, through the worthlessness of their captains and crews who have the greatest ignorance of the greatest things, men who have no knowledge of statesmanship, but think they have in every respect most perfect knowledge of this above all other sciences. (302b) (Fowler trans.)[12]

In short, double ignorance is not merely an epistemological or psychological menace. Rather, Plato is keenly aware that this unchecked life of double ignorance is the political danger par excellence.

12.2

In the *Alcibiades* I we see the threat of the combination of unchecked power and self-deception in the stubborn and overly ambitious youth who mistakenly thinks that his natural gifts – his affluence, physical prowess, and overall admiration from the masses – constitute his power over the Athenians. Intent on showing Alcibiades that none of these things prepares him to lead the polis, i.e., to truly care for others, Socrates first refutes the young man's various beliefs regarding his knowledge of leadership and justice, before eventually declaring that the boy is "married to ignorance of the vilest kind" (118b). Highlighting the boy's double ignorance and the danger of his chicanery, Socrates asks Alcibiades, "Then do you note that mistakes in action are due to this ignorance of thinking one knows when

---

[12] Again, think of the *Apology* where Socrates notably addresses the danger of double ignorance in the prejudices of his jurors, the thoughtlessness of his accusers, and the general failure of the Athenians to care for virtue and wisdom over mere appearances. Believing this life of pretense so dire, Socrates ends his defense speech by making a request of the jury, i.e., that if his sons don the cloth of conceit they should rebuke them (41e).

one does not?" (117d8–10). Appealing to Alcibiades' own conceit, his idea that what is valuable is his own image before the masses,[13] Socrates is able to convince him of the dangers of his double ignorance. Alcibiades is thus turned toward realizing that his ignorance might cause him to make politically noteworthy mistakes and tarnish his reputation and his consequent ability to seek the power he so desperately desires. Consequently, he admits that he must "take pains" with regard to himself.

Emphasizing their mutual need for inquiry, as Socrates admits that he too needs to be educated, that he too is similarly ignorant (124b-c), the philosopher ultimately identifies "taking care of oneself" with heeding the Delphic injunction γνῶθι σαυτόν. In so doing, he begins to offer images of how and why self-knowledge and self-care require both an admittance of ignorance and a commitment to caring not merely for the self but, more importantly, for others. Rather poignantly, Socrates compares the Delphic injunction with a command one would give an eye to see itself but with the caveat that this self-seeing only occurs in the act of the eye seeing itself in the eye of another (132c–133c). By gazing into the eye of another, the eye sees its constitutive activity. In other words, it is not the eye arrested in a mirror but only in the eye of another that one can observe the excellence of the eye (ἡ ὀφθαλμοῦ ἀρετή) (133b). Analogously, Socrates suggests that the soul must turn toward its beloved, focusing not on the beloved's outward appearance, reputation, or possessions but, rather, on the excellence of the beloved, what is markedly described as divine. As Socrates asks, "Can we call anything in the soul more divine than that part in which knowledge and thinking reside?" (133b). After Alcibiades agrees, Socrates continues: "Then this part of [the soul] is similar to the divine, and someone who looked at it and is able to grasp everything divine, god and intelligence, would have the best grasp of himself as well" (133c). In other words, Socrates suggests that what we see in the beloved is the divinity or good of the soul in its activity of knowing, an activity, as the analogy of the eye reflects, that cannot be done in isolation but, rather, can be carried out only with others who are similarly tending to knowledge and the divine.[14]

---

[13] Cf. Miller (1986) for analysis of the Socratic method of mimetic irony whereby Socrates mirrors the self-images of his interlocutors so as to expose them to the ridiculousness of their conceits.

[14] See Gordon (2012, 150–151). See further Renaud and Tarrant (2015, 64–71) for a concise summary of the debates concerning the interpretation of this enigmatic passage. Here, I am marrying the theocentric and anthropocentric interpretations so as to suggest an erotic account of how we become like the divine in Plato and Platonism. As many are well aware, in response to Socrates' highly enigmatic statements about the kinship of the soul with the divine, much of the Platonic tradition marries these remarks in the *Alcibiades* to the claim in the *Theaetetus* that one

This activity of seeing the divine part of soul with and within the other is based on Alcibiades' and Socrates' mutual recognition of ignorance. Insofar as Socrates has conspicuously framed the joint inquiry with both a discovery of ignorance and a mutual recognition of their need to come together to take pains over themselves, he has highlighted the origin of why we need to gaze at the other in the first place, why we must look to another and not merely ourselves. In tune with the *Phaedrus* and the *Symposium* as well as the *Republic* – where the human being is described as needy, as not self-sufficient (II.369a) – Plato's dialogues consistently iterate that human beings are erotic, that we are always, as Diotima insists, betwixt the divine and the mortal, the beautiful and the ugly, betwixt knowing and not-knowing. In this, then, the eye analogy should remind us that what Alcibiades sees in Socrates is not solely knowledge but also his admitted ignorance and his consequent commitment to the life of ceaseless examination. In turn, what Socrates sees in Alcibiades is not merely his stupidity and marriage to double ignorance. Rather, unlike Alcibiades' other lovers, Socrates looks past appearances into the divine power of the young man's soul and draws it out in conversation with him, draws it out by bringing the boy to a state of humility. In recognizing Alcibiades' complexity and caring neither for the blush of his youth nor for his political connections, Socrates converses "not with [his] face, it would seem, but with Alcibiades – that is, with your soul" (130e). Socrates seems to be stressing to the young boy that it is not with the face, not with the façade, not with the image you project to others that I converse. Rather, I converse with that "other" in you, that divine other that constitutes your power, your erotic longing as a being of *both* poverty and plenty, as one who is ignorant but possesses the seeds of wisdom and virtue in his soul. This is why Socrates believes that he is Alcibiades' first and only lover. Up until this point all his other lovers have cared only for an image of himself that he has created and nurtured, a puppet of beauty and power that he has unwittingly projected because he has been taught that reality is concerned only with images.[15]

In contrast, Socrates has known Alcibiades almost all his life and is aware of the boy's marriage to double ignorance, his doomed attraction to

---

should "become like god so far as is possible (ὁμοίωσις θεῷ κατὰ τὸ δυνατόν)" (*Tht.* 176b). See Plotinus, *Enneads* 5, 3 [49] 7.1–9, Iamblichus *De Mysteriis* 10.1.810 or Proclus, *In Alc.* 20.13–21.2 for direct identification of self-knowledge with becoming like god. For comprehensive discussions of the Platonic doctrine of ὁμοίωσις θεῷ, see Sedley (1997, 1999), Annas (1999), Armstrong (2004), and Baltzly (2004).

[15] Cf. the doxophilists of *R.* V.480e.

the masses and their love of appearances, but still sees the stirring of the good in the boy's curiosity, in his ambition and drive to obtain the best life. He loves Alcibiades as one who teeters on the verge of one kind of life or another. In other words, what this analogy suggests is that self-knowledge requires us to reflect on the complexity of the human condition, i.e., that our beauty, courage, and virtue are intimately wrapped up in their opposition, in the threat of slipping into the pursuit of distorted images of the self. In this, Socrates validates why the examined life is a ceaseless project, always requiring us to enter into conversation with others. The Socratic ἔλεγχος is not merely about testing beliefs for consistency. Rather, philosophical inquiry always exercises the soul, wrenches us to continuously expose our conceits, thus unveiling our power as beings who, despite ignorance, remain oriented toward realities outside our own solipsistic, and ultimately relativistic, understandings of the world.[16]

In this reading of the eye analogy, the *Alcibiades* seems to demand that the task of self-knowledge, self-care, and becoming like the divine cannot occur in isolation or without an honest recognition of confusion and perplexity, of the possibility of living a radically other form of life.[17] In short, knowing oneself requires that our gaze not be turned merely inward on our ambitions and pleasures in isolation from the world and others. Alcibiades will know himself, achieve his ambitions, and consequently care for himself when he sees himself in the eyes of Socrates, sees the genuine possibility that wisdom means living the life that mediates between ignorance and knowledge. As we shall discuss momentarily, this is the truly powerful and, even, pleasurable life that Alcibiades so desperately desires. Yet, as Plato so tragically reminds us throughout his corpus, Alcibiades'

---

[16] Consider Gordon (2012, 151), who writes on the erotic power of the eye analogy: "We might imagine the exquisitely handsome Alcibiades at the very moment when Socrates creates the image and wonder what transpires between them. Does he meet Socrates' eye? In that moment, a spark could be ignited in the young man that fuels his desires even further and inspires him to become this man's devoted boy. Or perhaps this is a moment during which Alcibiades cannot meet Socrates' eyes, ashamed of his shortcomings, a moment therefore unlike what he has experienced with any other lover or suitor before. If so, this moment might unveil Socrates' very real powers over Alcibiades and thereby substantiate his bold claims to power that begin their conversation. At the same time, too, the lover's gaze can be soothing, reassuring and consoling. The young man who aspires to so much, but beneath his bravado and pride retains a small, nagging doubt whether he can achieve his aspirations, could be comforted and encouraged by his powerful lover who promises so much and who will guide him in his quest. Either scenario is plausible, and perhaps each takes place in succession: Alcibiades first meets Socrates' eyes and then has to turn away. Regardless of Alcibiades' reactions, Socrates' creating the image of the lover and beloved intently gazing into each others' eyes further excites the drama with the power of eros."

[17] Cf. Scott (2000, 102), who emphasizes that self-knowledge requires understanding our ignorance so as to invite a radical transformation of one's life.

admission of ignorance and the consequent attempt to heed the Delphic oracle through joint inquiry will eventually be lost on the haughty youth. In the end, he will return to loving the appearance of himself as already beautiful and powerful in the eyes of the masses, an image that reflects back to him what he wants to see without the difficult work the Socratic lover demands. In the end, he will forget what he loved about Socrates–that what truly pleased him and satisfied his ambition, was the soul that accused him, that reminded him that he was living an imaginary life, that shamed him for his double ignorance but still invited him to pursue knowledge.

Ultimately, the doubly ignorant cannot love others; rather, they become obsessed, like those who stare in mirrors, with loving and caring for the image of themselves. This point is most evident in the *Laws* where the Athenian Stranger explicitly connects double ignorance with "excessive love of self" (V.731e) that blinds its possessor from tending to what should be loved, namely, the soul. This tragic condition compels the doubly ignorant to love what merely belongs to them instead of who they truly are:

> There is an evil, great above all others, which most men have, implanted in their souls, and which each one of them excuses in himself and makes no effort to avoid. It is the evil indicated in the saying that every man is by nature a lover of self, and that it is right that he should be such. But the truth is that the cause of all vice in every case lies in the person's excessive love of self. For the lover is blind in his view of the object loved, so that he is a bad judge of things just and good and noble, in that he deems himself bound always to value what is his own more than what is true; for the man who is to attain the title of "Great" must be devoted neither to himself nor to his own belongings, but to things just, whether they happen to be actions of his own or rather those of another man. And it is from this vice that every man has derived the further notion that his own folly is wisdom; when it comes about that though we know practically nothing, we fancy that we know everything; and since we will not entrust to others the doings of things we do not understand, we necessarily go wrong in doing them ourselves. Wherefore every man must shun excessive self-love. (V.731e–732b) (Bury trans. with minor alterations)

The connection between self-love and double ignorance leads to several important observations.[18] First, the Athenian emphasizes that self-love is a

---

[18] See Stalley (1983, 54) and Bobonich (2013, 103–14). For a discussion of self-love in Aristotle, consider Annas (1988). See Cicero *De finibus* 5, 28–29, and Plutarch *Moralia* 1.4.

problem that many excuse in themselves. For most, this indulgence is the acceptable vice of the soul. Many have grown accustomed to self-love as something inevitable and natural, and as such they do not shun it but, perhaps under certain conditions, revere such self-love as the highest kind of self-care. Of course, the Athenian will find this normalized self-love problematic because such erotic solipsism or auto-affection comes at the expense of pursuing what ought to be loved, the soul in its attunement to the Good or, as is the case in this passage, "to things just, whether they happen to be actions of his own or rather those of another man."

Second, the Athenian thinks self-love blinds us to the view of the object of love insofar as he sees only what belongs to him, *his* good versus *the* Good. In other words, unlike the eye analogy where we can see the soul in its erotic longing for knowledge, the self-lover cares only for his possessions.[19] In contrast, Socrates' eye analogy in the *Alcibiades* I requires an other for self-knowledge, an other who does not reflect our pretenses but rather – in her confessions of confusion, of not-knowing – reveals her authentic desire for transcendence, of wanting to be more than her perplexity, more than her ignorance. When we look to others we see that *my* good may be confused, that *my* good may not really be mine at all, may need to be questioned, and as such I begin to love myself as a being who, while ignorant, pursues knowledge with others.[20]

In the *Republic* and the *Symposium* Socrates very clearly lays out the idea that all, even the doubly ignorant, love the good and do everything for its sake (*R.* VI.505e and *Smp.* 206a). The problem with the desire of the doubly ignorant person is that it is misdirected because this person does not know herself and, as such, covers over her ignorance and need for inquiry. She fails to see herself in her erotic, needy state. Consequently, she fools herself into believing that her unexamined opinions will satisfy her desire for the good. This foolishness is fed by the fact that the doubly ignorant are pleased (recall this is one of the main conditions of error laid

---

[19] Cf. *Alc.* I 128d where Socrates differentiates between the self and what merely belongs to the self, in this case the body.
[20] Consider here the opposing image Socrates advances in association with his midwife analogy (*Tht.* 161a), i.e., that certain types of persons refuse to have their offspring examined and grow angry when they are taken from them. In other words, most care for ideas that are their own, clinging to them merely because they are their own, instead of caring for themselves. On the connection between knowledge of one's own ignorance and care for others, see Marina McCoy's Chapter 10 in this book.

out in the *Sophist*) by their own self-image and their unreflective beliefs about the good. Yet the rub for the doubly ignorant is that they fail to realize what would truly please them. For Socrates, recognizing our erotic condition allows us to turn ourselves to *reality* via the activity of inquiry and therein become "filled with the things that are appropriate to one's nature, satisfying those things which are in actual fact more real and would make us rejoice with true pleasure in greater reality and more truly" (*R.* IX.585b–e).

While this pursuit and ordering of the soul, through the philosophical life, is a ceaseless endeavor, the soul is fed by the pleasures of inquiry, sated by the process of thinking about and coming to understand what is real instead of what is imaginary. By contrast, think of the tyrannical soul of the *Republic*, whose eros and ambition ceaselessly consume finite pleasures and appearances. Since these pleasures are not substantial, i.e., they are not oriented toward the truly real, they are unable to satisfy the soul's need. In the end, the tyrannical soul's misdirected or vulgar eros will keep it mired in the world of appearances. As Socrates argues:

> They go neither beyond this point nor ever look up toward what is truly the upper region, nor are they conveyed that way. They are never filled with reality, nor have a taste of steadfast pure pleasure, but like cattle they are always looking downward, stooping themselves toward the ground, and they eat at a table and fatten themselves up and copulate, and in order to gain advantage in such things they trample over each other and kill each other with horns and hooves of iron on account of their insatiable desire, in that they are not filling the part of themselves which is real and continent with reality. (*R.* IX.586a4–b4)

Overall, tyrannical persons of double ignorance love their constructed images, the idols of themselves, while those of recognized ignorance love the soul in its reality, in its erotic state as always mediating between knowledge and ignorance. These latter individuals fill themselves with activities that demand confrontation and struggle, activities that require us to be confronted and loved by others who are in similar states. Contrariwise, the doubly ignorant fill themselves with vacuous images, projecting those shadows on walls for others to haphazardly think they know, and, as the arguments of the *Sophist* suggest, these (self-) image makers will suspect and, in some sense, know that they are empty, mere specters of persons. As such, the doubly ignorant sentence themselves to illusory associations and fellowships that merely reproduce solipsism, one that is incapable of the kind of Socratic friendship/love that will always threaten to dismantle our pretenses.[21] As the Athenian of the *Laws* argues, such persons "[G]row like unto men that are wicked, and, in so growing, to shun good men and good counsels and cut oneself off from them, but cleave to the company of the wicked and follow after them" (V.728b–c) (Bury trans.).

To conclude, the life of dissembling imitators, i.e., the life of double ignorance, is indeed concerned with the other. Yet this is only insofar as they are concerned with their own reputation before the other, i.e., their carefully crafted self-image as wise, as one not tainted by association with ignorance. Yet in reality they wander, they are "bewildered in spirit" (πλανᾶσθαι τὴν ψυχήν), neither knowing nor loving themselves in their erotic, in-between, condition. In contrast, Plato seems to want us to be transfixed by the other – by Socrates or friends/lovers like him – who calls "my" knowledge into question, who keeps "my" knowledge from merely being mine, from merely being idiosyncratic, in the etymological sense of the term "idiocy/idios" or "own." What we should discover in our erotic pursuits with others is that self-knowledge is not knowledge of "private" contents or our isolated/"inner" reflections. Unlike the mirror, the beloved's eye does not – or does not merely – refract my image, but it actually looks at me, both accusing me of ignorance and loving me for my wisdom, and in this I see that I too see them, that I accuse them, that I love them as a complex erotic being. In the eye of the other, I realize that I am also her possibility of self-knowledge, that I am also responsible for her being seen as a reality instead of an image. In this, we love one another as we are – creatures who can courageously turn from the life of dissembling images, of pretending we know when we do not, for the sake of becoming like the persons and objects we admire – selves who are what they are in loving, caring, and taking pains over other erotic others.

---

[21] For another good example of the connections between eros, double ignorance, and the possibility of friendship, see *Ly.* 217e–222a where, in contrast to the wise and utterly stupid, there are those who "while possessing this bad thing, ignorance, are not yet made ignorant or stupid, but are still aware of not knowing the things they do not know. Here, Socrates distinguishes the mere presence of ignorance from complete ignorance, while asserting that the mere presence of ignorance does not necessarily threaten a person's nature. Only when an agent makes himself *like* the thing he merely possesses does this mere presence become malignant. A similar idea is expressed in the *Theaetetus* (176d–177a).

CHAPTER 13

Philebus, Laws, *and Self-Ignorance*

Harold Tarrant

13.1

There are many reasons to explore the pages of Plato's latest creative phase for clues as to his thinking on self-knowledge. However, ever since Denyer proposed that the *Alcibiades* I is a rather late dialogue, written by Plato after events at Peparethos in 361 BC,[1] those interested in testing such a theory should be prepared to reflect on how far the acknowledged late dialogues agree with the *Alcibiades* on the subject of self-knowledge, which is arguably the key question the dialogue sets out to tackle.[2]

When Renaud and I were tackling the reception of the *Alcibiades* among the Neoplatonists, two passages stood out as having been influential on their discussions of self-knowledge (or, more accurately, self-ignorance).[3] *Laws* IX.863c–d influenced the whole Neoplatonic discussion of the difference between Socratic ignorance and the more serious ignorance shown by Alcibiades (according to *Alc.* 117a–118b) by providing the terminology of "double ignorance" for the latter and "single ignorance" for the former.[4] This may be seen particularly in Olympiodorus' discussion of that passage at *In Alc.* 123.20–125.23 (cf. 128.6–131.32). The distinction assists Olympiodorus in mapping Alcibiades' progress in the dialogue, for at this point he becomes aware of his lamentable condition, double ignorance becoming single ignorance.

The other passage of considerable relevance was from *Philebus* (48c7–e11), where mention of the Delphic inscription is followed by a threefold

---

[1] See Denyer (2001, 23–24, 152).
[2] See Renaud and Tarrant (2015, 13–22) and Werner (2013, especially 308–309). I have been reflecting on the problem of the *Alcibiades'* authorship and date for some time, but I am very dubious about whether the dialogue can be *wholly* authentic (Renaud and Tarrant 2015, 260–269), without rejecting the notion of a Platonic core, possibly arising from material that Plato had used for a sympotic performance (Tarrant 2018).
[3] See Renaud and Tarrant (2015, 35 and n. 23, 161–164).
[4] For a detailed analysis of these two kinds of ignorance, see Danielle Layne's Chapter 12 in this book.

division of self-ignorance: ignorance about one's external goods, ignorance about one's body, and ignorance about one's state of soul.[5] Porphyry makes use of this passage in his four-book work on the Delphic command "Know yourself" (275F Smith). He cites the division of self-ignorance early in this fragment, before moving to material more dependent on the *Alcibiades* (131a–b, 133d–e), and follows that with words that allude to *Philebus* 50b3: "the tragicomedy of the lives of the foolish." The division of self-ignorance had been fairly simple, corresponding to the distinction between soul, body, and externals: one can be mistaken about one's wealth, about the quality of one's physique, or about the quality of one's inner person. In a nutshell, one can think oneself wealthier, of superior physique, or superior in virtue to what one really is. But, says *Philebus* 49a, of these last it is the ones who have an inflated view of their own wisdom who are the worst.

It is very easy to imagine some influence of the *Philebus* over the *Alcibiades*. In the very opening of the latter dialogue (104a–c) we have a discussion of the physical attributes, and less importantly the wealth (c2) of the young man, showing him to be able to assess these attributes correctly. Obviously, we shall see him later being completely mistaken about the degree to which he has the knowledge to qualify him for rule. Less directly, the dialogue also raises issues about his wider excellence (134a–d), for Socrates implies that he does not yet possess it, seeing that its acquisition will be important for his self-care and for his leadership of the city.

If we look closely, however, we shall find that the *Alcibiades* does not recognize knowledge about one's physique or about one's wealth as *self-*knowledge at all. One's bodily attributes are not one's *self* but what belongs to that self: not *me* but *mine*. One's external possessions belong to what belongs to one's self: not *mine* but *something still more remote* (131a–c, 133c–e). But without knowing me I am unable to recognize what my belongings are or what belongs to my belongings. Self-knowledge is always concerned with the soul, and mistakes about the body and externals are inevitable if one cannot acquire knowledge of the self (133d–e).

To be fair, the *Philebus* had never claimed that mistaken assessments of one's wealth or physique were independent of any assessment of one's

[5] Since sketching out this chapter, I have been delighted to see that Moore (2015a, 185–215) devotes a whole chapter to the *Philebus* in a book on self-knowledge and views the dialogue more widely as relevant to the views of Plato's Socrates on self-knowledge; the common thread in Moore's book is Socrates. It is particularly useful for what is common to the depiction of Socratic discussions of self-knowledge, whereas my emphasis will be on Plato (including an imitator, if the *Alc.* I is not by Plato), looking for differences and shifts of emphasis.

inner attributes, but it never questioned it either. And it is hard to believe that the *Philebus* regarded self-assessment in all three spheres to be a matter of a single *technê* as the *Alcibiades* claims (133d12–e2). This all-or-nothing approach to valuable knowledge, coupled with the craft analogy, is much more typical of what we usually think of as the "Socrates" of the early dialogues, and one does not expect such simplicity later. Yet what needs to be recognized is that all the emphasis in the *Philebus* is on self-ignorance and that its whole dispute between the side of pleasure and the side of knowledge, which involves an elaborate classification of knowledge at 55c–58e, seems to take virtually no account of self-knowledge, even though the Delphic injunction was mentioned.

But there is more. At 19c Protarchus, after declaring that it is great for the sensible man (σώφρων)[6] to be able to recognize everything, affirms that a "second sailing" would be to avoid escaping one's own notice. What could "escaping one's own notice" be if not a failure of self-recognition? What does Protarchus, a relatively astute interlocutor, have in mind? He is essentially accusing Socrates of failing to honor his promise to assist them in their search for the greatest good for human beings, and not because he is intending to disappoint them, but because he does not realize that his present tactics are unproductive given the nature of his audience. Socrates is apparently being accused of a lack of self-knowledge. The Neoplatonists made every effort to credit Socrates with a considerable degree of self-knowledge in spite of his protestations at *Phaedrus* 229e about his lack of it, and similar hints even in the *Alcibiades* (124b–c, 127e). Their sole surviving commentary on the *Philebus*, that of Damascius, passes silently over this passage. Self-deception is not a charge that is easily leveled against the Socrates of the so-called early dialogues, for it is the very antithesis of Socratic knowledge as described in the *Apology*, where the self-deceivers are the recipients of his elenctic attention. But there seems in the *Philebus* to be no insistence on Plato's part that his "Socrates" should occupy the moral and intellectual high ground.

13.2

The emphasis on self-ignorance in the *Philebus* is actually accompanied by considerable interest in a variety of experiences that can happen to us

---

[6] Because the term means literally "safe-minded" and in view of its frequent connection with self-knowledge, I prefer to use a translation that suggests a quality of mind, albeit one that has strong ethical implications. Hence I shall avoid the common translation "temperate" here.

without ever registering with our senses (cases of nonsensation, 33d–34a, 43a–c), and in particular with seemingly pleasurable experiences that on closer inspection turn out not to be pleasurable at all (36e–44a). These are likely to accompany various kinds of judgment and can certainly involve some kind of self-deception. This in turn owes much to Plato's interest here in the complexities of psychology, an interest that is now no longer so directly intertwined with a particular educational mission. Plato's Socrates in this dialogue sometimes seems a somewhat reluctant participant in the quest, so that thoughts of the Delphic injunction at 48c no longer bring to mind any particular Socratic processes (such as elenchus or midwifery) as possible ways of remedying the fault,[7] but merely stimulate the deeper analysis of the way that comedy affects us. It may indeed be said that in the *Philebus* Socrates continues to retain that serious worry over people's overestimation of their own cleverness (or "wisdom," *sophia*), but there is a special venom reserved for that kind of self-delusion about one's expertise that belongs to people who also have considerable power (49b1–c5), a venom that far exceeds that which applies to the comic self-delusion of those who are fundamentally lacking in the strength to harm the fabric of society, and are therefore able to be mocked with impunity – unlike the powerful sort who cannot be challenged.

This division between powerful and weak among the people who have a false conceit of their own wisdom is reiterated again in the *Laws* passage (IX.863c6–d1), and it promises to be important in the setting of penalties for serious crimes, which is to follow,[8] perhaps as indicators of whether we are dealing with injustice or simply with injury, and if injustice, whether it is willing or not; all this the judges must take into consideration. Naturally it is the type with power that the lawgiver is to be most concerned about, for double ignorance can in that case be the source of especially dangerous crimes. Once again, there is no sign that Plato's treatment of the assumption of knowledge has anything notably "Socratic" about it.

Furthermore, it is in fact questionable whether Plato is interested in quite the same problem concerning people's false conceit of knowledge that Socrates had discussed in the *Apology*. There, of course, there had been three different classes of people among whom Socrates had discovered a false opinion about their own knowledge or wisdom: politicians, poets,

---

[7] Most obviously at *Ap.* 21a–23c and *Chrm.* 164e–167a, but also at *Alc.* I 124a–b; cf. (without mention of Delphi) *Tht.* 210c, *Sph.* 230a–e.

[8] It seems this will be the case at IX.864b8–c2, but it is difficult to see how far that division is actually respected in the imposition of the laws to which the Stranger returns at IX.864c10–11.

and ordinary professional people who knew a trade (21c–22e). While it is often difficult to be sure on whose behalf Socrates in the *Apology* thought he was acting,[9] it seems to me that his concern was for those people *as individuals* rather than for the society of which they were part,[10] and consequently there was no great difference between the politicians (the most powerful group) and the others. Socrates' mission in that dialogue might involve any of his fellow-citizens without distinction.[11] No great distinction was apparent between people who were firmly convinced that they had special expertise and people who merely assumed that they knew things without giving it a great deal of thought: between people like Euthyphro and Protagoras, for instance, and Crito or Charmides. Anybody's assumption of knowledge, whether or not it was backed by a massive ego and strong convictions, could be enough to set Socrates looking for an elenchus. But in *Laws* the emphasis has switched from an ethical one to a political one, and the mission of curing every individual of ills that affect them has given way to a mission of correcting society's ills.

13.3

In this respect, one might have difficulty here seeing quite where curing Alcibiades' self-ignorance belonged. Clearly Socrates' interest in him in the *Alcibiades* I was intensely personal, even though he had premonitions of what might befall Alcibiades in the public arena later. That his concern was not for Athens' well-being seems obvious from the fact that he saw himself in competition with the *demos* regarding it as a rival lover able to corrupt the object of his affections (132a, 135e). It is true that Alcibiades was making dangerous assumptions in the *Alcibiades* about his knowledge of

---

[9] His service was the *result* of a personal curiosity about the Delphic response (21b–c), and so to some extent it was *for himself*, and yet it remained in a very real way service *to the god* (28d–30a). No speech in the law courts could afford to neglect any public benefit that resulted from the speaker's behavior, and so the god's business is a benefit practiced "in the city" (30a7) and the human benefactor is like a gadfly settling "upon the city" (30e3, e6). If the city should kill Socrates, then the best hope would be for another to come and "care for" them (31a7), since he is like a god's gift "to the city" (31a8–9). However, the elenchus always operates on individuals, and Socrates does not claim that he does this *because* the city needs it, and he practices the elenchus on foreigners as well as locals (30a4–5), but rather more on locals *as they are closer in kinship to him*, not because the city benefits more from curing locals. At *Meno* 84c8 we are offered a clear case of Socrates' elenchus having benefited a foreign individual, and it is arguable that in the *Apology* too the benefit, while widespread, is largely offered to the Athenians as individuals, not to the collective.

[10] This follows from Socrates' description of his mission as giving the same kind of private encouragement to virtue as a father or elder brother might offer (*Ap.* 31b3–5).

[11] See 23b3–6 (καὶ τῶν ἀστῶν καὶ τῶν ξένων ἄν τινα οἴωμαι σοφὸν εἶναι.), 29d6 (ὅτῳ ἂν ἀεὶ ἐντυγχάνω ὑμῶν), cf. 31b3–4 (ἰδίᾳ ἑκάστῳ προσιόντα).

fairness and unfairness, but most of us do make such assumptions very early in life (cf. 110b–c).[12] Moreover, this is not something about which the lad has strong convictions – rather, he thinks that he has picked up the relevant knowledge in the same way that people pick up the Greek language from those around them (110d–111a). Certainly he makes no extravagant claims either to have made some personal discovery or to have had especially eminent teachers on questions of fairness and the like. While he suffers from double ignorance insofar as he thinks he knows things that he does not know, it is not any inexcusable pride in his assumed knowledge that makes this double ignorance so shameful, but rather the fact that he is rushing to test it in public life (118a–c). While there is no doubt that the author of the *Alcibiades* sees double ignorance as especially troublesome if combined with power, for which reason Socrates is seen to be diverting the young man from public life at this stage, he does not attempt to see Alcibiades' problematic ignorance as anything unusual (118b8–c2). There is nothing in the *Alcibiades*' treatment of ignorance and of self-knowledge that would cause one to relate it closely to the hiatus-avoiding dialogues (*Sophist, Statesman, Timaeus, Critias, Philebus, Laws*, and (if genuine) *Clitophon*).

One particular word that leaps from the page at *Philebus* 49a2 and d11 is *doxosophia*, referring to "wisdom" as part of one's image, whether or not that wisdom is a sham – as it must be here, since it is a false impression of wisdom. The only other occurrence of that word is at *Sophist* 231b6, where the so-called sophistry of noble lineage (ἡ γένει γενναία σοφιστική, 231b8) is seen as practicing the exposure of vain conceits of wisdom. Rowe (2015) has recently weakened, or perhaps modified, the link between this quasi-sophistry and Socrates' practice, but in any case this is clearly later thinking about what the elenchus, rightly used, could achieve rather than a straight description of how it had functioned earlier. At *Laws* IX.863c5, in place of *doxosophia* we meet its two-word equivalent *doxa sophias*, but the meaning is probably little different.[13] The false mask of wisdom that certain people adopt becomes increasingly important in Plato's latest works and is

---

[12] Compare the accusations of cheating made even in his sleep by the similarly competitive "Pheidippides" at the beginning of Aristophanes' *Clouds* (25).

[13] Other relevant close conjunctions of *dox-* and *soph-* found at *Euthphr.* 305d3–5 (τὰ νικητήρια εἰς δόξαν οἴσεσθαι σοφίας πέρι), *Phdr.* 275a6 (σοφίας ... δόξαν) and 275b2 (δοξόσοφοι), *Lg.* 701a6 (σοφίας δόξα). With two relevant passages in *Epin.* 976b5 (πρὸς δόξαν σοφίας) and c7–8 (ὁ σοφὸς ὄντως ὢν καὶ μὴ μόνον δοξαζόμενος) this seems to confirm that the concept of *doxosophia* gained increasing importance in Plato's later works. There seems to be little technical sense in the *Euthydemus*, but by the story of Theuth in *Phaedrus* a technical ring begins to be heard that recurs in *Sophist, Philebus*, and *Laws*.

particularly liable to be referred to in contexts where people deceive themselves (and others) in assuming their own expertise in a variety of seemingly important areas. If the *Alcibiades* I had really been written by Plato between 361 BC and his death in 347 BC, then one might legitimately have expected some such terminology there too, especially where Alcibiades is exposed as having culpable ignorance himself. As things are, neither the terminology nor the concept seems to be present.

This should not come as a surprise. Among the reasons Renaud and I gave for being wary about whether Plato would have wanted to revisit Socrates' relationship with Alcibiades in the years 361–347 BC are the following:

1. Plato seems no longer to favor simple solutions in his late period, and is normally led into considerable levels of complexity.
2. Plato is suspicious of homoerotic attraction in his later works.
3. Not only the aging Plato but also his senior pupils seem to lack interests relevant to the *Alcibiades* I.[14]

None of this is compelling, for too little about the working of the Academy during this period is known, but one might have thought that the *Alcibiades* I ought at very least to have some connections with Plato's later works on questions of self-knowledge. Those works do show a common concern with any stubborn and erroneous conviction that one possesses wisdom or some important branch of knowledge. They do not appear to have as deep a reservation about the simple assumption that one has such knowledge.

13.4

Now I do not wish to suggest here that the *only* reason for looking at issues surrounding self-knowledge in the so-called late dialogues is to be able to date the *Alcibiades* I. Another is the possibility that it can tell us something important about the dispute between those who accept a developmentalist account of Plato's philosophy and those who believe *either* that a single coherent system of philosophy underlies all Plato's works *or* that each dialogue has to be considered as a discrete product whose relevance is confined to its chosen characters in their particular dramatic situation. For either of these sharply contrasting hypotheses would undermine the assumption that Plato's philosophy developed over the course of his total

---

[14] Renaud and Tarrant (2015, 264).

output in such a way that there are distinct groups of dialogues that are best studied together.

Now it is clear that Plato often makes a strong connection between sensibleness (*sōphrosunē*) and self-knowledge. The identification of the two is clearly being made by Plato's Critias at *Charmides* 164c–165b, and while what follows in that dialogue shows that it is somewhat problematic, it is perhaps uncontroversial to claim that Plato had explored such ideas at length in this dialogue because he was genuinely interested in them. Certainly Socrates in the *Alcibiades* I, after hinting at the identity of the two at 131b4, makes it quite explicit at 133c18–19, and Alcibiades is not tempted to challenge it. Part of the reason why Critias and Alcibiades were attracted to this concept of sensibleness is that it was backed by popular belief, for, as Timaeus tells us (*Ti.* 72a), "it has been well said since olden times that to act out and recognize one's own business and one's self belongs only to the sensible man."[15] Nor is there any real gulf between associating sensibleness with self-knowledge and an alternative account of the virtue that presumes it to be self-control, assuming that this latter requires one to *recognize* the object of control.

Despite the approval given to the idea that only sensible people (there meaning people of sound mind) can play their own parts and recognize themselves in the *Timaeus*, one needs to recognize that there is no real interest in the late dialogues in self-knowledge *as a key to any of the virtues*. Let us take, for example, sensibleness. Plato still remains very concerned to promote this virtue in those late dialogues that have much moral or political content. The language of *sōphrosunē* remains common.[16] But where is the corresponding interest in promoting self-knowledge? If the two remained closely linked in Plato's mind, one would expect this to emerge somewhere, for these dialogues occupy no small part of the *corpus*.

[15] Quoted also by Denyer (2001, 206, cf. 222).
[16] Figures for hiatus-avoiding dialogues, including the *Epinomis*, which also reflects the language of the Academy during Plato's last years, are as follows:

Table 13.1

Dialogue	Sph.	Plt.	Ti.	Criti.	Phlb.	Laws	Epin.
σωφροσύνη	0	1	1	0	1	14	1
σώφρων	1	7	2	0	3	29	3
σωφρονεῖν	0	0	0	0	3	19	1

Where is the connection with the Delphic injunction? Admittedly, there is the oblique allusion to it in the old saying approved at *Timaeus* 72a, but this occurs in a physiological discussion rather than an ethical one. We have seen how Delphi is used to introduce types of self-ignorance in the *Philebus*. In the *Laws* the most relevant passage that I can find runs as follows:

> Friends . . . it's difficult for you to know for now what's yours and further-more [to know] yourselves, as the Delphic inscription also puts it. Hence I, as lawgiver, lay down that neither you nor this property are your own belongings, but it all belongs to your entire family both past and future, and even more do the entire family and property belong to the city. (XI.923a2–b1, my translation)

This announcement by the lawgiver, discussing the rules of inheritance, eliminates knowing what is yours (important at *Alc.* 133c–e), because your property is your family's and the whole family, including you, belong to the state. Yet that is less important than the fact that the law-giver is, if anything, *discouraging* his citizens from making the effort to know either themselves or what belongs to them. Presuming that he remains keen to promote sensible behavior, the link between such behavior and self-knowledge would appear to have been broken. That is the overall impression that we receive from *Laws*: that a system of virtues is encouraged that owes little to what Socrates had thought to be the first lesson of all in the *Phaedrus* (229e4–230a1): the lesson of self-knowledge.

But had the link still been there in the *Philebus* perhaps? At 19c, as we have seen, Protarchus declared that it is a fine thing for the sensible man (σώφρων) to be able to recognize everything, before affirming that a "second sailing" would be to avoid escaping one's own notice. He is in fact suggesting that Socrates is trying to get them to examine a number of complex peripheral issues, while forgetting what he has actually promised them. Much as if he had worried about the rationalist interpretation of myths in the *Phaedrus* instead of trying to understand himself better, so here too he is forgetting himself in favor of obscurities. Protarchus may perhaps be *encouraging* Socrates to be a little more heedful of Delphi, and by the choice of the term σώφρων he too seems to be influenced by the traditional connection between sensible behavior and self-knowledge, just as Timaeus had apparently been. But should we detect any more than this here? Does Plato still retain that commitment to self-knowledge that had been credited to Socrates at *Phaedrus* 229e?

Let us return briefly to the *Sophist*. After the Stranger's description of the state to which those with false conceits are reduced by the questions of the "sophist of noble lineage," Theaetetus declares that this state, in which they have been purged of the obstacles that prevent their learning, is the "best and most sensible (σωφρονεστάτη) of states" (230d5–6). But it is essentially a state *without impediments to knowledge* rather than a state of any particular knowledge: it is a state where one believes one knows only what one does know (230d3–4). It implies no insights into the self, such as Socrates appeared to want in the *Phaedrus* when asking questions that seemed to search for the essence of his own soul (230a3–6), and it may not involve any knowledge at all. At *Philebus* 19c, in suggesting that the inquiry may progress if Socrates does not forget himself, what Protarchus is demanding from Socrates is not any special insight but just the keeping in mind of his promise! It is that rather than omniscience that Socrates should be aiming at.[17]

So Plato in his later years was not working with a positive conception of self-knowledge that identifies it with the awareness of some deeper truths about one's own nature, but with one that made it the absence of any exaggerated ideas of one's own knowledge and ability. That is why the Delphic influence is now found coupled with attacks on self-deception rather than on the promotion of any positive excellence. Something has changed in the way Plato views these matters. It is not a huge shift, but it has considerable implications for his ethics insofar as the close connection with virtue has disappeared, and it is indeed a sign of the development of his thinking, particularly on psychology. While I should be most reluctant to see such changes of emphasis, which affect the beliefs of the majority of us as we get older, as a proof that any particular developmentalist hypothesis concerning Plato is correct, I do believe that it shows that we may be able to map subtle changes of viewpoint, as also of language, in the works of almost any philosopher whose output spans a few decades. My thesis here, then, is that the latest dialogues work with an essentially negative view of what self-knowledge is, i.e., a state of freedom from those false convictions that are accompanied by the belief that one knows. Such a state may have positive benefits, but it does not involve a deep awareness of the very core of our being or lay the foundations for virtue.

13.5

One may now compare the attitude toward self-knowledge and the perils of ignorance found in the late dialogues with those encountered in the

---

[17] Strictly, perhaps, it is that rather than omniscience that the σώφρων should be aiming at (19c2), but the overall effect is to suggest that Socrates, *if he is* σώφρων, will settle for the more modest path.

Alcibiades II. A majority view holds that this dialogue followed its longer namesake and takes up many of its themes.[18] The most trusted criterion of the lateness or otherwise of Plato's genuine dialogues, the rates of hiatus, would place the *Alcibiades* II (in the unlikely event of its being genuine Plato) between the "late" dialogues and their "early" or "middle" predecessors, with a hiatus rate of around 12.8 per hundred word breaks,[19] as opposed to between 6.4% and 10.0% for late dialogues and between 26.6% and 15.7% for all other dialogues.[20] For comparison's sake the equivalent rate for the *Alcibiades* I is 19.2% up to 120a and 18.2% from 120a to the end, both parts falling within the range for parts of the *Republic* (19.9%–16.0%)[21] and comparable with most other doubtful dialogues in this part of the corpus.[22]

I offer these figures to show that it is most unlikely that the *Alcibiades* II is a genuine early or middle dialogue of Plato. The figures suggest that the author is not consciously trying to adopt the more artificial style associated with the development of rhetorical theory, since he is content to produce the natural conversational style of Socrates, but that at the time of writing the avoidance of the more awkward cases of hiatus was now something that came naturally. The number of quotations from tragedy and epic also suggest an author with strong literary interests who did not want his dialogue to be free of literary polish. Whatever the case, it does not seem

---

[18] See Thesleff (1982, 377), quoted by Renaud and Tarrant (2015, 102); also Johnson (2003, xviii n. 9); somewhat more cautious is Hutchinson in Cooper (1997, 596).

[19] I give my own figures, since Janell's figures, even with the additions provided by Brandwood (1990, 156), omit most works of doubtful authenticity; they also give figures per page rather than per hiatus opportunity. Word breaks involving any punctuation have not been included in my figure, which would therefore vary slightly from editor to editor. Total hiatus, including cross-punctuation cases, rises to 15.7% for *Alcibiades* II, as opposed to between 17.1% and 27.3% for early and middle dialogues and between 6.0% and 10.3% for late dialogues.

[20] The figure of 26.6% is the final part of the *Parmenides* where literary concerns are surely very far from Plato's mind, the early part being still high at 23.9%; 15.7% is for *Phaedrus* where literary and rhetorical concerns are important, as also for *Menexenus* (16.1%); all parts of the *Republic* fall between 20% and 16%.

[21] Books 2, 6, and 10 were split for this purpose, separating off the beginning of the discussion of the state, the Sun-plus-Line material, and the Myth of Er, respectively. Results were as follows: I, 19.9; IIa, 16.3; IIb, 17.5; III, 16.6; IV, 18.5; V, 16.6; VIa, 16.0; VIb, 17.5; VII, 16.5; VIII, 16.4; IX, 17.4; Xa, 19.1; Xb, 16.8.

[22] *Hipparchus* 18.6%; *Amatores* 17.4%; *Theages* 19.8%. These rates would be a little low for undisputed dialogues held to be early (usually 20%–22%), but that for *Laches* too is only 18.1% and *Gorgias* around 19.5%. In the two latter cases, the presence of rhetorical material may account for the difference, but there is little such material in the dialogues of disputed authorship. I have no complete figures for *Minos* but a 645-gap sample yielded a rate of 22.9%.

at all likely that the *Alcibiades* II could precede the *Alcibiades* I or be any earlier than Plato's late dialogues.[23]

In spite of the frequency of passages that recall the *Alcibiades* I in one way or another, the *Alcibiades* II does not make happiness dependent on self-knowledge, but rather on the knowledge of the good (146b–147a), as one might perhaps expect from *Laches* 199c–e or from *Republic* VI.505b8–10. It is far from obvious that one would search for the good inside oneself or in a mirror of oneself as in the *Alcibiades* I.[24] Yet like *Philebus* and *Laws* the *Alcibiades* II does highlight the problems of self-ignorance (143a–b). As I argued with Renaud, Alcibiades is able to observe what a huge problem *ignorance* can be for people.[25] Accordingly they must be on their guard against making decisions based on ignorance. He includes himself here and believes that because of ignorance "we lose sight of ourselves (λελήθαμεν ἡμᾶς αὐτούς) as we carry out and – worse still pray for – things that are really bad for ourselves (ἡμῖν αὐτοῖς)." The first-person plural reflexives strongly suggest that it is a kind of self-ignorance that Alcibiades is concerned with. People fool themselves, but "everybody would think he is capable of this, to pray for what is best rather than worst for himself (αὐτὸς αὐτῷ)." Alcibiades again brings in the idea of fooling oneself at 148b1–2: one must be careful "so that one does not escape one's own notice praying for bad things in the belief that they are good (ὅπως μὴ λήσει τις αὐτὸν εὐχόμενος μὲν κακά, δοκῶν δὲ τἀγαθά)." Hence he treats these dangers *both* as a failure of self-knowledge *and* as a failure of fundamental moral knowledge.

But what is this failure of self-knowledge? In the *Alcibiades* I the "self" had been one's soul rather than a body (130e), so that self-knowledge became soul-knowledge: an appreciation of our inner identity. And the soul's self-knowledge became knowing its own inner "self" and the source of its intellectual powers (133b7–c7). This knowledge would bring with it an awareness too of what belongs to "us" and what does not, indeed of the goods and evils that belong to us (133c21–23). Yet the *Alcibiades* II seems unaware that the soul is one's "self" at 141c1–3 when maintaining that Alcibiades (the person) would not give up "his soul"[26] (as if his *possession*) in return for imperial power, and it appears to use the

---

[23] Note that Aronadio (2008, 56), who rejects authenticity, argues that the work should still be dated in Plato's lifetime, not after 350 BCE.

[24] On the key 'mirror' passage at 132e–133c, see Tarrant (2015).

[25] Renaud and Tarrant (2015, 105–106).

[26] I acknowledge that word *psuchê* need mean little more than "life" on occasions, but surely it would have to mean more in this context to anybody who had accepted the lessons of the *Alcibiades* I.

same kind of concept of self-knowledge as the *Philebus* and the *Laws*: a state of freedom from those false imaginings that are accompanied by the belief that one knows.

Admittedly the *Alcibiades* I had recognized the problems of such imaginings and seen them as the supreme and most reprehensible ignorance (117b–118b), but there was no suggestion that its removal was all that was to be done. Knowing one's self required a specific awareness, and even some kind of "reflective" technique that would enable one to achieve it. The Alcibiades who has been relieved of his false opinions by the elenchus and finally admits his ignorance still does not have that self-knowledge required for the moral and political tasks ahead. By contrast, in the *Alcibiades* II the removal of the mist from Alcibiades' soul will bring him already to the task of telling good from evil (150d–e). Self-knowledge here seems to imply little more than the awareness that one knows nothing of much significance. As in the late dialogues, this state has positive benefits but involves no deep awareness of the core of our being and lays no foundation for virtue. Hence, it would seem that the *Alcibiades* II preserves the rather negative view of self-knowledge that we have seen in the late dialogues.[27]

13.6

The negative view of self-knowledge in the late dialogues has a further consequence for my view of the *Alcibiades* I. As has recently been pointed out, this is the dialogue where we find the ignorance approved by Socrates repeatedly described in terms of *knowing* what one does not know (117c2–3, 117c4, 117d4–5, 118a1).[28] Whereas in the late dialogues, as we have argued, Delphic or Socratic self-knowledge has involved no positive knowledge at all, here at the climax of Alcibiades' refutation in the first part of the dialogue, states of awareness of one's own ignorance are treated as if they were themselves states of knowledge. Only thus indeed can self-knowledge play the necessary role of underpinning the virtues required for both private and political life at the end of the dialogue, where self-knowledge is required not only for knowledge of one's own concerns

---

[27] This is perhaps not the place to go further still and argue that it has a negative attitude to knowledge in general, and yet some have seen it as somehow connected with the New Academy. It is in general much more conscious than one expects in a "Socratic" work that much knowledge can fail to be beneficial at all without some *moral* knowledge that tells one how to apply it (143b–147b).

[28] Kurihara (2012). The same verb (εἰδέναι) is used for the act of recognition and the fact of nonrecognition in the last three cases.

but also for knowledge of other people's concerns and those of the city (133e–134b). In this way, self-knowledge comes to play the role of a Socratic super-art, enabling the exercise of other arts that will be required for the acquisition of private and communal happiness (134c–e). Whereas dialogues like the *Sophist*, *Philebus*, and *Laws* (supported by the author of the *Alcibiades* II) had seen the acquisition of self-knowledge in terms of the expulsion of false beliefs following the recognition that one does not know them, eliminating obstacles to knowledge and correct behavior but not of itself supplying anything beyond this, the *Alcibiades* I makes it a genuine step forward and a fertile source of further knowledge in its own right. According to commonly accepted chronology, the late dialogues have diminished the role that Socrates had afforded to self-knowledge in the *Phaedrus*, whereas the *Alcibiades* I has magnified it.

Hence, if the *Alcibiades* I were really a work of Plato (or the Academy) contemporary with the late dialogues, then he or his school would appear to have moved simultaneously in opposite directions on a central question of ethics. Here the author has sought to build further on the role afforded to self-knowledge explaining exactly how it is fundamental to successful conduct; elsewhere Plato has allowed it to become little more than the removal of the mists of delusion, removing an obstacle to success but scarcely securing it. Though there are those unitarians who could offer explanations of even this kind of anomaly, it seems to me safer to find some other context for the *Alcibiades* I, rejecting the theory that it is a product of Plato's own late period.

Bibliography

The following is comprised of both cited sources from the chapters in this collection and additional sources directly or indirectly concerning the theme of self-knowledge in Platonic philosophy, supplemented by the editors in hopes of providing further orientation for future research on the topic.

EDITIONS OF PLATO AND OTHER ANCIENT AUTHORS

Aeschylus. 1977. *The Oresteia*. Translated by Robert Fagles. New York: Penguin Books.
Anonymous. 2011. *Prolegomena to Platonic Philosophy*. Translated by L. G. Westerink. Wiltshire, UK: Prometheus Trust.
Anthologie Grecque (Anthologie Palatine). 1960. Vol. 4. Edited by Pierre Waltz. Paris: Belles Lettres.
Aristotle. 1936. *Physics*. Edited by W. D. Ross. Oxford: Clarendon Press.
      1957. *Metaphysica*. Edited by Werner Jaeger. Oxford: Clarendon Press.
      1957. *On the Soul. Parva Naturalia. On Breath*. Translated by W. S. Hett. Cambridge, MA: Harvard University Press.
Aronadio, Francesco, ed. 2008. *Dialoghi spuri di Platone*. Torino: Unione tipografico-editrice Torinese.
Bailly, Jacques. 2004. *The Socratic Theages: Introduction, English Translation, Greek Text and Commentary*. Hildesheim: Georg Olms Verlag.
Burnet, John, ed. 1900–1907. *Platonis Opera*. 6 vols. Oxford: Clarendon Press.
Burnyeat, Myles F. 1990. *The Theaetetus of Plato*, trans. M. J. Levett, revised by Myles Burnyeat. Indianapolis, IN: Hackett Publishing.
Cooper, John, ed. 1997. *Plato: Complete Works*. Indianapolis, IN: Hackett Publishing.
Denyer, Nicholas, ed. 2001. *Plato: Alcibiades*. Cambridge: Cambridge University Press.
Dover, Kenneth, ed. 1980. *Plato: Symposium*. Cambridge: Cambridge University Press.
Duke, E. A., Hicken, W. F., Nicholl, W. S. M, Robinson, D. B., and Strachan, J. C. G., eds. 1995. *Platonis Opera: Tomus I*. Oxford: Clarendon Press.
Euripides. 1960. *Iphigenia in Tauris*. In *Greek Tragedies*. Vol. 2. Translated by David Green and Richmond Lattimore. Chicago, IL: University of Chicago Press.

Gill, Mary L., and Ryan, Paul, trans. 1996. *Plato: Parmenides*. Indianapolis, IN: Hackett.

Hamilton, Edith, and Cairns, Huntington, eds. 1961. *Plato: The Collected Dialogues, Including the Letters*. Princeton, NJ: Princeton University Press.

Herodotus. 1992. *The Histories*. Translated by Walter Blanco. New York: W. W. Norton & Co.

Hesiod. 2000. *Works and Days*. In *Homeric Hymns, Epic Cycle, Homerica*. Translated by Hugh G. Evelyn-White. Cambridge, MA: Harvard University Press.

Hippocrates. 1978. *Hippocratic Writings*. Translated by J. Chadwick and W. N. Mann. New York: Penguin Books.

Homer. 1996. *The Odyssey*. Translated by Robert Fagles. New York: Penguin Books.

1997. *Iliad*. Translated by Stanley Lombardo. Indianapolis, IN: Hackett Publishing.

Johnson, David M., trans. 2003. *Socrates and Alcibiades: Four Texts*. Newburyport, MA: Focus.

Joyal, Mark. 2000. *The Platonic Theages: An Introduction, Commentary and Critical Edition*. Stuttgart: Franz Steiner Verlag.

Olympiodorus. 1982. *Commentary on the First Alcibiades of Plato*. Edited by L. G. Westerink. Amsterdam: Hakkert. Original edition, 1956.

2016. *On Plato First Alcibiades 10–28*. Translated by Michael Griffin. London: Bloomsbury Academic.

Pindar. 1882. "Fragment 131." In *Selected Odes*. Translated by Thomas D. Seymour. Boston, MA: Gin, Heath, & Co.

Plato. 1914. *Apology*. Translated by H. N. Fowler. Cambridge, MA: Harvard University Press.

1914. *Phaedo*. Translated by H. N. Fowler. Cambridge, MA: Harvard University Press.

1921. *Theaetetus*. Translated by H. N. Fowler. Cambridge, MA: Harvard University Press.

1924. *Meno*. Translated by W. R. Lamb. Cambridge, MA: Harvard University Press.

1925. *Symposium*. Translated by H. N. Fowler. Cambridge, MA: Harvard University Press.

1926. *Laws*. Translated by R. G. Bury. Cambridge, MA: Harvard University Press.

1927a. *Charmides*. Translated by W. R. Lamb. Cambridge, MA: Harvard University Press.

1927b. *Alcibiades I*. Translated by W. R. Lamb. Cambridge, MA: Harvard University Press.

1932. *Gorgias*. Translated by W. R. Lamb. Cambridge, MA: Harvard University Press.

1970. *Symposium*. Translated by Suzy Groden. Amherst: University of Massachusetts Press.

1973. *Laches and Charmides*. Translated by Rosamond Kent Sprague. Indianapolis, IN: Bobbs-Merrill & Co.

1991. *Republic.* Translated by Allan Bloom. New York: Basic Books.

2003: *Rempublicam.* Edited by S. R. Slings. Oxford: Clarendon Press.

Plotinus. 1966. *Enneads.* Translated by A. H. Armstrong. Cambridge, MA: Harvard University Press.

Proclus. 1899–1901. *Procli Diadochi in Platonis rem publicam commentarii.* Edited by W. Kroll. 2 vols. Leipzig: Teubner (reprint, Amsterdam: Hakkert, 1965).

1971. *Commentary on the First* Alcibiades *of Plato.* Translated by William O'Neil. The Hague: Martinus Nijhoff.

1995. *The Platonic Theology.* Translated by Thomas Taylor. Wiltshire, UK: Prometheus Trust.

2007. *On Plato Cratylus.* Translated by Brian Duvick. London: Bloomsbury Academic.

Sophocles. 1994. *Philoctetes.* In *Sophocles,* volume II. Translated by Hugh-Lloyd Jones. Cambridge, MA: Harvard University Press.

Sprague, Rosamund Kent, ed. 1972. *The Older Sophists.* Indianapolis, IN: Hackett Publishing.

Thucydides. 1900. *Historiae: Tomus Prior.* Edited by H. S. Jones. Oxford: Clarendon Press.

West, Thomas G., and West, Grace Starry, trans. 1986. *Plato: Charmides.* Indianapolis, IN: Hackett Publishing.

Yunis, Harvey, ed. 2011. *Plato: Phaedrus.* Cambridge: Cambridge University Press.

SECONDARY LITERATURE

Adam, James. [1902] 1963. *The Republic of Plato.* Cambridge: Cambridge University Press.

Adorno, Theodor. 1982. "Freudian Theory and the Pattern of Fascist Propaganda." In *The Essential Frankfurt School Reader.* New York: Bloomsbury Academic.

Ambury, James M. 2011. "The Place of Displacement: The Elenchus in Plato's *Alcibiades I.*" *Ancient Philosophy* 31 (2): 241–260.

2014. "Socratic Character: Proclus on the Function of Erotic Intellect." In *The Neoplatonic Socrates,* edited by Danielle A. Layne and Harold Tarrant, 109–117. Philadelphia: University of Pennsylvania Press.

2015. "Plato's Conception of Soul as Intelligent Self-Determination." *International Philosophical Quarterly* 55 (3): 299–313.

Annas, Julia. 1981. *Introduction to Plato's Republic.* Oxford: Oxford University Press.

1985. "Self-Knowledge in Early Plato." In *Platonic Investigations,* edited by Dominic O'Meara, 111–138. Washington: Catholic University of America Press.

1988. "Self-Love in Aristotle." *The Southern Journal of Philosophy* 27: 1–18.

1999. *Platonic Ethics, Old and New.* Ithaca, NY: Cornell University Press.

Armstrong, John M. 2004. "After the Ascent: Plato on Becoming like a God." *Oxford Studies in Ancient Philosophy* 26: 171–83.

Asmis, Elizabeth. 1986. "Psychagogia in Plato's *Phaedrus*." *Illinois Studies in Classical Philology* 11: 153–172.

Avnon, Dan. 1995. "Know Thyself: Socratic Companionship and Platonic Community." *Political Theory* 23: 304–329.

Ballard, Edward. 1965. *Socratic Ignorance: An Essay on Platonic Self-Knowledge.* The Hague: Martinus Nijhoff.

Baltzly, Dirk. 2004. "The Virtues and 'Becoming like a God': Alcinous to Proclus." *Oxford Studies in Ancient Philosophy* 26: 297–322.

Baracchi, Claudia. 2014. "One Good: The Mathematics of Ethics." *Graduate Faculty Philosophy Journal* 25 (2): 19–49.

Belfiore, Elizabeth S. 2012. *Socrates' Daimonic Art: Love for Wisdom in Four Platonic Dialogues.* Cambridge: Cambridge University Press.

Benardete, Seth. 1953. "The Daimonion of Socrates: A Study of Plato's *Theages*." Master's thesis, University of Chicago.

   1984. *Plato's Sophist.* Chicago, IL: University of Chicago Press.

   2007. *Plato's Theaetetus: Part I of the Being of the Beautiful.* Chicago, IL: University of Chicago Press.

Benatouïl, Thomas. 2006. Faire usage: le pratique du stoïcisme. Paris: Vrin.

Benitez, Eugenio, and Guimaraes, Livia. 1993. "Philosophy as Performed in Plato's *Theaetetus*." *The Review of Metaphysics* 47 (2): 297–328.

Benson, Hugh. 2003. "A Note on Socratic Self-Knowledge in the *Charmides*." *Ancient Philosophy* 23: 31–47.

Bentley, Russell. 2005. "On Plato's *Phaedrus*: Politics beyond the City Walls." *Polis* 22: 230–248.

Bersani, L., and Phillips, A. 2008. *Intimacies.* Chicago, IL: University of Chicago Press.

Biral, A. 1997. *Platone e la conoscenza di sé.* Roma-Bari: Laterza.

Blondell, Ruby 2002. *The Play of Character in Plato's Dialogues.* Cambridge: Cambridge University Press.

Bobonich, Christopher. 2013. *Plato's Laws: A Critical Guide.* Cambridge: Cambridge University Press.

Bosanquet, Bernard. 1895. *A Companion to Plato's Republic for English Readers.* New York: Macmillan.

Bowery, Anne Marie. 2007. "Know Thyself: Socrates as Storyteller." In *Philosophy in Dialogue: Plato's Many Devices*, edited by Gary Alan Scott, 82–110. Evanston, IL: Northwestern University Press.

Boyle, A. J. 1974. "Plato's Divided Line. Essay II: Mathematics and Dialectic." *Apeiron* 8: 7–21.

Brandwood, Leonard. 1990. *The Chronology of Plato's Dialogues.* Cambridge: Cambridge University Press.

Brickhouse, Thomas C., and Smith, Nicholas D. 1983. "The Origin of Socrates' Mission." *Journal of the History of Ideas* 44: 657–666.

   1984. "The Paradox of Socratic Ignorance in Plato's *Apology*." *History of Philosophy Quarterly* 1 (2): 125–131.

   1989. *Socrates on Trial.* Princeton, NJ: Princeton University Press.

   1994. *Plato's Socrates.* Oxford: Oxford University Press.

Brill, Sara. 2016. "Greek Philosophy in the 21st Century." *Oxford Handbooks Online.* Last modified June 2016. Available at www.oxfordhandbooks.com/ view/10.1093/oxfordhb/9780199935390.001.0001/oxfordhb-9780199935 390-e-70?rskey=TYtNSl&result=1.

Brown, Eric A. 2000. "Justice and Compulsion for Plato's Philosopher-Rulers." *Ancient Philosophy* 20 (1): 1–17.

Bruell, Christopher. 1997. "Socratic Politics and Self-Knowledge: An Interpretation of Plato's *Charmides.*" *Interpretation* 6: 141–203.

Brunschwig, Jacques. 1996. "La Déconstruction du «Connais-toi toi-même» dans l'Alcibiade Majeur." *Recherches sur la Philosophie et le Langage* 18: 61–84.

1999. "Revisiting Plato's Cave." *Proceedings of the Boston Area Colloquium in Ancient Philosophy* 19: 145–173.

Burger, Ronna. 1980. *Plato's Phaedrus: A Defense of a Philosophic Art of Writing.* Tuscaloosa: University of Alabama Press.

Burkert, Walter. 1985. *Greek Religion.* Cambridge, MA: Harvard University Press.

Burnet, John. 1923. *The Socratic Doctrine of the Soul.* Oxford: Oxford University Press.

Burnyeat, Myles F. 1997. "Culture and Society in Plato's *Republic.*" *The Tanner Lectures on Human Values* 20: 217–324. http://tannerlectures.utah.edu/_ documents/a-to-z/b/Burnyeat99.pdf.

2000. "Plato on Why Mathematics Is Good for the Soul." *Proceedings of the British Academy* 103: 1–81.

Cain, Rebecca Bensen. 2007. *The Socratic Method: Plato's Use of Philosophical Drama.* New York: Bloomsbury Academic.

Capra, Andrea. 2014. *Plato's Four Muses: The Phaedrus and the Poetics of Philosophy.* Washington, DC: Center for Hellenic Studies.

Carone, Gabriella. 1998. "Socrates' Human Wisdom and *Sōphrosunē* in *Charmides* 164cff." *Ancient Philosophy* 18: 267–286.

Carvalho, John. 2014. "Socrates' Refutation of Apollo: A Note on Apology 21b7–c2." *Journal of Ancient Philosophy* 8: 40–56.

Chroust, Anton-Hermann. 1965. "The Organization of the *Corpus Platonicum* in Antiquity." *Hermes* 93 (1): 34–46.

Cobb, William S. 1992. "Plato's *Theages.*" *Ancient Philosophy* 12: 267–284.

Cooper, J. M. 1999. *Reason and Emotion: Essays on Ancient Moral Psychology and Ethical Theory.* Princeton, NJ: Princeton University Press.

Cornford, Francis M. 1932. "Mathematics and Dialectic in the Republic VI–VII (II)." *Mind* 41 (162): 173–190.

Courcelle, Pierre, 1974. *Connais-toi toi-même de Socrate à Saint Bernard.* Paris: Etudes Augustiniennes.

Cross, R. C., and Woozley, A. D. 1964. *Plato's Republic: A Philosophical Commentary.* London: Macmillan.

DeHaas, Frans. 2010. "Know Thyself: Plato and Aristotle on Awareness." In *Ancient Perspectives on Aristotle's De Anima*, edited by Gerd van Reel and Pierre Déstree, 49–70. Leuven: Leuven University Press.

Detienne, Marcel. 1999. *The Masters of Truth in Archaic Greece*. Translated by Janet Lloyd. New York: Zone Books.

Dillon, John M. 2003. *The Heirs of Plato: A Study of the Old Academy, 347–274 B.C.* Oxford: Oxford University Press.

Dixsaut, Monique. 2002. *Métamorphoses de la Dialectique dans les Dialogues de Platon*. Paris: Vrin.

Dorter, Kenneth. 1990. "Diaresis and the Tripartite Soul in the Sophist." *Ancient Philosophy* 10: 41–61.

Eisenstadt, Michael. 1981. "A Note on *Charmides* 168e9–169a1." *Hermes* 109: 126–128.

Ferrari, G. R. F. 1987. *Listening to the Cicadas: A Study of Plato's* Phaedrus. Cambridge: Cambridge University Press.

Forster, Michael. 2007. "Socratic Ignorance." *Oxford Studies in Ancient Philosophy* 32: 1–35.

Foucault, Michel. 1978. *The History of Sexuality*, volume 1. New York: Vintage Books.

Freud, Sigmund. 1990. *Group Psychology and the Analysis of the Ego*. Translated by J. W. W. Strachey. New York: Norton Press.

Friedländer, Paul. 1958. *Plato: An Introduction*. New York: Harper.

  1964. *Plato*, volume II: *The Dialogues First Period*. Translated by Hans Meyerhoff. New York: Pantheon.

  1969. *Plato*, volume III: *The Dialogues, Second and Third Periods*. Translated by Hans Meyerhoff. London: Routledge and Kegan Paul.

Gadamer, Hans-Georg. 1980. *Dialogue and Dialectic: Eight Hermeneutical Studies on Plato*. Translated by P. Christopher Smith. New Haven, CT: Yale University Press.

  1986. *The Idea of the Good in Platonic-Aristotelian Philosophy*. Translated by P. Christopher Smith. New Haven, CT: Yale University Press.

German, Andy. 2017. "Is Socrates Free? The *Theaetetus* as Case Study." *British Journal of the History of Philosophy* 25 (4): 621–641.

Gerson, Lloyd P. 1992. "The Ignorance of Socrates." *Proceedings of the American Catholic Philosophical Association* 66: 123–135.

  2003. *Knowing Persons: A Study in Plato*. Oxford: Oxford University Press.

  2015. "Ideas of Good?" In *Second Sailing: Alternative Perspectives on Plato*, edited by Debra Nails and Harold Tarrant, 225–242. Helsinki: Societas Scientiarum Fennica.

  2016. "The 'Neoplatonic' Interpretation of Plato's *Parmenides*." *International Journal of the Platonic Tradition* 10 (1): 65–94.

Giannopoulou, Zina. 2015. "Self-Knowledge in Plato's *Theaetetus* and *Alcibiades I*." *Boston Area Colloquium for Ancient Philosophy* 30: 73–93.

Gill, Christopher. 1985. "Plato and the Education of Character." *Archiv für Geschichte der Philosophie* 67: 1–26.

  2007. "Self-knowledge in Plato's *Alcibiades*." In *Reading Ancient Texts*, volume I: *Presocratics and Plato*, edited by Suzanne Stern-Gillet and Kevin Corrigan, 95–112. Leiden: Brill.

Gill, Mary L. 2012. *Philosophos: Plato's Missing Dialogue*. Oxford: Oxford University Press.

Gonzalez, Francisco J. 1995. "Self-Knowledge, Practical Knowledge and Insight." In *The Third Way: New Directions in Platonic Studies*, edited by Francisco Gonzalez, 155–188. Lanham, MD: Rowman and Littlefield.

1998. *Dialectic and Dialogue: Plato's Practice of Philosophical Inquiry*. Evanston, IL: Northwestern University Press.

Gooch, Paul W. 1971. "'Vice Is Ignorance': The Interpretation of Sophist 226a–231b." *Phoenix* 25: 124–133.

Gordon, Jill. 1999. *Turning toward Philosophy: Literary Device and Dramatic Structure in Plato's Dialogues*. University Park, PA: Pennsylvania State University Press.

2012. *Plato's Erotic World: From Cosmic Origins to Human Death*. Cambridge: Cambridge University Press.

Graver, M. 2008. *The Stoics on Emotions*. Chicago, IL: University of Chicago Press.

Griswold, Charles. 1981. "Self-Knowledge and the 'ἰδέα' of the Soul in Plato's *Phaedrus*." *Revue de Métaphysique et de Morale* 86 (4): 477–494.

1986. *Self-Knowledge in Plato's Phaedrus*. New Haven, CT: Yale University Press.

Grote, George. 1888. *Plato and the Other Companions of Sokrates*, volume 1. London: J. Murray.

Habermas, Jürgen. 1992. "Themes in Post-Metaphysical Thinking." In *Philosophical Interventions in the Unfinished Project of Enlightenment*, edited by Axel Honneth, Thomas McCarthy, Klaus Offe, and Albrecht Wellmer, 28–53. Cambridge, MA: MIT Press.

Hackforth, Reginald. 1942. "Plato's Divided Line and Dialectic." *Classical Quarterly* 36: 1–9.

1946. "Moral Evil and Ignorance in Plato's Ethics." *Classical Quarterly* 40: 118–120.

Hadot, Pierre. 1995. *Philosophy as a Way of Life*. Translated by Michael Chase. Malden, MA: Blackwell.

Halper, Edward. 2000. "Is Knowledge of Knowledge Possible? *Charmides* 167a–169d." In *Plato: Euthydemus, Lysis, Charmides. Proceedings of the Fifth Symposium Platonicum*, edited by Thomas Robinson and Luc Brisson, 309–316. Sankt Augustin: Akademia Verlag.

Howland, Jacob. 2004. *The Republic: The Odyssey of Philosophy*. Philadelphia, PA: Paul Dry Books.

Hyland, Drew A. 1981. *The Virtue of Philosophy: An Interpretation of Plato's Charmides*. Athens, OH: Ohio University Press.

1995. *Finitude and Transcendence in the Platonic Dialogues*. Albany, NY: State University of New York Press.

2011. "*Aporia*, the Longer Road, and the Good." *Graduate Faculty Philosophy Journal* 32 (1): 145–175.

Irwin, Terrence. 1995. *Plato's Ethics*. Oxford: Oxford University Press.

Johnson, David. 1999. "God as the True Self: Plato's *Alcibiades I*." *Ancient Philosophy* 19: 1–19.

Johnson, Marguerite, and Tarrant, Harold, eds. 2012. *Alcibiades and the Socratic Lover-Educator*. London: Bloomsbury Academic.

Joyal, Mark. 1990. "Anacreon Fr. 449 (P.M.G.)." *Hermes* 118. Bd., H. 1: 122–124.

Kahn, Charles H. 1996. *Plato and the Socratic Dialogue: The Philosophical Use of a Literary Form*. Cambridge: Cambridge University Press.

2013. *Plato and the Post-Socratic Dialogue: The Return to the Philosophy of Nature*. Cambridge: Cambridge University Press.

Kamtekar, Rachana. 2004. "What's the Good of Agreeing? Homonoia in Platonic Politics." *Oxford Studies in Ancient Philosophy* 26: 131–170.

Kang, Chol-Ung. 2008. "Socratic Eros and Self-Knowledge." *The Journal of Greco-Roman Studies* 32: 79–102.

Kirk, Gregory. 2016. "Self-knowledge and Ignorance in Plato's *Charmides*." *Ancient Philosophy* 36: 303–320.

Klein, Jacob. 1989. *A Commentary on Plato's Meno*. Chicago, IL: University of Chicago Press.

Korsgaard, Christine, 1999. "Self-Constitution in the Ethics of Plato and Kant." *Journal of Ethics* 3: 1–29.

Krämer, H. J. 1990. *Plato and the Foundations of Metaphysics: A Work on the Theory of the Principles and Unwritten Doctrines of Plato with a Collection of the Fundamental Documents*. Translated by J. R. Catan. Albany, NY: State University of New York Press.

Kraut, Richard. 1991. "Return to the Cave: *Republic* 519–521." *Proceedings of the Boston Area Colloquium in Ancient Philosophy* 7: 43–62.

1992. "The Defense of Justice in the *Republic*." In *The Cambridge Companion to Plato*, edited by Richard Kraut, 311–337. Cambridge: Cambridge University Press.

Kurihara, Yuji. 2008. "Plato on the Ideal of Justice and Human Happiness: Return to the Cave (*Rep.* 519e–521b)." *Philosophical Inquiry* 30 (3–4): 77–86.

2012. "Socratic Ignorance, or the Place of the *Alcibiades I* in Plato's Early Works." In *Alcibiades and the Socratic Lover-Educator*, edited by Marguerite Johnson and Harold Tarrant, 77–89. London: Bloomsbury Academic.

Landazuri, Ortiz De. 2015. "The Development of Self-Knowledge in Plato's Philosophy." *Logos (Madrid)* 48: 123–140.

Larivée, Annie. 2012. "Choice of Life and Self-Transformation in the Myth of Er." In *Plato and Myth: Studies on the Use and Status of Platonic Myths*, edited by Catherine Collobert, Pierre Destrée, and Francisco J. Gonzalez, 235–257. Leiden: Brill.

2016. "Le pouvoir protreptique de l'amour. Éros, soin de soi et identité personnelle dans le *Banquet*." In *Plato in Symposium: Selected Papers from the Tenth Symposium Platonicum*, edited by Mauro Tulli and Michael Erler, 380–385. Sankt Augustin: Academia Verlag.

Lavecchia, Salvatore. 2012. "Selbsterkenntnis und Schöpfung eines Kosmos. Dimensionen der *Sophia* in Platons Denken." *Perspektiven der Filosofie* 35: 115–145.

Layne, Danielle A. 2009a. "In Praise of the Mere Presence of Ignorance from Plato to Erasmus." *The Proceedings of the American Catholic Philosophical Association* 83: 253–267.

2009b. "Refutation and Double Ignorance in Proclus." *Epoché* 13 (2): 347–362.

2015. "Involuntary Evil and the Socratic Problem of Double Ignorance in Proclus." *The International Journal of the Platonic Tradition* 9: 27–15.

2018. "Proclus on Socratic Ignorance, Knowledge, and Irony." In *Socrates and the Socratic Dialogue*, edited by Alessandro Stavru and Christopher Moore, 816–834. Leiden: Brill.

Lear, Jonathan. 1992. "Inside and Outside the *Republic*." *Phronesis* 37 (2): 184–215.

Lee, Edward N. 1973. "'Hoist with His Own Petard': Ironic and Comic Elements in Plato's Critique of Protagoras (*Tht.* 161–171)." In *Exegesis and Argument: Studies in Greek Philosophy Presented to Gregory Vlastos*, edited by E. N. Lee, A. P. D. Mourelatos, and R. M. Rorty. Assen: Van Gorcum.

1976. "Reason and Rotation: Circular Movement as the Model of Mind (Nous) in Later Plato." In *Facets of Plato's Philosophy*, edited by William H. Werkmeister, *Phronesis* Supplement 2: 70–102.

Lee, Mi-Kyoung. 2005. *Epistemology after Protagoras.* Oxford: Oxford University Press.

Lennox, James. 2009. "Bios, Praxis and the Unity of Life." In *Was ist 'Leben'? Aristoteles' Anschauungen zur Entstehungsweise und Funktion von Leben*, edited by Sabine Foellinger. Stuttgart: Franz Steiner.

2010. "Bios and Explanatory Unity in Aristotle's Biology." In *Definition in Greek Philosophy*, edited by David Charles, 329–355. Oxford: Oxford University Press.

Levy, David. 2018. "Socrates' Self-Knowledge." In *Socrates in the Cave: On the Philosopher's Motive in Plato*, edited by Paul J. Diduch and Michael P. Harding, 77–106. New York: Palgrave Macmillan.

Liddell, Henry George, Scott, Robert, and Jones, Henry Stuart. 1996. *Greek English Lexicon.* Oxford: Clarendon Press.

Lisi, Francisco. 2016. "Sophistischer und Philosophischer Sprachgebrauch bei Platon." In *Platon und die Sprache*, edited by Dietmar Koch, Irmgard Männlein-Robert, and Niels Weidtmann, 62–81. Tübingen: Narr Francke Attempto Verlag.

Long, Anthony 2001. "Ancient Philosophy's Hardest Question: What to Make of Oneself?" *Representations* 74: 19–36.

2014. *Greek Models of Mind and Self.* Cambridge, MA: Harvard University Press.

Lott, Micah. 2012. "Ignorance, Shame and Love of Truth: Diagnosing the Sophist's Error in Plato's *Sophist*." *Phoenix* 66 (1–2): 36–56.

Mackenzie, Mary Margaret. 1988. "The Virtues of Socratic Ignorance." *The Classical Quartley, New Series* 38 (2): 331–350.

Marrin, Brian. 2017. "What's Next in Plato's *Clitophon*? Self-Knowledge, Instrumentality, and Means without End." *Epoché* 21 (2): 307–320.

Marrou, H. I. 1965. *Histoire de l'Éducation dans l'Antiquité*, 6th edition. Paris: Éditions du Seuil.

Matthews, Gareth. 2003. *Socratic Perplexity and the Nature of Philosophy*. Oxford: Oxford University Press.

May, Hope E. 1997. "Socratic Ignorance and the Theraputic Aim of the *Elenchos*." In *Wisdom, Ignorance and Virtue: New Essays in Socratic Studies*, edited by Mark McPherran, 37–50. Edmonton: Academic.

McCabe, Mary M. 1994. *Plato's Individuals*. Princeton, NJ: Princeton University Press.

2007. "Looking Inside Charmides' Cloak: Seeing Others and Oneself in Plato's *Charmides*." In *Maieusis: Essays on Ancient Philosophy in Honor of Myles Burnyeat*, edited by Dominic Scott, 1–19. Oxford: Oxford University Press.

2010. "Banana Skins and Custard Pies: Plato on Comedy and Self-Knowledge." In *Plato's Philebus: Selected Papers from the Eighth Symposium Platonicum*, edited by John M. Dillon and Luc Brisson, 194–203. Sankt Augustin: Academia Verlag.

2011. "'It Goes Deep with Me': Plato's *Charmides* on Knowledge, Self-Knowledge and Integrity." In *Philosophy, Ethics and a Common Humanity: Essays in Honour of Raimond Gaita*, edited by Christopher Cordner, 161–180. London: Routledge.

2013. "Waving or Drowning? Socrates and the Sophists on Self-Knowledge in the *Euthydemus*." In *The Platonic Art of Philosophy: Festschrift for Christopher Rowe*, edited by George Boys-Stones, Dimitri El Murr, and Christopher Gill. Cambridge: Cambridge University Press.

McCoy, Marina. 2008. *Plato on the Rhetoric of Philosophers and Sophists*. Cambridge: Cambridge University Press.

McCoy, W. James. 1975. "The Identity of Leon." *The American Journal of Philology* 96 (2): 187–199.

McKim, Richard. 1985. "Socratic Self-Knowledge and 'Knowledge of Knowledge' in Plato's *Charmides*." *Transactions of the American Philological Association* 115: 59–77.

McPherran, Mark. 1996. *The Religion of Socrates*. University Park, PA: The Pennsylvania State University Press.

Migliori, M., Napolitano, L. M., Fermani, A., eds. 2011. *Inner Life and Soul: Psychē in Plato*. Sankt Augustin: Academia Verlag.

Miller, Mitchell. 1986. *Plato's Parmenides: The Conversion of the Soul*. University Park, PA: Pennsylvania State University Press.

1999. "Figure, Ratio, Form: Plato's Five Mathematical Studies." *Apeiron* 32: 73–88.

2015. "Making New Gods? A Reflection on the Gift of the *Symposium*." In *Second Sailing: Alternative Perspectives on Plato*, edited by Debra Nails and Harold Tarrant, 285–306. Helsinki: Societas Scientiarum Fennica.

Moore, Christopher. 2014. "How to 'Know Thyself' in Plato's *Phaedrus*." *Apeiron* 47 (3): 390–418.

2015a. *Socrates and Self-Knowledge*. Cambridge: Cambridge University Press.

2015b. "Socrates and Self-Knowledge in Aristophanes' *Clouds*." *Classical Quarterly* 65: 2.

2015c. "Self-Knowledge in Xenophon's *Memorabilia* 4.2." *Classical Journal* 110 (4): 397–417.

Morris, T. F. 1989. "Knowledge of Knowledge and Lack of Knowledge in the *Charmides*." *International Studies in Philosophy* 21: 49–61.

Morrison, J. S. 1977. "Two Unresolved Difficulties in the Line and Cave." *Phronesis* 22: 212–231.

Moss, Jessica. 2012. "Soul-Leading: The Unity of the *Phaedrus*, Again." *Oxford Studies in Ancient Philosophy* 43: 1–23.

Murdoch, Iris. 1977. *The Fire and the Sun*. Oxford: Oxford University Press.

Naas, Michael. 2015. "American Gadfly: Plato and the Problem of Metaphor." In *Plato's Animals: Gadflies, Horses, Swans and Other Philosophical Beasts*, edited by Jeremy Bell and Michael Naas, 43–59. Bloomington, IN: Indiana University Press.

Nails, Deborah. 2002. *The People of Plato: A Prosopography of Plato and Other Socratics*. Indianapolis, IN: Hackett Publishing.

Nehamas, Alexander. 1992. "What Did Socrates Teach and to Whom Did He Teach It?" *The Review of Metaphysics* 46 (2): 279–306.

Nicholson, Graeme. 1999. *Plato's Phaedrus: The Philosophy of Love*. West Lafayette, IN: Purdue University Press.

Nightingale, Andrea. 2010. "Plato on Aporia and Self-Knowledge." In *Ancient Models of Mind: Studies in Human and Divine Rationality*, edited by Andrea Nightingale and David Sedley, 8–26. Cambridge: Cambridge University Press.

Nikulin, Dmitri. 2012. *The Other Plato: The Tübingen Interpretation of Plato's Inner Academic Teachings*. Albany, NY: State University of New York Press.

North, Helen. 1966. *Sōphrosunē: Self-Knowledge and Self-Restraint in Greek Literature*. Ithaca, NY: Cornell University Press.

Notomi, Noburu. 1999. *The Unity of Plato's Sophist*. Cambridge: Cambridge University Press.

Nussbaum, Martha. 1979. "The Speech of Alcibiades: A Reading of Plato's *Symposium*." *Philosophy and Literature* 3: 131–172.

Opsomer, Jan. 1997. "Plutarch's Defence of the *Theages*: In Defence of Socratic Philosophy?" *Philologus* 141 (1): 114–136.

Pangle, Thomas. 1987. "On the Theages." In *The Roots of Political Philosophy: Ten Forgotten Socratic Dialogues*, edited by Thomas Pangle, 147–174. Ithaca, NY: Cornell University Press.

Politis, Vasilis. 2007. "The *Aporia* in the *Charmides* about Reflexive Knowledge and the Contribution to Its Solution in the sun Analogy of the *Republic*." In *Pursuing the Good: Ethics and Metaphysics in Plato's Republic*, edited by Douglas Cairns, Fritz-Gregor Herrmann, and Terry Penner, 231–250. Edinburgh: Edinburgh University Press.

Principe, Jade. 2006. "The Ascent as a Return to the Cave." *Rhizai* 2: 219–239.

Radke, Gyburg. 2003. *Die Theorie der Zahl im Platonismus: Ein systematisches Lehrbuch*. Tübingen/Basel: Francke.

Rappe, Sara. 1995. "Socrates and Self-Knowledge." *Apeiron* 28: 1–24.

Reeve, C. D. C. 2006. *Philosopher-Kings: The Argument of Plato's Republic*. Indianapolis, IN: Hackett Publishing.

Remes, Pauliina. 2013. "Reason to Care: The Object and Structure of Self-Knowledge in the *Alcibiades* I." *Apeiron* 46: 270–301.

Renaud, François, and Tarrant, Harold. 2015. *The Platonic Alcibiades I: The Dialogue and Its Ancient Reception*. Cambridge: Cambridge University Press.

Renz, Ursala, ed. 2016. *Self-Knowledge: A History*. Oxford: Oxford University Press.

Rider, Benjamin. 2011. "Self-Care, Self-Knowledge, and Politics in the *Alcibiades* I," *Epoché* 15: 395–413.

Robinson, Richard. 1953. *Plato's Earlier Dialectic*. Oxford: Clarendon Press.

Roochnik, David. 2002. "Self-Recognition in Plato's *Theaetetus*." *Ancient Philosophy* 22 (1): 37–51.

Rossellini, Ingrid. 2018. *Know Thyself: Western Identity from Classical Greece to the Renaissance*. New York: Doubleday.

Rowe, Christopher. 2011. "Self-Examination." In *The Cambridge Companion to Socrates*, edited by Donald Morrison, 201–214. Cambridge: Cambridge University Press.

2015. "Plato, Socrates, and the *genei gennaiai sophistikê* of *Sophist* 231b." In *Second Sailing: Alternative Perspectives on Plato*, edited by Debra Nails and Harold Tarrant, 149–168. Helsinki: Societas Scientiarum Fennica.

Ryan, Paul. 2012. *Plato's Phaedrus: A Commentary for Greek Readers*. Norman, OK: University of Oklahoma Press.

Sayre, Kenneth M. 1969. *Plato's Analytic Method*. Chicago, IL: University of Chicago Press.

Schmid, W. Thomas. 1998. *Plato's Charmides and the Socratic Ideal of Rationality*. Albany, NY: State University of New York Press.

Schmitt, Arbogast. 2008. *Die Moderne und Platon: Zwei Grundformen europäischer Rationalität*. Stuttgart: Poeschel.

Schultz, Anne-Marie. 2013. *Plato's Socrates as Narrator: A Philosophical Muse*. Lanham, MD: Lexington Books.

2015. "Socrates on Socrates: Looking Back to Bring Philosophy Forward," *Proceedings of the Boston Area Colloquium in Ancient Philosophy* 30: 123–141.

Scott, Gary Alan. 2000. *Plato's Socrates as Educator*. Albany, NY: State University of NY Press.

Scully, Stephen. 2003. *Plato's Phaedrus*. Newburyport, MA: Focus Publishing.

Seaford, Richard, Wilins, John, and Wright, Matthew, eds. 2017. *Selfhood and Soul: Essays on Ancient Thought and Literature in Honor of Christopher Gill.* Oxford: Oxford University Press.

Sedley, David. 1997. "'Becoming like God' in the *Timeaus* and Aristotle." In *Interpreting* the Timaeus-Critias: *Proceeding of the IV Symposium Platonicum*, edited by Luc Brisson and Tomás Calvo, 327–339. Sankt Augustin: Academia Verlag.

1999. "The Ideal of Godlikeness." In *Oxford Readings in Philosophy: Plato* (2 vols.), edited by Gail Fine, 359–383. Oxford: Oxford University Press.

2004. *The Midwife of Platonism: Text and Subtext in Plato's Theaetetus.* Oxford: Oxford University Press.

Seeskin, Kenneth. 1986. *Dialogue and Discovery: A Study in Socratic Method.* Albany, NY: State University Press of New York.

Sichel, Betty. 1985. "Self Knowledge and Education in Plato's Allegory of the Cave." *Proceedings of the Annual Meeting of the Philosophy of Education Society* 41: 429–439.

Smith, Nicholas D. 1997. "How the Prisoners in Plato's Cave Are 'like Us.'" *Proceedings of the Boston Area Colloquium in Ancient Philosophy* 13: 187–204.

Smyth, Herbert W. 1963. *Greek Grammar.* Cambridge, MA: Harvard University Press.

Stalley, R. F. 1983. *An Introduction to Plato's Laws.* Indianapolis, IN: Hackett Publishing.

Stern, Paul. 1999. "Tyranny and Self-Knowledge: Critias and Socrates in Plato's *Charmides.*" *American Political Science Review* 9 (2): 399–412.

2008. *Knowledge and Politics in Plato's Theaetetus.* Cambridge: Cambridge University Press.

Strauss, Leo. 1959. *"What Is Political Philosophy?" and Other Studies.* Westport, CT: Greenwood Press.

Tarrant, Dorothy. 1958. "The Touch of Socrates." *The Classical Quarterly* 8 (1–2): 95–98.

Tarrant, Harold. 2003. "Review of Joyal, *The Platonic Theages.*" *Phoenix* 57 (1–2): 154–156.

2005. "Socratic *Synousia*: A Post-Platonic Myth?" *Journal of the History of Philosophy* 43 (2): 131–155.

2007. "Olympiodorus and Proclus on the Climax of the Alcibiades." *The International Journal of the Platonic Tradition* 1 (1): 3–29.

2012. "Improvement by Love: From Aeschines to the Old Academy." In *Alcibiades and the Socratic Lover-Educator*, edited by Marguerite Johnson and Harold Tarrant, 147–163. London: Bloomsbury Academic.

2015. "Where Did the Mirror Go? Plato [?] *Alcibiades I* 133c1–6." *Elenchos* 36: 361–372.

2018. "The Socratic Dubia." In *Socrates and the Socratic Dialogue*, edited by Alessandro Stavru and Christopher Moore, 386–411.

Taylor, A. E. 1932. *Socrates.* London: Methuen.

Thein, Karel. 2011. "L'âme, l'homme et la connaisance de soi dans le *Premier Alcibiade*." *Chôra* 9–10: 171–202.

2012. "Imagination, Self-Awareness, and Modal Thought at *Philebus* 39–40." *Oxford Studies in Ancient Philosophy* 42: 109–149.

Thesleff, Holger. 1982. *Studies in Platonic Chronology.* Helsinki: Societas Scientiarum Fennica.

Tschemplik, Andrea. 2008. *Knowledge and Self-Knowledge in Plato's Theaetetus.* Lanham, MD: Lexington Books.

Tsouna, Voula. 2001. "Socrate et la connaissance de soi: quelques interpretations." In *Figures de Socrate,* edited by André Laks and Michel Narcy, 37–64. Villeneuve d'Ascq: Presses Universitaires de Septentrion.

Tuozzo, Thomas M. 2001. "What's Wrong with These Cities? The Social Dimension of Sophrosyne in Plato's *Charmides*." *Journal of the History of Philosophy* 39 (3): 321–350.

2011. *Plato's Charmides: Positive Elenchus in a "Socratic" Dialogue.* Cambridge: Cambridge University Press.

Vegetti, Mario. 2013. "Dialectics: Configurations and Functions." In *The Painter of Constitutions: Selected Essays on Plato's Republic,* edited by Mario Vegetti, Franco Ferrari, and Tosca Lynch. Sankt Augustin: Academia Verlag.

Vernant, Jean-Pierre. 1990. "The Myth of Prometheus in Hesiod." In *Myth and Society in Ancient Greece.* Translated by Janet Lloyd. New York: Zone Books.

Vlastos, Gregory. 1989, December 15. "Divining the Reason." *Times Literary Supplement Historical Archive* 1393. Accessed September 9, 2016.

1991. *Socrates: Ironist and Moral Philosopher.* Ithaca, NY: Cornell University Press.

Von Fritz, Kurt. 1963. *Philosophie und Sprachlicher Ausdruck bei Demokrit, Platon und Aristoteles.* Darmstadt: Wissenschaftliche Buchgesellschaft.

[1932] 1969. *Platon, Theaetet und die Antike Mathematik.* Darmstadt: Wissenschaftliche Buchgesellschaft.

Warnek, Peter. 2005. *Descent of Socrates: Self-Knowledge and Cryptic Nature in the Platonic Dialogues.* Bloomington, IN: Indiana University Press.

Werner, Daniel. 2012. *Myth and Philosophy in Plato's Phaedrus.* Cambridge: Cambridge University Press.

2013. "The Self-Seeing Soul in the *Alcibiades I*." *Ancient Philosophy* 33: 307–331.

Westra, Laura. 1992. "Knowing the Self in Plato, Plotinus, and Avicenna." In *Neoplatonism and Islamic Thought,* edited by Parvis Morewedge, 89–110. Albany, NY: State University of New York Press.

White, David A. 1993. *Rhetoric and Reality in Plato's Phaedrus.* Albany, NY: State University of New York Press.

Zuckert, Catherine. 2009. *Plato's Philosophers: The Coherence of the Dialogues.* Chicago, IL: University of Chicago Press.

Index of Names

Page numbers in **bold** identify references to be found in the footnotes of these pages.

Index of Subjects

Page numbers in **bold** identify references to be found in the footnotes of these pages.

Index of Passages

Page numbers in **bold** identify references to be found in the footnotes of these pages.